FINDING YOURSELF

in the

NEW TESTAMENT

FINDING
YOURSELF

NEW
TESTAMENT

FINDING YOURSELF

in the

NEW TESTAMENT

Best-Selling Author
AL CARRAWAY

CFI
An imprint of Cedar Fort, Inc.
Springville, Utah

This is not an official publication of The Church of Jesus Christ of Latter-day Saints. The opinions and views expressed herein belong solely to the author and do not necessarily represent the opinions or views of Cedar Fort, Inc. Permission for the use of sources, graphics, and photos is also solely the responsibility of the author.

ISBN 13: 978-1-4621-4361-0

Published by CFI, an imprint of Cedar Fort, Inc.
2373 W. 700 S., Suite 100, Springville, UT 84663
Distributed by Cedar Fort, Inc., www.cedarfort.com

Library of Congress Control Number: 2022943184

Cover design by Shawnda T. Craig
Cover design © 2022 Cedar Fort, Inc.
Edited and typeset by Valene Wood

Printed in Colombia

10 9 8 7 6 5 4 3 2 1

Printed on acid-free paper

Dedicated
to the reader

Other books by Al Carraway

Wildly Optimistic
More than the Tattooed Mormon
My Dear Little One
Cheers to Eternity
Rooted: Scripture Study Journal

Contents

Finding Yourself In . . .

CONTENTS

Finding Yourself in . . .

Mary and the Angel

Matthew 1 & Luke 2

Mary was from a peasant family, living a typical life of a Jewish girl in a rural village, far from the religious center of Jerusalem. We don't know much of her personal life previous to the angel visitation, but we can assume she would have worked and helped her mother and other woman in their community with cleaning, weaving, collecting water, and gathering firewood to pull their weight in their insignificant village. And we know that she was espoused to Joseph, which was more than just engaged to him, it meant that they were already legally bound together.

Because of Isaiah's prophecy, for centuries, many young Jewish women had dreamed and wondered, "Will I be chosen as the mother of the Messiah?" But it is likely that Mary was not one of them because she knew and made comment on her "*low estate.*" As Nathaniel even asked, "Can there any good thing come out of Nazareth?"[1] Which makes Mary all the more relatable when it comes to bridging the gap of how we see ourselves

---

1. John 1:46

versus how God sees us. What we think we are worthy of versus what He already has strategically and profoundly planned for us.

God passed by the rich and noble families of the Jewish people, and went instead to an insignificant village, to a poor virgin bound to a poor carpenter. He sent an angel to reveal the truth of who she really was and what was in store for her. I see myself in what she must have been feeling, our times we feel insignificant, unqualified, or less than, I have been there often.

And this was not something Mary asked for. Unlike Zacharias and Elizabeth, this was not a result of faithful prayers. This came to Mary under very different circumstances, not to fulfill petition, but to show God's will for her. This was God intervening for a complete redirection and life change when everything was on the line. I can see myself in her with this, being shown and asked to do something different than what I had in mind. How many times I have been asked by God to do something but I'd say, "*This isn't what I asked for,*" as I struggled to know why or if I was going to move forward with it. *I didn't ask* to move across the country. I didn't ask for several bouts of unemployment. I didn't ask for serious health complications when I was pregnant with my third child. I didn't ask to be houseless as a family of five when our house fell through after we already drove across the country.

I can see myself in the course correction and in the sacrifice. I have been there often. Deep sacrifice and life-changing direction change is not foreign to me. I have been there when I got baptized at age twenty; a choice that cost me my family. It was them or God. But could you even choose? Could you choose a God you just met over those you've always had? Were raised by? Loved by?

I see myself in Mary when she was asked to sacrifice and to leave behind. When God asked me to move away from the only way of living I knew of, in New York, to across the country to a place I had never been before, where I didn't know a single person. And to find out my journey following the Spirit did not mean it would be easy and definitely not smooth. Doing what God asked of me meant that what to come was even harder. I see that with Mary, too. I was ripped away from anyone I've ever known and loved, in a new state by myself, only to be treated so painfully by others when getting there, because of things I could not change— *my appearance*. Despite my faith and actions, I still hear from others that God could never love someone like me, *"I mean look at you."*

And Mary. Having to move forward with things she cannot change, having to walk around with the appearance of sin, assuming public shame she would have likely endured as an unmarried mom-to-be.

Joseph was told to *fear not*, but that fear had so many logical layers to it. It wasn't just fear of what other people would think of him, nor was it just fear of being a father to a baby that was conceived without him. It was also fear of Mary's life. If Joseph was not the father while they were already bound together by law, that would fall under adultery. Joseph was in fear of what would happen to her. She'd be ostracized, shamed, divorced, and no one would go near her. She'd be a tainted, impure woman all her days. Being a "just man," Joseph would try to *protect* her by divorcing "her quietly," precisely so that she would not be potentially stoned, just like another familiar bible woman we know of. I see myself in Joseph. Having layers of logic, weight, and fear of what God has brought me. I have been there often.

We see a girl trying to grasp and understand her unique call from God in a moments time. And with all of that—the seeming insignificance of her life thus far, the different, the course correction, the sacrifice, the potential punishment. With everything on the line, Mary responded, *"I am the handmaid of the Lord. Let it be done unto me according to your word."* Mary didn't hesitate; she didn't ask for a sign, nor proof, neither more time to think. Considering all that was required to this poor, unsuspected Jewish girl of an insignificant village, *I am the handmaid of the Lord*—I am someone who does the will of God—is what she commits to no matter what was required of her, even if it meant losing everything. A commitment that comes that readily with that steep of sacrifice and change can only come from a commitment that was made long before any angel appears to her. And instead of being burden by the task and uncertainty ahead, she "*rejoices!*" She considers herself "*blessed.*" Almost as if it is a privilege to be part of it all, even the hard and unwanted ache that is going to follow. In fact, Simeon even prophesied to Mary that "a sword shall pierce through thy own soul also."[2] And yet, she "*magnifies the Lord.*"

"*Let it be done unto me.*" *Let* it happen to me. Allowing God to be God; giving Him the opportunity to show her just how great He really is. And what is it that happens when we allow God to be God? Something we never imagined for ourselves. Something greater. *How?*

Mary trusted, believed, and then acted regardless of not knowing the details of *how* she would fulfill what she was given; "How?" was the only question she asked.

"*The Lord is with thee,*" is how. And the "*power of the highest shall overshadow thee,*" is how. "*Nothing is impossible,*" is how. And Gabriel, telling her about Elizabeth who is 6 months pregnant in her old age, was not just another item on a list of miracles, but seeing His hand in her life also showed Mary that it wasn't just her. It meant she wasn't alone.

Little did humble Mary know what exactly would all unfold. Turns out humble, poor, and seemingly no different than any other young Jewish girl, is one of the few women mentioned in scriptures and the only woman whose life and ministry were prophesied about centuries before her birth. She wasn't sinless or perfect, she was a regular woman who allowed God to take her somewhere better and making something more of her. And because of that, she became Jesus's first disciple. Early Christian churches gave Mary the title of *theotokos*, the "bearer or mother of God," as a reminder of the important part that she played in the Father's plan. She is one who is now even mentioned in the Quran *more often* than in the Bible— two of the longest chapters

---

2. Luke 2:35

being named after her and her family—because of how highly esteemed she is by so many.

She wasn't *just* someone that birthed the Savior of the World, although quite the feat on its own. Because of moving forward with God and God's will, she was part of something so much bigger than that one moment. A whole life and a life hereafter that was full of blossoming magnifications. Regardless of others and regardless of the cost, she allowed God to use her in an extraordinary way. God calls ordinary men and women and uses them in extraordinary ways to help build His kingdom and give them something better.

There are times I know we wonder, well who am *I? I'm no different than anyone else, I don't have much. I come from little and can't seem to see anything significant about me.*

But little do *we* know. Little do we know what we are capable of doing and becoming and what will blossom and magnify because we are His. The entire purpose and existence of God is to bring us to the better and make us better. And regardless of how we see ourselves, regardless how others see us, regardless of our situations, our backgrounds, the sacrifices, and the unexpected, we are deserving of everything better and blossoming simply because we are His.

When we feel unfit, unworthy, and fearful, let us see ourselves in Mary. Although seemingly ordinary living in insignificance, Mary was in fact part of the royal lineage of David, just as the Messiah was prophesied to be born to. And for us, regardless of where we are and what we are doing, we really are in fact offspring of God,[3] direct lineage to the most powerful Being to ever exist. And little do we know what's in store; the greater magnifications that come when we allow God to be God, simply because we are His. And He is showing us who we really are and what is in store for us. And *it is* grand! Better than what we had in mind for ourselves.

---

3. Acts 17:29

God may bring us to something hard. He may bring to us something that is not what we asked for, but we are part of something so much bigger than the right now, so much bigger than what's right here. We are not alone. There are others. God *is* with us. He gives us *power*. We, every one, have reason to *rejoice*. So "*fear not.*" Absolutely *nothing* is impossible.

Finding Yourself In . . .

Zacharias and Elizabeth

Luke 1

Unlike Mary who was visited by an angel for something she did not specifically seek after, Zacharias and Elizabeth spent most of their lives petitioning and pleading to the Lord their desires to have a child. They could qualify to say that they were dealt a poor hand in life—to want something so passionately but be barren and to have the option not even logically be on the table for them. Life, and time, kept passing them by with what appears to be an unanswered and impossible desire, and they find themselves well into old age. Even if Elisabeth wasn't barren, they were now far too old where that wouldn't have mattered. How many other things to be stacked against them with their deep yearnings?

Zacharias was a Jewish high priest who served in the temple The priests with the Aaronic Priesthood serving in the temple were organized into a group, or course, of 24, each group holding about 1,400 men. Zachariah was in the eighth course; and when it was their courses turn, would serve for a week straight in the temple. During which, priests wouldn't see their families, abstain from wine and most foods, and bathe often. And knowing just how many high priests serving there paints the picture of just how rare it was to be chosen to enter the sanctuary of the Lord—where the holy of holies was right there, separated by a veil—and burn incense on the gold alter. The privilege of officiating the burning of incense in the temple might only come once, or possibly never in the lifetime of a priest.

But that's exactly where Zacharias found himself. Absolutely a very humbling and important day for him, absolutely a very solemn occasion. A multitude of priests were bowing in prayer outside while waiting for Zacharias to finish praying and burning the incense inside. Noticeably to those priests, Zacharias was taking longer than normal, because as we know, it was then an angel of the Lord appeared to him. *"Thy prayer is heard . . .and thou shalt have joy and gladness."*

Opposite to Mary's response to the angel, Zacharias asks for a sign, and is struck dumb for he *"believest not my words which shall* [will] *be fulfilled."* Being struck dumb may seem like punishment to hesitation to believe, but *what if* it wasn't. *What if* it was a tool that was used to have him, and others, *believe* and be shown the power and reality of God!

Despite all odds, despite logic, despite passing time, Elisabeth was with child. In hiding until a reunion with Mary, where the babe leapt in her belly bearing testimony before he was even born that Jesus is the Christ, a start of what John would do his whole life—proclaim and prepare for Jesus's coming.

Through the *tender mercy of our God,* the *"hand of the Lord"* was with them and they were *filled.*

Tradition implied and friends assumed the miracle baby would be named after the father, Zacharias. John was a new name and a new route. Which can also imply the lesson that we don't have to do what has always been done. How things have always gone may not always be right. Following divine counsel should hold more weight than potential peer pressure or social norms.

Through John, Zacharias, and Elisabeth, we are clearly shown that we should never give up on our righteous desires. But this lesson is more than getting what we want, because we are all well aware that we will not always get what we are pleading for. We just read about Mary who wasn't asking for what was brought to her; both however show that they lead to *greater* things and both illustrate the reality that God is actively part of both situations.

Whatever God is giving you, He will sustain you in it. A lot of things that will come up in our lives may very well not make logical sense; but is that not more of a witness that it didn't come from us, but from *Him?* How easy it is when we are not getting what we are pleading for—especially righteous, good things—to say God is not listening, God does not care, or He is not there at all. We are shown that through even decades of passing time, our prayers *are always heard* and our desires are always known. And whatever it is that God brings us to, whether our answered petitions or the unexpected, it *will* in fact lead to *joy* and *gladness*! Living a life of what may seem to be ignored desires and missed blessings, Zacharias was still living a life that had him in the right places doing the right things. Waiting on the Lord will never be in vain.

We are shown the reality that regardless of what comes our way, regardless of passing time and logistics of our narrowmindedness, through the "*tender mercy of our God, the hand of the Lord*" is in fact with you through it all. He comes to you, bringing "*light to them that sit in darkness,*" to "*guide our feet into the way of peace.*" God's words will be fulfilled. And you *will* be *filled*.

Finding Yourself in . . .

The Birth of Christ

Matthew 2 & Luke 2

THE JOURNEY TO BETHLEHEM

Leaving Nazareth, a little town of little importance as far as trade and commerce goes, Mary and Joseph start their travel to the city of David. Fulfilling prophecy in Micah, Mary rides on a donkey to Bethlehem because Christ was of the house and lineage of David.

The journey was at least (approx.) 90 miles, but perhaps even farther than that if they went around Samaria, like most Jews did. Why? Well in short, Samaritans hated Jews.

Great with child, it is highly likely Mary was in labor during this long and uncomfortable travel. Russell M. Nelson said it was likely "camped out several nights because their journey would have required three to four days."[1] Having been in labor three times myself, I dread and ache picturing what Mary felt these

---

1. https://www.churchofjesuschrist.org/study/ensign/2011/12/
   the-peace-and-joy-of-knowing-the-savior-lives?lang=eng

last days of pregnancy while being required to continuously and uncomfortably travel and sleep on the outdoor ground.

And after thinking of physical fatigue, my mind goes into how she must have been feeling outside of her physical fatigue and discomfort. It was so much more than even that. I think of all the opportunities that came up that didn't work out for them, how it must have crushed their spirits and optimism. I think of the relief she must have felt when she finally approached an inn, *could this be a blessing for her to ease her discomfort finally?* How badly she wanted a place in the inn but was denied. How heartbreaking it must have been, already tried and tired, when it didn't work out.

Was it because Mary was being punished? Did she do something wrong? *No way.* Not at all.

But God had something else in mind: *a manger.* It may not have seemed perfect to Mary and Joseph—not what they had in mind at all. But it was all a part of Heavenly Father's plan and even prophecy. Russell M. Nelson said, "When they reached Bethlehem, the time came for the birth of the Holy Child."[2] Jesus could have been born any one of those days traveling. But He wasn't born until the time and place were what Heavenly Father needed.

Could you imagine if Mary and Joseph didn't keep going? Or if they were accepted into the inn? Would the shepherds have found them? Would they have been there to bless others and to fulfill the plan and prophecies?

Surely the birth of Christ was perfect in every way. So we, too, should wait for our *"manger,"* our something better according to what God has strategically planned for us, rather than settling for who knows what, with our limited narrow-mindedness. Wait for our perfect something, according to Him. I know it can be hard and full of discomfort, just like Mary experienced. But

---

2. https://www.churchofjesuschrist.org/study/ensign/2011/12/
the-peace-and-joy-of-knowing-the-savior-lives?lang=eng

when we see opportunities pass, we can learn from her to keep going, knowing there *is* something else to come.

You are not being punished. Your efforts are not in vain. Everlasting struggle is not in God's cards for you. And when it is His time, it will happen—relief and blessings and the something greater that God surely bring to us, because that's God's entire purpose, to bring us to better things. It will not just bless you but profoundly help and bless others because of it, because you waited, because you trust Him, because you know that "*he will not fail thee.*"[3]

And so, the Savior of the world was born in a manger. Prophecy fulfilled. And He would be Mary's son and also her Savior. And following the angel's counsel, they named the baby Jesus. Which comes as no surprise, Jesus meaning Savior, the name rightfully given to Him whose whole purpose is to come to *save* His people. His entire purpose is to save *you*. He is a Savior that choose to come and be born during a genocide and be born as a minority, a refugee. He chose to be born to a poor, unwed teen from a town that was said nothing good could come out of. He chose to be poor, to carry every pain, and to be powerless. He chose to be misunderstood, abused, betrayed, and killed. Because He chose us. He came down from heaven to carry, to lift, to forgive, to strengthen, to save every one of us every single step of the way because He chose and *loves* us. *Fear not for behold I bring you good tidings of great joy.*

LAMBS AND SHEPHERDS

Every firstborn male lamb was considered holy and was set aside for sacrifice for Passover. They would literally be wrapped tightly . . . *swaddled* . . . in specially designated temple cloths to prevent them from damaging, dirtying, or hurting themselves, and they would be laid in a manger to keep them contained while waiting to be examined for blemishes.

---

3. Deuteronomy 31:8

They could be taken to Jerusalem and purchased by people wanting to present a sacrifice before the Lord to atone for their sins. When the angel appeared to the shepherds in the fields, he told them that they would find the newborn King wrapped in swaddling clothes and laying in a manger. *"Let us now go even unto Bethlehem"* was their response, knowing where He would be found because swaddling clothes were only used in one particular location and for one particular purpose. And without hesitation, they left in haste, they hurried, they waited not, and they *made known abroad* about the birth of the Messiah, they told many of their Savior.

And you know, maybe it was cool that they saw the babe in the manger. But to me, it's more impactful knowing that they left their flocks. Them having the *most important* job there was: raising and watching the lambs that would be sacrificed for Passover—the ones that strictly needed to be *perfect* in *all* ways, without blemish. If anything were to happen to those sheep, it would cost the shepherds their lives. Leaving them could result in death.

And yet, they willfully abandoned the flock, and left the most important job there was, knowing what it would cost them. Because to them, even the most important job wasn't as important as it was to find and follow Christ. Because to them, it was more important to be closer to Him, than it was to live. Because to them, they knew to truly live came from Him, the light and the *life* of the world.

THE WISE MEN

Where is the child that is born, for we have seen the star. We don't know how many wise men came in total, but there is more of what we *do* know. We know that from long tradition, wise men were called *magi*, which is a word used to describe learned priests and holy men. We can gather that the wise men, however many there were, were holy men and priests trained and seasoned in interpreting ancient scriptures. In their knowledge, they were likely anxiously awaiting and watchful for the Messiah to come.

Recognizing the star with great excitement, the wise men started their journey. Again, we don't know when they arrived, but it was not when the family of three was still at the manger. What we do know is that they came at least forty-days *after* Jesus's birth, after when He was presented to the Lord in the temple, a requirement for the firstborn male of every family. Traditionally, every firstborn male shall be *dedicated to the Lord*. Every mother was required a burnt offering—a lamb, or a pair of doves or pigeons, and present the Lord with their new firstborn male baby.

"*Herod the Great*" was no respecter of persons with his ruthless violence and cruelty, putting to death anyone that hinted a threat to him or his rule and power. Rumors of the birth of a *King of Jews* reached Herod and the search for Christ begun. Cue the wise men, who were secretly inquired by Herod, on what they knew of this *king* and about when in time they saw this star appear. The wise men were directed by Herod to Bethlehem and told the wise men to return when they learned of his whereabouts so that Herod *the Great,* could go *worship* the babe as well. *Eyeroll*

Days, weeks, or months after the 40-day presentation to the Lord, the wise men found Mary, Joseph, and baby Jesus in a house and presented their gifts. Their travel, their faith, their studies, their sacrifices, were not in vain. Because there they were. And there the Savior of the World was. And they worshipped Him. A great model of what we should do, spending our time studying, learning, seeking, sacrificing, and worshipping.

Being warned of God in a dream, the wise men were told not to return *into their country* their original route and so left another way. Following their departure, the Lord appeared to Joseph telling them to flee to Egypt until further instruction. After it was apparent the wise men were not returning, Herod ruthlessly ordered the slaughter of all the children that were in Bethlehem aged two and under. And the Savior of our souls was divinely saved and protected to continue out His mission. One that only existed because of God's love *for you.*

THE STAR

'Twas the night before Christmas! And all the believers were going to be killed. If we momentarily leave the New Testament and hop over the 3 Nephi, every single believer was going to be murdered if the star signifying the birth of Jesus did not appear. They quite literally needed Christ in order to live. Awaiting the sign which had been spoken of by Samuel the prophet, and now the believers are down to that very night for it to appear. Scripturally it's said that, "*the time is past, and the words of Samuel are not fulfilled; therefore, your joy and your faith concerning this thing hath been* vain."

There's no way for you to know how often I have felt that way. But I do have a hard time keeping track of all the times I have seen myself in this. Passing time causing me to doubt and wonder if my efforts and faith were in vain. "*There were some who began to say that the time was past for the words to be fulfille*d." How easy and tempting it is to second-guess and doubt what we are promised as time passes. Passing time has this strange effect that seems to dim our promises and blessings. It can drain our energy, our hope, our optimism, our faith. Passing time can sometimes make us feel we have nothing to show for our efforts. I see myself in the times that are like this, where I feel my efforts and my faith have been in *vain.* Ongoing seasons with little or no change, continuing without answers that haven't come yet, it can all stretch us thin.

Yet even when time and logic may suggest otherwise, "*a new star did appear, according to the word.*" At a time that was worthy of them wondering where God was in any of this, before it was ever too late for them, that exact "*night shall the sign be given, and on the morrow come I into the world, to show unto the world that I will fulfil all that which I have caused to be spoken.*" He came. Christ literally came before it was too late. Light literally came and drove out the dark. *"There was no darkness in all that night, but it was as light as though it was mid-day,"* and *"it had come to pass, all things, every whit, according to the words of the prophets."*

Regardless of circumstances and time, promises and prophecy *were* fulfilled. And they were blessed. They were *saved*.

The Lord *will, and does,* fulfill all the words that He has caused to be spoken by His prophets. In ancient days and to us. Passing time does *not* dim blessings promised to us. He *is* mindful of us, of our circumstances, and our *time.* The right things will never come *too late.* We *will* be blessed. We *will* be saved. We will, and *do,* have light!

I once taught a Christmas Sunday school lesson where, before class, I taped a star on the wall of a classroom. It wasn't hidden and it wasn't small. But no one knew I put it there, so no one looked for it. As my lesson was ending and class time had run out, I asked who had noticed the star I taped on the wall. Not one hand went up. But just because they didn't notice it, didn't change the fact that it was there. In times of the unwanted and uncertain, it is easy to focus on all that is going wrong, or all that is *not* happening or changing. And even if we may not be noticing God, and the blessings and help that *is* there, it doesn't change the fact that they are.

I know the weight that comes from not knowing how or when things will work out. But where we don't find an ending to a trial quite yet, we find ease and added strength. Where we can't find answers to prayers quite yet, we find comfort and reassurance. Where we don't see promised blessings quite yet, we find love and help and continued guidance. No, maybe He doesn't come and take our situation away, and maybe He doesn't come in the way we were hoping and expecting, but light will always be there because Christ will always be here.

And like the star when Christ was born, and like the star in my classroom, and like the many, many ways He tries to get our attention every day, just because we may not see them, doesn't mean they are not there. Just because they may be different, doesn't mean that He is not there.

And like the star to the wise men and the shepherds, we will, *and do,* have light that guides us! We do, and will always have, Him. The light and life of the world. A light that *shineth in darkness.* A light that cannot be dimmed. And like the believers in 3 Nephi who need Christ in order to live, *so do we,* to truly live.

Seeing Yourself in . . .

The Boy Jesus at the Temple

Luke 2

Although there is a gap between His birth and Jesus being found as a boy in the temple, we can assume it would have been what happened to any Jewish boy His age. Jesus was Jewish and was raised practicing and participating in Jewish traditions, cultures, and beliefs. That absolutely implies that His childhood was spent actively learning, studying, and preparing as it was required of that by all Jewish boys. Jesus as a boy was well taught in the law and with the scriptures to prepare to reach age of accountability and adulthood, where they would then take on more and better responsibilities within their religious practices. In Jewish culture, age *thirteen* has always been that age. We can know that Jesus had a deep understanding of God.

Biblically, Jewish men were required to attend the religious celebrations surrounding the Feast of the Passover in Jerusalem, which is likely why Jesus and His family were there, celebrating and participating in their Jewish beliefs. Approaching thirteen, Jesus may have been preparing for, and in the process of, what we call today, a Bar Mitzvah. The title wasn't used back in biblical days, nor was it celebrated the same way, but that age has always been the law and practice to further their vocation and advance in status. *Bar* means "son" in Aramaic, and *Mitzvah* means "commandment" in Hebrew, it is when they become a "son of the commandment."

Which also means at that age, they will advance in status and finally participate in the observances of the Jewish faith. It's finally being able to be called up to do an *aliyah*, which is reciting a prayer before and after the Torah reading, as well as for the first time, allowed to finally read from the Torah itself. They will then be trusted as a witness and become obligated to bear his own responsibility and all the commandments of God. Before the age of thirteen and without a childhood of dedication to learning, they would not be ready or allowed to do those things. This is similar to boys in The Church of Jesus Christ of Latter-day Saints, reaching a certain age and understanding to receive the Aaronic Priesthood and then being able to have more responsibilities and new ways to participate, like pass the sacrament.

I find it so exciting to know that, of all the ages Jesus teaching in the temple as a boy could have happened, that it happened at the age of *twelve*. Although during preparation for Jewish boys it is not uncommon to *talk* to elders on teachings, it *is* worth pointing out that He was *teaching them* in the temple. Different, impressive, and significant to do as a young boy, absolutely nods to His path towards growing into our Savior. But also, significant to note that He was teaching *before* the age He was deemed ready—before He was even really able and allowed to do so. And with Joseph Smith Translation, we learn even underage and unfit, they were *hearing Him* and asking *Him* questions.

To participate in the celebration and feast of Passover, multitudes of people came from distant provinces in large companies and caravans, mostly for needed safety against violence. Scriptural wording of *"after the custom of the feast"* and *"fulfilled the days"* nods towards the celebration's duration, which was seven days, symbolic of the time that passed when their people fled for their freedom from the Egyptians up until the parting of the Red Sea. Mary and Joseph knowing somewhat of Who Jesus was to become because of prophesies and their angel, wise men, and shepherd experiences, Jesus being found in the temple teaching on His own, was further confirmation and further witness. Showing His love and dedication to both of His Fathers, He was coming into His own, learning and blossoming into who God intended Him to be.

Regardless of being raised a normal, mortal Jewish boy, it has always been within Jesus to be among us, to help our understanding, to grow in knowledge of our God, and to be our Savior.

An incredible truth lays within that sentence. But we can also see ourselves in another lesson we can pull from this experience. Investing to study, dedicating time to learning, *increasing in wisdom and stature* leads to growing into our own divinity. It leads to learning more about ourselves and who God wants us to become.

Finding Yourself in . . .

The Baptism of Jesus

Matthew 3, Mark 1, Luke 3 & John 1

Sometimes we get it skewed and backwards, repentance, that is. The word alone sometimes has this negative weight and a reminder of everything we are doing wrong. The adversary absolutely exploits and skews to get us to linger longer in that inaccurate perspective to get us to sit still, to stand still, to stop. He gets us to feel bad about our efforts so that we stop making them. But repentance isn't punishment, nor is it condemning. But the reality is, repentance is quite possibly the most optimistic and freeing thing there ever is! The *privilege* we have to change. To try again. To start again. Over and over. And *ohhh*, would it stink so bad if we couldn't. Repentance means all is *not* lost, it means things can change, it means *we* can change. We *can* improve. Because of the privilege to repent, to change, every passing second is a chance to turn it all around. We do not have to be who we were. We are not stuck; we are not stagnant. We are not living linear, this is not final, we are not done. It means we have a God of commas, not periods. Repentance isn't to condemn a sinner, but to encourage all of us to experience exactly the reason Jesus found worthy enough to allow Himself to be abused and killed.

John the Baptist's life's mission and great purpose was to speak and teach of such thing. Like all religious teachers in this day, they would be trained in the schools and authorized with an attained license from chief priests. They would wear certain clothing and robes and live a fine life within the church. John, however, did none of those things. Not in *their* ways, but God's ways. Wearing not fine linens and robes, but camel's hair and loin cloths. Not partaking of feasts, but eating locusts and honey. Not appearing in synagogues or temple courts, but retreating and staying in the wilderness. He spent many years away from men in preparation for what his life's mission was to be—preparing the way of the Lord and bringing people to the privilege of repentance and remission of sins. The ability and privilege of change, of improvement. Multitudes of people would travel out to him, confused if *he* was Christ himself, but always pointing and preparing them to One that is *"mightier than I* that *cometh."*

Nazareth continued to be the home for Jesus during the eighteen-year gap in the scriptures. He continued to increase in wisdom and knowledge and grow even more into His role of the Messiah. Emerging from Nazareth at the age of thirty, He reunited with His second cousin, John the Baptist, in the River of Jordan. Confused at his baptismal request, *"I have need to be baptized of thee. And comest thou to me?"* Although we are unsure how long it's been since they were together last, but perhaps also from spiritual dedication of seeking, John immediately recognizes Him as sinless. A perfect man was baptized by someone who was not. Setting an example, proving the importance of following a covenant path, and showing us that *there is more.* There is more to come, there is more to receive, there is more to take part in, bigger and better things are on this path. *He* is on this path.

Only a handful of times does God our Father speak in scripture, all of which have been pivotal moments for mankind, and *this* is one of them. God, in His humility and without any need for focus and attention on Himself, speaks of Jesus, *"This is my beloved son, hear him."* We have a biblical account of the Godhead—Christ in the water, Holy Ghost as a dove descending, and the voice of God, your Father, speaking. And He is *"well pleased."* But it also shows that God is mindful. He is aware of what we are doing.

"I indeed have baptized you with water: but he shall baptize you with the Holy Ghost." When I was confirmed a member at the age of 20, that was a physical difference for me. The contrast was *huge,* and it was real, and well surpassed, even *tripled,* the feeling I felt when I was actually baptized. Going your entire life to not have the gift of the Holy Ghost, twenty years of contrast, to then receiving it, it was night and day for me. It's been an anchor to me. But since 2009, doubt has come. A longing has come and pleadings for me to *feel* the Spirit has come. *I wish I felt the spirit more often than I do* has come to me. Maybe you, too? This account reinforces my anchor that the Holy Ghost actually has come to us. *But what if*—the Spirit *is* guiding and speaking and directing us *so seamlessly* because of the promise of it always being with us, that we don't even know what it's like to *not* have it? *What if*—we're so used to working with it for so long, we don't give it full credit? *What if*— we unconsciously overlook it and take it for granted because it's ingrained in us so well—just like He promised. How beautiful that is, to have it part of us like that.

I'm good at unconsciously limiting our limitless God. I subconsciously tell myself *how* the Spirit should come to me; *I* tell myself *how* the Spirit should feel. I put this box around it all, and when it's not in big obvious ways, I say the Spirit is not there. Cue the longings and the pleadings.

But although I may not *recognize* the Holy Ghost as often as I would like, it doesn't change the reality that it *really is* always with us and participating and working. The consistent, constant, subtle ways—small ways, unnoticeable ways. How beautiful it is, to experience His promise so smoothly and seamlessly.

I wonder how life could blossom if we stripped down some layers of second-guessing and standing still, and took confidence in the resources and promises He has given us? I wonder how different our life could be if we took greater confidence in being a *confirmed* member and moved forward knowing God's promises do not fail us. To move forward knowing God does not fail us. Knowing that following Jesus down the covenant path does not fail us. What a *thrill* it is to keep moving forward through it all. Seeing it all unfold. Life blossoming in new ways, His ways.

How beautiful that is. Simply to be part of it all.

Finding Yourself in . . .

Jesus in the Wilderness

Matthew 4 & Luke 4

Immediately after His baptism and the heavens opening, Jesus was *driven* by the *Spirit* into the wilderness to be with God. He purposely withdrew from people and the distractions of His community to better learn of, and from, His Father. Weeks and weeks of seclusion and fasting to learn and to listen. As we know at the end of this forty-day experience, Christ goes and teaches in the synagogue where He finally, and publicly, speaks of who He really is. "*I am He,*" He will say. "*This day is this scripture fulfilled.*" *I am the fulfilment of this prophesy of Isaiah.* Christ leaves His forty days of temptation from the adversary to seek out His disciples. Our Savior of the world leaves from this experience ready to begin His work and to fulfil His mission on earth.

And knowing what would shortly come to be, not just with Christ, but for all of us, the adversary came wearing many different hats of temptations. In the wilderness, he went to Jesus trying to sell, distract, and alter Jesus's direction with all that is appealing here in this life. Physical appetites, materialism, popularity, vanity, *power*. Although He was sinless, Jesus was capable of sinning; such effort of temptation would not have been happening if there was no possibility of His yielding and the possible derailing of His calling by the adversary. Christ was hungered, He was physically weak, and the tempter strategically exploited the appeals of the human side of Christ. From the high place on the temple, to the high place of a mountain, Christ was shown visuals from a bird's eye view of all the wealth, treasure, and bounty of this world, and told to *take*. *"All these things will I give thee, if thou wilt fall down and worship me."* In the wilderness, Satan tried to skew, distract, and get Jesus to doubt who He was and to abandon the love, relationship, and calling from God. Forty relentless days in Jesus's weakness, feeling so deeply all the lures of men, the adversary showed Him *everything* wanted by man in desperate attempts to stop Him, to put an end to all that He will do. Jesus created a bread called manna for the Israelites when they wandered in the wilderness for forty *years*, the adversary tempted Jesus to do the same for Himself to fulfill His bodily needs easily. But the adversary was not the master over Jesus. Christ could have saved Himself from the cross, He could have fed and nourished His famished body in the wilderness. But He didn't.

So what could have caused Jesus to not only turn away but leave the wilderness with such a resolve to finally start His work and put in motion all that would unfold?

You.

Saving you. Getting you back. Giving you everything. He was motivated, strengthened, and dedicated *to you*. Him creating this world, Him coming here, the miracles, the lessons, the temptations, struggles, sacrifices, His death, it was always about and for you. And He never lost sight of that. He never lost sight *of you*.

And with all that, we also are given a template on how to better recognize the lures of the adversary in our own life and pursuits. When we are becoming a new person, when we are making the time and effort, when we are fulfilling our greater purpose, Satan absolutely will try to lure us away and convince us that his ways are better than the path we are on. He comes to us in our weak times, in our vulnerable times, and exploits it, disfigures it, skews it. He asked the savior, *"If thou be the Son of God, command this stone that it be made bread," "If thou be the Son of God, cast thyself down from hence."* Which come back again to Him while Jesus was nailed to the cross, *"If thou be the king of the Jews, save thyself . . .if thou be the Christ . . ."* The adversary wasn't asking those question for proof of *who* Jesus was, He knew *who* He was and what He is capable of doing. The adversary wasn't trying to learn more of Him; he was trying to stop it, trying to get Christ to doubt *Himself.* He gets in our mind with similar *if* questions to retreat, and second-guess, telling us that we should be different, or that things should be different. *If* you were better at *this,* if you were more of *that, if* you were different, *if* you had more of, *if only . . .*

All good things come from God, including thoughts and feelings. Good could not exist without God. Every feeling of happiness, every feeling of comfort, hope, forgiveness, feelings of strength, of laughter, of lifted weight, protection, change, guidance, only exists because God exists. It is from and because of God.

Every thought we have, even if fleeting, that tells us we can make it through another day, to just hold out a little longer and to keep going. Moments when we think, *Ah, okay*! Those moments that we can't really explain, moments when our hearts beat just a little bit faster. Goosebumps moments. Moments when we feel our eyes water and we know if we blink, tears will fall. Moments when we feel our souls jolt and dance within us. That is us experiencing and feeling God. It is God participating in our personal lives showing us that He is there.

In contrast, it is the adversary that makes us feel anything that is *not good,* thoughts and feelings included. If it is not good, it is not of God. If it is not God, it is not truth, it is not reality.

Feelings of, *I'm not worth it, why bother, I'm the exception, I'm a bad person, I'm not worthy to pray, it is hopeless, I am helpless, all is lost,* is not good. Therefore, not God, therefore, not truth, therefore not reality. Even when our lives need correcting, it is never done in a way to discourage us, but to build us up and motivate us. With correction coming from God, it comes coupled with reassurance and hope and comfort, rather than the contrast of shame or hopelessness. Anything that brings us away from God is the tempter's itinerary, trying to lure us away from all that is different than what we have and who we are. Jesus going to the wilderness *not* to confront Satan, but to seek and commune with His father shows us temptation and the adversary will come to us simply as a result of being here on earth. Just think of how he got Adam and Eve to hide and retreat in the garden from the only ones that could help them. His attempts all intend to get us to stop, to slow, to retreat, to alter direction away from growing into the successful, thriving person God intended us to become all along. During Jesus's time with Satan, *"angels ministered unto him."* During our time in our wilderness that we walk through, and our time spent with the adversary, He sends us help. We do not struggle alone nor without help and guidance and unseen strength.

It was always about You.

It will always be about saving you. Getting you back. And giving you everything. And He'll never lose sight of that. He'll never lose sight *of you.*

Finding Yourself in . . .

The Miracle of the Fish

Matthew 4, Luke 5 & Mark 1

I will always say passing time is one of the hardest things I am called to go through. Time keeps passing with little or no change and your optimism and faith have been worn thin and exhausted and you are sure that your efforts are in vain. A full night, a full season, a full chance at success and progress, has passed by Peter, and not a single fish has come. He was *washing his nets*, he was done, he was stopping, he was out of time and there was nothing left to do that he hadn't already done. And with all that time and effort, he still came up fruitless. I know what Simon, turned Peter, must have been feeling because I have been Peter so many times. Exhausted, thin, discouraged, and absolutely I am mad from effort and having to move on with little or no change, having to move on with *not one fish*.

After forty days of no edible substance and being hounded by Satan, Jesus does not leave with confusion or doubt, but with drive and focus to finally, and publicly, put into motion His work as our Savior. *This* is when it is time to really begin His work and to fulfil His mission on earth. Jesus leaves from the wilderness of temptations and goes directly to the synagogue and speaks of who He really is. *"I am,"* He will say. *"This day is this scripture fulfilled."* I am the fulfilment of this prophesy of Isaiah. He leaves His forty days with the adversary and directly seeks out His disciples.

Jesus returns to Galilee, and He is returning in *power.* The *power of the Spirit* is with Him. And not only does He return with power and the Spirit, but He returns *anointed* by God. Anointed means Christ Messiah. He returns as the *Christ!* *"The spirit of the lord is upon me because he hath anointed me."* He returns as God's "personal representative in *all* things pertaining to the salvation of mankind."[1] And with all that, the learned in the synagogue only saw Him as a son of a carpenter. Despite returning as the anointed Christ with great power and spirit, they were so upset with Him and what He was claiming to be and what He was teaching, they *"thrust him out."* And not just out of the synagogue, they drove Him out of the city and led Him *"unto the brow of a hill . . .that they might cast him down."*

But *"passing through the midst of them, he went his way"* and He kept teaching, and then found Simon turned Peter and Andrew. We can gather that Peter wasn't *just* a fisherman, he was a *skilled* fisherman that had enough success to have turned it into a business of sort. We know this because he had multiple ships with people that worked for or with him, which means, he knew what he was doing.

Jesus was teaching on one of Peter's smaller boats. After His words, Jesus yelled out to a very skilled-in-the-art fisherman, Peter, while he was washing his nets. While he was packing up, giving up, as the night came to an end with defeat. *"Let down your nets"* was not something I would have wanted to hear. All that passing time, the entire night, consumed with expert effort, and who is to tell me to simply *let down* my net? A *carpenter*? No, thanks. Would I have responded that way? I know my blunt self would have absolutely said something expressing my pride and

---

1. Bible Dictionary, "Anointed One."

logic. *Already did, thanks. I know what I'm doing. I know how to do my job.*

I am Peter, not just with passing time and no fruit for my efforts, but being asked by Him to do something that doesn't make any logical sense. I am learning to respond more often the way Peter did, *"Nevertheless . . . I will."* Despite what doesn't make sense, despite my fatigue, despite passing time, *"I will."* And what happens when we do that? *Magnification.* Both our ships filled and sinking, kind of magnification. Everything that He asks of us will always lead to something much better than what we had in mind, even if on our way to them it's on a path longer than anticipated, or an unwanted or unexpected path. Jesus didn't ask anything different than what they weren't doing already themselves. The difference was, they did it *with* Christ. *Christ is the difference.*

Simon Peter fell down at Jesus's knees, *"Depart from me for I am a sinful man." "Fear not, from henceforth thou shalt catch men."* Men. People. Souls. Fish are nothing. But to Peter, what was more important than his entire career, trade and life's support? *Him.* This is your reminder that you have *much* greater things that lay ahead. There is so much more than what's *right here.*

They brought their ships back to land, *"forsook all,"* abandoned and renounced it all, straightway leaving their nets, *"and followed Him."* Because *with Him* leads to greater things, greater magnifications. And they're not just leaving behind nets and boats, they're leaving behind everything, they're leaving behind a different way of life, *their* old ways, old habits, traditions, their way of thinking. I was turning 21 when I learned about that difference that Christ really does make. But *following Him* absolutely is one of the most intimate things we could ask someone. Intimate because it's completely personal, it's a person in their entirety. Extended the invitation to be baptized is asking them to change almost everything—not just what they do, but even the way they think. It's a complete transformation of their entire life, which created their entire being of existence on this earth that they know of. When we ask someone to get baptized, we're asking them to leave behind or change years of habits, many traditions, and sometimes family—their parents, their siblings . . . friends. I had to leave behind all of them to *leave my net*.

It's an invitation to hit a restart button, but sometimes it's restarting and resetting things they love and will miss. It's overcoming, relearning, rewiring, and a deep, deep reconstruction of themselves. It can be overwhelming to gain a testimony, you know? Change is extremely scary when you have such a long history and contrast of life filled with decisions, plans, paths, and dreams that you're learning are completely out of sorts with the Lord's will. Thinking of everything you need to be doing better with or stop doing altogether is exhausting in itself. You have racing thoughts of fear of what this could mean for your life now and how unexpected and unknown and scary whatever the next steps are, because you have no idea what even happens next.

Nevertheless . . . I will.

Jesus called every single one of His disciples with, "*come and see*." Because "*thou shalt see greater things.*" Greater. Those in the synagogue and Peter in the boat were both learned and skilled in their ways, yet one drove Him away and one drove close to Him. One was prideful and dismissive, and one was humble. One stayed in their own ways with their own wisdom, and one received *greater things*. The difference was one did it *with* Christ. Even with passing time and fatigued efforts and sacrifice and redirection, *Christ is the difference.*

"*Thou shalt catch men*" means Jesus has something bigger in mind for us. In all areas of our life. Something of greater importance and greater meaning. Fish are nothing. If He wanted fish, He could get fish.

He wants you.

So *come. And see.* See the *greater things.*

Seeing Yourself in . . .

Water Turning to Wine

John 2

When I met the missionaries passing on the street, I listened to them only at first because I felt bad my friend had been so rude to them. I didn't want God to be real because that would mean I would have to change. I didn't want to change. I loved who I was and what I was doing, and I didn't want anything or anyone to change that. If I changed, I wouldn't be me anymore. That's what I thought. At 21, I had this idea of how my life would go because I was in charge to pick my life for myself. I feel safer and I'm more comfortable when I am in charge.

It shouldn't be, but giving your life to God is hard. Because giving it to the most powerful Being to ever exist does not mean we always get what we want. If we give it to Him, what is He going to do with it? It could mean uncharted, unmarked, and unwanted paths. It could mean giving up comfort or passions, and unexpected outcomes. If I am in charge and if things go *my* way, then I'm able to better control unmet expectations and disappointments.

But life, and this miracle of water turning into wine, isn't about getting what we want. It's about becoming something different, something new, something *better*.

The Law of Moses required ceremonial cleansing, so these water pots that Jesus used were extremely common. They were filled with running or living water because it was considered pure. They were always made of stone because the vessels for purifying could not be subject to corruption and become impure; clay and pottery in ancient times would however, through absorption. This "living water" would be stored in these large stone water jars, which would function like a reservoir to hold this ritually clean water, then later it would be used for purification to symbolically become spiritually clean and holy. Absolutely never would these be used to drink out of, nor would storing any other liquid in it even be a thought.

"Woman," a term of high respect in those days, *"mine hour is not yet come."* In other words, *I haven't started my formal mission yet.* I'm not sure that Mary knew what Jesus would have specifically done to help in this situation because this was His first recorded miracle. She didn't quite know what He was truly capable of doing until the miracles and events that would follow this one. But this shows that she knew enough of what was promised of who He would be, His ability to help, and do that which we cannot do on our own.

One of the most powerful things we can ever learn for ourselves is exactly what Mary showed. *I don't know what He will do with it, but I know that He will be there for me to help make it better.*

We all know they ran out of wine, and we all know that traditionally the best wine was served first. But how truthful it is, that with Him, something better is possible and is coming. And how profoundly symbolic to think what was used for purification, making one holy, is what Jesus used for His first recorded miracle that started His mission as our Savior. The Messiah's first public miracle and it's one of purification and holiness and *change*.

How fun to think it could also be symbolic that Jesus is literally filling something that is practiced because of the Law of Moses, when He Himself fulfills the actual Law of Moses. Filling, and then changing, replacing, water to wine symbolically representing the change and the replacing of old ways and old laws to new ones. To His. How beautiful to realize that just a few days earlier, Satan tempted Jesus in the wilderness to provide for His impoverished, fasting body, and didn't. And now here He is, providing to supply a luxury for others because of His deep love and dedication for us.

Jesus left the wilderness and went directly to the synagogue to, for the first time publicly, say who He is. And now has the time come to show who He is. And what does He do? He changes water into wine. The best wine they had tasted. The change is that to something better, something that was known for joy, celebration, and covenant blessings. It's a transformation into the best that has ever been and could ever be.

We already talk about John the Baptist dedicating his life to teaching the power and privilege of repentance, of change. And here Jesus is, with His first public miracle, demonstrating exactly that. The power and ability to change, to improve. And how fitting it is for Peter and Andrew who just left behind their old ways and just at the start of being and doing things differently. A privilege and gift that can only come from and because of Jesus. Doing what Jesus did to the water, to them, to us—a transformation into someone better with a life's change that will lead to a life that is better.

I may not have wanted the change, but I did change, and I still am changed, because that is what happens when Christ becomes a reality to you; you change because then you want to, and because then, you *can*. And it has been a blossoming transformation of purification and holiness. I am not who I ever once have been. But my gosh, am I *better*. Like water to wine, He changes us into something significant and precious, something of greater worth. Continuously coming into who I was meant to be all along, and *what a feeling*. Could you trade that?

There have been too many times to even begin to keep track of all the things I would ask and plead for, and not get. Most of which, I was given was unexpected and even unwanted. But it was everything I was resistant to, everything I was fighting against, that has brought me to *everything* I have now. My favorite things have come because I didn't get what I originally wanted.

So no, this miracle and this life isn't about getting what we want because that's not what living here on earth is about. Mary didn't demand specifically for Jesus to make more wine. She just knew turning to Him, He would be there with the best way to help and do that which we could not do ourselves. As we continue to turn to Jesus, we'll be profoundly grateful things didn't go our own way because we will find a better version of ourselves, living our best life, experiencing things we didn't even know were available to us, with new knowledge and talents we wouldn't have wanted to go any further in life without.

We may not know what He's going to do when we turn to Him, but one day we will pause and look around, and we'll see where we are, what we've gained along the way, the something different and the something much better. And we'll wonder why we hadn't done better all along turning to Him. Experiencing the power and privilege of change.

Your *hour* has *come*. Turn to Him and be *filled* with living water and allow Him to do that which we cannot do alone. Allow Him to take you somewhere better. Allow Him to replace the old and transform to new. Something better is possible and is coming.

In verse thirteen starts His forward movement of His mission right when the *Jew's Passover was at hand*. Exactly three years from this moment, starting His mission, the Lamb of God will be back at this time of Passover, but to finish His mission. To present Himself to be sacrificed that we might be saved because of His deep love and dedication for you.

Seeing Yourself in . . .

Nicodemus

John 3

Iwas raised Catholic. My grandmother was ordained a Carmelite, a higher order within the religion. It was a pretty big deal. My mom and aunt went to an all-girls catholic school with nuns and Latin classes. I grew up going to church often, even bible summer camp, like most other New Yorkers in my area. At a young age, I even have vivid memories of midnight mass and prepping for my confirmation in seventh grade. The older I grew, the more our efforts and beliefs turned into an obligatory attendance only on Easter and Christmas, and after my last milestone in junior high, there was no reason to go back because we got all our boxes checked. I grew up with knowledge of Jesus, but what I was supposed to do with any of it, I had no idea nor desire. They were nothing more than stories of someone's life, no different than the story of a neighbor's life, both of which I didn't care to learn more about.

I thought religion was something people only turned to when something was going wrong in their life. Religion and the idea of God was only there to serve as a mental comfort to those lacking or struggling or missing. Ever since my seventh grade catholic confirmation, I left behind all religious ways and gave not one moment thinking of the idea of something bigger than me. If you asked me, I was never seeking nor searching nor lacking. I was content, I was happy; I felt satisfied with myself, and I didn't need anything or anyone to alter that.

Meeting the missionaries after graduating college was not orchestrated by me, but simply a passing on the sidewalk. I didn't need them or their supposed God. But feeling bad for how my friend had poorly treated them, I listened out of obligation. Absolutely, I invited them back to learn more because it was incredibly fascinating to me to learn of others and what makes them do the things that they do. I would have them come and I would listen just out of curiosity, I just had so many questions. The more I saw from them, the more questions I had. I always masked my growing curiosity with trying to prove the missionaries wrong, that nothing would happen with my pathetic and awkward efforts because it was all just in their heads. But regardless of not wanting it to change me, others noticed before I ever did. They noticed a different countenance. I would get asked often what I was doing differently because I looked *good*. But nothing ever clicked and terrified me more than when I found myself *defending* the Church, saying to others, "Well, actually they don't believe that. They believe this." Small progress all stemmed from so many questions that I had, trying to grasp it all, trying to see if I could even puzzle piece it into this life that I loved. This life that I felt was always satisfying and fulfilling. My first realization of change came from defending. That, for me, is what put in motion better efforts, better intentions, better seeking; all of it leading to a better life with better purpose and better direction with Him.

A great debate—Nicodemus. He almost always comes with a question to ask of ourselves and of others, which side are you on? Was he a seeker on his way to conversion? Or was he a coward who couldn't bring himself to be all in and fell short? Either way you land, there is something important to learn for ourselves on both sides. Nicodemus sat in a powerful sect among the Pharisees as a *ruler of the Jews*, a member of the Sanhedrin. Jesus called Nicodemus "the teacher of Israel," a term indicating that he was recognized as the master religious teacher in Israel. He was well educated in the laws with years of training and studying for his ranking, his entire life was around these certain ways and certain teachings and grew to be a high example of them to others. Most Pharisees saw Jesus as a threat to their position of power and control over the Jews; most of their efforts, as we know, were seeking to destroy, not learn from. Nicodemus sought after Jesus though. He was moved by genuine inquiry and perhaps a spiritual pull and Nicodemus acted on it. Meeting with the Savior at night likely because to be seen when sitting in his position of a leader posed great risk. Potential excommunication and even death if he spoke out to loudly. But Nicodemus wasn't ready to sacrifice for whom he has yet to learn of. Can we blame him? To Nicodemus, prior to meeting with Him one on one, Jesus was just a great teacher. And prior to my questions, Jesus was just a neighbor with stories. It's hard to be willing to sacrifice and change inside out for someone we have yet to learn of who they really are.

"*Rabbi*," Nicodemus addresses Christ—*my master*—in other words, I know that you have "*come from God.*" Already setting himself apart from other Pharisees because they did *not* believe that Jesus Christ was sent by God. They all witnessed the same miracles as each other, but Nicodemus was in tune enough to recognize the light of Christ, that is within us all, ignite and see it differently than they. Jesus repeatedly teaches on being *born again*, to become new, to become different, a spiritual rebirth with the Savior of the world and of our souls. In effect, Jesus is inviting Nicodemus to go to Him, to be renewed, revived, restored, and spiritually to become His. God "*sent not his Son into the world to condemn the world; but that the world through him might be saved.*" *Save*! Jesus repeatedly teaches to believe. If we believe, we will *not perish*. If we believe we will have "*everlasting life.*" If we do not, we shall *not see life.*

There's definite irony when we look at the teachings Nicodemus received from Jesus— following Jesus, believing

Him, and allowing Jesus to change us. And did he? We don't know for sure. Some say it was pride, or ignorance in his lack of immediate understanding. Maybe it was. But if that were the case, do we not all have a little bit of Pharisee within ourselves? A little spiritual pride or showmanship where we think we've got it all together or at least we want it to appear like we do? Here may be a man who struggled in the same ways we do, a little stuck in our ways, perhaps little hints of self-righteousness. But at the same time, he still went to and found Jesus. We sometimes struggle being like the Pharisees, but deep in our hearts we want to follow the Lord. Is Nicodemus showing us that we, too, can break away from our Pharisee like qualities?

So, was he among those who "*loved darkness rather that light*"? Did he not have courage to face criticism? Did his comfortable life of power hold him back? Was his superior training blinding him? Was he rationalizing and rejecting? Did he love the praise of man more than the praise of God? Was he not keeping his spark of interest alive? I personally give Nicodemus grace when he finds confusion and curiosity in his questions to Jesus, as it does in fact challenge his personal life of upbringing and knowledge, as it did mine. Not rejecting but pondering and processing. I do see myself in him in this moment, asking and learning something new and different than what we were originally taught and based our whole lives around. Nicodemus may not have *immediately* left his net, but neither did I. But it did lead him to *defend*, as did I. Defending was another step in my conversion, which was very much a process. Was it the same for him?

In front of his fellow Pharisees who were just talking and accusing of deception, Nicodemus does speak up, "*Doth our law judge any man, before it hear him, and know what he doeth?*" He is not only defending but trying to save, buying Jesus more time. Nicodemus is requesting that Jesus not be condemned without a hearing. "*Art thou also of Galilee?*" I wonder if the Pharisees noticed a difference in his countenance like others did with me? Was that another step in his conversion or was it too little and not enough of what he actually could have done?

The pain that is attached to Nicodemus's story is the pain of the "could haves." What could have been if he did follow Jesus sooner than when he potentially may have? Did he fall short, did He miss out? This for certain, Jesus could have made for him something greater than he ever could have on His own. Greater than the worldly praise, tasseled garments, and high position. Perhaps Nicodemus could have taken the place of Matthew as an apostle. Could you imagine the impact Nicodemus could have had with his talents and conversion? Could you imagine the mass amount of people he could have been able to connect with as an example and pioneer for them to follow behind? Perhaps the saddest words in life are *it might have been.*

We do not hear of Nicodemus again until after Jesus was crucified, which could imply that nothing significant worth noting for him had happened in-between. No big awakening to the truthfulness to change his ways, no big ah-ha moment to change his current life. But Nicodemus was there during Jesus's passing. He was there during Passover week, a particularly high day for Jews under the Law. Nicodemus had important obligations elsewhere. He was not preparing himself for this high Sabbath by making sure he was meticulously and ceremonially clean, but by choosing to deliberately make himself ceremonially unclean by preparing a dead body for the grave. Nicodemus served as a mortician for the Savior, bringing one hundred pounds of aloes and myrrh and preparing His body for burial. We see a very different Nicodemus, who was once afraid to come to Jesus in the day, is now there, regardless of what others thought of him or his reputation as a Pharisee.[1]

We don't know what happens to Nicodemus after this to bring us to any definitive side of where he was as a convert or a coward. We don't know if he went to the Savior at His death fully converted, ready to serve His master, or if he arrived filled with guilt and regret and did what little he could that was left to try and help with His anguish. This much we do know, He was there

---

1. See John 19:39.

doing the most sacred acts when everything was on the line for him to lose, and all of our efforts and sacrifices are honored and magnified no matter where we are on the path. And this much we do know, once we have an encounter with the Savior, our lives will undoubtably never be the same.

John is the only one who writes about Nicodemus, and he leaves us hanging on the fate of how the rest of his life unfolded. Did what happened at the cross lead to his change? Did he retreat and stay put? Perhaps the greater lesson to learn comes from not knowing. An open ending so we can see with him the choice in ourselves of what to do with this Jesus who is called Christ. Exposure to truth is not enough, it centers on the courage to follow and believe Jesus. And are we? Is there part of us that needs to overcome tendencies of a Pharisee? Are we acting upon the knowledge being offered us? Is there a part of us that stays a little longer in fear over faith? Do we contemplate our worldly possessions and perception to others more than we should?

"I ask of you . . .have ye spiritually been born of God? Have ye received his image in your countenances?"² We do not have to live in the pain of the could haves. Because of Jesus, we can and should be born again, we can and should be renewed and revived, we can and should change into something different, something undoubtably better than what we can do for ourselves. When we move forward to believe and follow, we will be brought back to the Savior of the World and of our souls and be called His. *"Have ye experienced this mighty change in your hearts?"* How will your story end? What will you do with this Jesus who is called Christ? Are we going to let what happened on the cross change us?

---

2. Alma 5:14

Finding Yourself in . . .

The Woman at the Well

John 4

I think of the man with palsy who had himself some good group of friends to lift him up and help him to move forward to where he needed to go. That story comes with a little bit of a sting because there were so many times where I wish I'd had that, but I didn't. Getting baptized caused a long season of loneliness for me. With family angry in silence, friends who left, new areas in new states where I didn't know anyone, and where my new community people who were so turned off by me. I had eight years of living by myself with no roommates, no one could walk in on me crying in the depths of struggle. What then? Who then?

And what of times not only of physical loneliness, but times when I felt alone spiritually? Unanswered prayers. Unfulfilled fasts. Passing time. Unwanted and uncharted paths. Times when I have pleaded to feel the Spirit and I just didn't in that moment. We all have these moments when we feel alone, literally and/or emotionally. And we are certain that no matter our efforts, there's no way to properly express to anyone what we're really feeling. Challenges are obviously hard on its own but feeling by yourself in them is what makes them even more difficult. Times when I felt lost, and out of sight of God. Alone. Unnamed and unimportant.

As history goes, we know for centuries the Samaritans hated the Jews, and at the time of Christ, it had developed into a most intense hatred. So much so that Jews would completely avoid a direct route from Judea to Galilee and purposely travel a much longer route out of the way, just to keep their distance from Samaria. But it wasn't just that they hated and avoided them, to the orthodox Jews, the Samaritans were considered more unclean than a gentile of any other nationality. If a Jew even ate food prepared by a Samaritan, it was as great of an offense as it was to eat the flesh of swine.

Not much more could have been stacked against the woman at the well. A Samaritan alone would have been pushed far from the actions and attention of Jesus. But she was also a female in a society where women were both demeaned and disregarded. So not only is she hated and unclean regardless of gender but degraded is also added. Her list of offenses continues to increase against her as her actions add a history of sin and adultery to even have the other women in her community and social class look down upon her as well.

Maybe it didn't make sense to go to a well alone at the heat of the day because it was always done in groups of people later when it was cooler. But seeing that it was highly likely that the women at the well was outcast in her community and by other women, we can understand potentially why she had gone alone when she did. Maybe the woman at the well, as she intentionally planned to be alone drawing water at noon day, was thinking of the weight of her burdens. Maybe she was thinking about how she wished she could change things and how she wished things were different. I don't doubt she needed a step away from her life of shame, judgment, and poor decisions. Perhaps she was thinking of how she was only there because she wanted to be alone. Or maybe because she deserved to be alone. We don't know who she is, she's not named in the scriptures, but how much we can relate to her. Times when it seems we're disregarded, alone, and out of sight. Unnamed, unimportant, undeserving, unfit, unclean, unworthy.

Then comes Jesus on that shorter course. Then comes Jesus, a Jew, on the direct but the unexpected, uncharted, and even unsafe path. Pulled in that direction by inspiration and duty; "*he must needs go,*" are His words. It's interesting and beautiful when I think of all the experiences of healing and forgiveness that came from Jesus were most times initiated by the ones going to Jesus and asking themselves. But here we see Jesus already at the well and it is Him that speaks to her first. "*Give me to drink.*" Jesus, waiting and willing.

Hesitant and shocked, understandably so, she asks Jesus *how.* How is it that you're turning to *me*? How is it that you are in need of someone like me?

Being at Jacob's well, highly esteemed for its unfailing source of water, their exchanges back and forth lead to profound truths about living waters more powerful than even that. "*Who it is that saith to thee, Give me to drink; thou wouldest have asked of him, and he would have given thee living water.*" Responding with, if you knew who I was, you would be asking me for a drink. Living water, blessings that flow from heaven to us through Christ that are cleansing and sustaining. "*Art thou greater than our father Jacob, which gave us this well?*" Or we could reword for our lives, are you actually greater than what good is already here? Jesus answered her with truths and promises that "*whosoever drinketh of the water that I give him shall never thirst*" because the water the He gives is from a well of "*everlasting life.*" Just as water is essential for our physical life, His living water is essential for our eternal life, our salvation, to never thirst because it is all sustaining and never ending. His living water that he freely offers to all—"*if anyone thirsts, let him come to me and drink*"—be filled, be sustained, and be nourished by Him.

Anyone? Even someone with so much stacked against them? Even the unnamed? The unworthy? Maybe as she heard of the extended promise that she can have this unfailing living water, she was thinking how all of her sins disqualify her. Could the feeling of condemnation have been whispering the lie that she is the exception for who she is or what she's done?

Jesus is all knowing, He knows everything about her. He knows that she has "*had five husbands*" as well as someone else at that moment who wasn't her husband. And yet, He still offers to her. He knew her, He knew her secrets, the depths of her soul, and He stills sits with her, He still teaches her. He stays with her for *two days*. Her encounter with Jesus is the longest between the Messiah than any other individual in the gospel of John. Jesus declared Himself to her that He is the Messiah, "*I that speak unto thee am he.*" There were multiple times Christ chose not to respond with who He is, and yet the Samaritan woman was worth telling this incredible truth to.

In nearly every way, Jesus is an anomaly; He deviates from what is standard or expected, He chooses to love the least lovable people, and He chooses to use the least likely characters. She who had neither title, nor position, nor formal education, nor a stainless past, becomes a witness of the Messiah. A marginalized, sinful, outcast, unclean Samaritan female of a despised race was deserving of Him. Not only does she have an intimate one-on-one encounter with Christ, but also receives revelation and eternal salvation. She was experiencing the living water welling up inside of her that moved her to renewal. No longer was she paralyzed by her past or by fear or shame or judgment, as she runs into the city telling those who looked down on her to "*come, see.*" And they did! "*They went out of the city, and came unto him . . . And many of the Samaritans of that city believed on him for the saying of the woman, which testified.*" Her actions and testimony bring a *city* of people to Jesus. And "*many more*" believed.

It's easy to be consumed with guilt and regret from what we are lacking and all that is wrong, but maybe it was those things that led her to be with Jesus. The weight and loneliness we feel from who we are or what we may have done, are hard realities. But although the effects of feeling those things are real, being hidden from and out of sight of God is not.

We may feel alone and burdened. We may feel disenfran-chised and think we are the exception. We may spend a lot of time in the sun alone at our wells, but regardless of what and where, Jesus will and does travel forbidden, uncharted paths to get to us. On purpose. Even, and especially, when everyone else may fail us. He meets us where we are and teaches and renews. He comes to us because He doesn't lose sight of us. Regardless of what we have done or haven't done, regardless of if we are tire-lessly trying to do what's right or on a long road of shortcomings and sins, He comes to us. And He stays with us. And although they are unnamed in the scripture, He knows them. He knows the depths of our soul and still His invitation to drink from His living water and experience His love and power to be saved is for *anyone* who thirsts. And what we think is a painful moment alone with a weight we wouldn't know how to explain to anyone else, could turn into an intimate one-on-one moment with the Savior, if, like the woman at the well, we are willing to listen and if we are willing to be taught.

The unworthy and unnamed are deserving of Him who is unfailing. Because of exactly who she was and what she did, we know that we can be anything and still be worth it to Him. Because Jesus went to her, He will come to us. Because Jesus offered Himself to her, He offers Himself to us. Because Jesus cleansed and renewed her, He will cleanse and revive us. Because He used her as a tool for His work, He is in need of you, as well. And in our times of doubt that He would ever want to spend time with us, let us take His counsel, *believe me.*

Jesus *is* here, waiting and willing.

Finding Yourself in . . .

The Man with Unclean Spirits

Luke 6

As resistant as I am to not write about the miracle of healing in this experience, there's also another incredibly powerful truth that lies here that deserves attention.

Jesus went into Capernaum, which is the north end of Galilee, on the Jewish Sabbath, which is Saturday, and the first thing they did was enter into the synagogue and Jesus taught. "*They were astonished at his doctrine,*" because Jesus taught differently than "*the scribes,*" the religious leaders and teachers who interpreted the gospel for Jews. And as we know, in the synagogue was the man with an "*unclean, evil spirit.*" Which is interesting to note, that Jesus's first public confrontation and defeat with the powers and influence of evil, takes place in a place of worship for the people of God. And doesn't the evil spirit *testify* of Christ! The evil spirits testify *of* Christ and *to* Christ! "*I know who thou art, the holy one of God.*"

Satan and the third of the hosts of heaven that followed him, do not have a veil over their memory like we do. They know Christ, they know what His purpose is and they know what

He'll be doing. Like Satan with Jesus in the wilderness asking all of those *if* questions, he wasn't asking those questions for proof of who Jesus was. He wasn't trying to learn more of Him, he was trying to derail Him. The adversary, those evil forces in this world, they know who we are. They know what we are trying to do and work towards. And absolutely they will be here to try and stop us. Absolutely they will try to distract, skew, confuse, and destroy.

"Leave us alone; what business is it of yours what we do, thou Jesus of Nazareth? art thou come to destroy us?" Are you really going to ruin our opportunity to dictate and influence people?

Jesus rebuked them to be silent, to depart—and they did obey, obligated to obey Jesus's single command to leave. There was no great fight, no showdown, no battle, no going back and forth, just a single command. *"The unclean spirit had torn him, and cried with a loud voice, he came out of him."* They left screaming loudly by tearing and throwing the man around to the ground. But with the voice of His single command, they left. And it could not be more apparent that Jesus's word provokes Satan's wrath because Jesus, His kingdom and His followers, absolutely are the most significant threat to what Satan is trying to accomplish— derailing and destroying our potential and our purpose to receive the greater things.

Amazed is the word that was used. Those in the synagogues wondered in amazement, *"What thing is this? . . . for with authority commandeth he even the unclean spirits, and they do obey him."* Here we see Jesus for the first time publicly show that He is more powerful, not just when the adversary came against Himself like in the wilderness, but in *our* lives, too. Christ is more powerful, and we have that power, we have power over the adversary. So, learning to recognize his evil spirits and his snares holds important weight for us to exercise our power that we do in fact have over Satan to cast him out.

What has been helpful for me recognizing God is to better recognize the adversary. All good things come from God, including thoughts and feelings. Every feeling of happiness, every feeling of comfort, hope, forgiveness, feelings of strength, of lifted weight, protection, change, guidance, only exists because God exists. Us feeling the Spirit is us experiencing God, that is the tool He uses. It is from and because of God. Every thought we have, even if fleeting, that tells us we can make it through another day, to just hold out a little longer and to keep going. Moments when we think, *ah, okay!* Those moments that we can't really explain, moments when our hearts beat just a little bit faster. Although I am struggling, I laughed today. That is good. That could not have happened if God was not real. Me laughing is me experiencing God.

In contrast, this should make it a little easier to recognize the adversary. Anything that is *not* good, thoughts and feelings included, is not God, it is not how God communicates to us. If it is not good, it is not God. If it is not from God, it is not truth, it is not reality. Feelings of, *I'm not worth it, why bother, I'm not worthy to pray, it is hopeless, I am helpless, all is lost,* is not good. Therefore, not God; therefore, not truth. Even when our lives need correcting, it is never done in such a way to discourage us, but to build us up and motivate us. With correction coming from God, it comes coupled with reassurance and hope and comfort, rather than the contrast of shame or hopelessness.

Anything that keeps us from acting, from doing, from moving forward, from trying again, is Satan's itinerary. Just think of how he got Adam and Eve to hide and retreat in the garden from the only ones that could help them. He is dangerously subtle by not getting us to do anything "bad," but getting us to do nothing. The adversary gets to me the most by standing still. To stay idle. To sit a little longer in our questions, sit a little longer in our problem solving. Recognizing the adversary could be taking a step back and asking ourselves, *Are we moving forward? How am I talking to myself? Am I filled with hope and encouragement regardless of what season am I in? Or am I overwhelmed with weight? What does my next step look like even if that step is small?* The sooner we can recognize the adversary, the faster we can cast Him out—a literal power that is ours, a power he has to obey. Joseph Smith said, "The devil has no power over us only as we permit him."[1] We're allowed to feel deflated, we're allowed to struggle, we're allowed to feel sad or upset. But it's up to us whether or not to choose to live there. The adversary will stay as long as we allow him to. The initial feeling from escaping Satan's grasp and influence may be uncomfortable like the man in the synagogue, but we have what we need to get rid of any unnecessary weight that the adversary causes to slow us down. *You* have *power.* You have Jesus.

And as we continue to turn to Him and give Him the opportunity to show us how great He is, we will strengthen our conviction to able to better confess, *I know who thou art, the holy one of God.*

"Immediately his fame spread abroad throughout all the region round about Galilee." And *immediately* Jesus leaves and, just a few yards away from the synagogue where this happened, He enters Peter's house to *rebuke* yet again only moments after rebuking the evil and unclean spirits in the synagogue. *Immediately* healing Simon's mother-in-law leads to that entire night of one-by-one healing of others by Him. Jesus is showing us with this day and an entire night of miracles, His ability and dedication to us for overcoming the adversary and healing.

---

1. Joseph Smith, "Discourse 5 January 1841, as Reported by Unidentified Scribe," *The Joseph Smith Papers,* https://www.josephsmithpapers.org

Finding Yourself in . . .

Healing at Peter's House

Matthew 8

After casting out the evil and unclean spirits from that man in the synagogue, Jesus *immediately* leaves to travel only yards away to Peter's house with Peter, Andrew, James, and John, the newly called disciples. After rebuking only minutes before, He walked out one door and into the next, *rebuking* by a single command, yet again. Peter's mother-in-law laid with *"great fever,"* which has been said that because of the marsh-like surroundings in Capernaum, it was a bit of a hotspot for fevers and malaria. I only note that part for a potential connection of our surroundings living in a fallen world, and its effects on us. Jesus stood over her, *"and took her by the hand,"* rebuked the fever (commanded the fever to leave), and it left her. Just like that, at the sound of Jesus's single command, her serious illness left her. He *"lifted her up"* and *"immediately"* she arose and ministered unto them.

Isn't it profound to realize this miracle of healing happened in a *home* by the touch of hands? Accessing Jesus's power to heal is ours and can be accessed right in our homes by the touch of hands on our head. And what does she do after she is healed?

What does she do after her experience with Jesus, and she has been changed? She served Him. He raises us up and we repay Him by serving Him—by living as He would want us to.

And one of my favorite parts of Jesus's time in Peter's home is what happens next. Healing that man, then healing Peter's mother, was just the start to the miracles in that day. As dinner approached, people by the masses showed up to Peter's house seeking change and relief. He spent the entire night healing *all* of them, every single one of them that came to Him, one by one. *"As the sun was setting, all they that had any sick . . .he laid his hands on every one of them, and healed them."* He healed them *all*. Healing a man to healing a woman to healing a child to healing an unbeliever. Jesus cares about every single one of us. The entire night, one by one, personally, and individually. He has time for you simply because you are His. And there is nothing He can't heal and there is no one that He won't save. He turned, and He turns, no one away. Jesus is our great physician both body and soul. He heals; He restores. *All* of us. And although they are unnamed in the scriptures, He *knows* them. He knows *you*.

"As the sun was setting" is my favorite part of that. Sometimes we can be put off from reading so frequently the word *immediately* when those in the scriptures are being healed, when we feel that has not been the case for us. *The sun was setting,* and it was getting late into the evening, late into a season of struggle, late into our life, and that struggle is still there. That has been me many times. *The sun was setting* are those times when light seems to be dimming or that our opportunity for things to change has passed us by, that it is too late. But even if it is late into the night, late into our season, late into our life—even if the sun is setting, your one-by-one Savior *does* come.

We do not have to wait for a new morning, a new week, a new chapter, a new season! Right now, even if it's late into the night, we can hit the reset button. It's the whole point of Christ willingly allowing Himself to be killed. We may be in a hard season right now, but seasons don't last forever. Just because things haven't worked out yet doesn't mean they won't. We will find peace to our soul. Everlasting struggle just isn't in God's cards for us. Because of Jesus, right now, in this life, in this season, even *while the sun is setting*, our great physician is here to *heal*. And maybe Jesus won't always take our struggle away completely. But He does in fact come with hands pierced with love, dedication, and power to *lift* you higher. And He does in fact come with relief, with comfort, with guidance, hope, strength, forgiveness, and love. It is not too late; you are not too far gone. He will never look at you like a waste of time. There is nothing He cannot fix and no one He will not save. Simply because you are His.

And even when the sun is setting and it seems as though darkness will overcome, Jesus does in fact come with *light*. *"I am the light of the world: he that followeth me shall not walk in darkness."*[1]

The sun always rises, and you are always His.

---

1. John 8:12

Finding Yourself in . . .

The Sermon of the Mount

Matthew 5 & 6

I'm currently in a season that I don't love being in. I like to think that I've really learned to embrace and welcome the unwanted and unexpected that God brings me, but then the time keeps passing with little or no change and I start to get tired. And frustrated. Just this morning I was on the floor of my kitchen feeling exactly that, the long and tired season that seems to drag on and it's thinning. Been feeling that I've done it wrong and that my right things are also fruitless things, and then it starts to sting when others are in a season of reaping when you're still sowing; stings when others are feasting and you're in a famine. Sometimes we wonder that maybe we're doing it wrong. Sometimes we start to wonder if we're doing the right things or as many things, or if we're failing or falling or that our calling in life isn't grand enough or our impact isn't deep enough. Absolutely Satan exploits and capitalizes on our long seasons and gets us to skew our perspective on God in our personal lives.

We are told to be *"perfect even as your Father which is in heaven is perfect,"* and the adversary comes to us with weight and pressure and tells us that we will never be enough, we are disappointing, we aren't deserving, why bother? He is quick to remind us of all our shortcomings and reoccurring mistakes and skews beautiful realities to use them against us to get us to stop trying. Skewing, shaming, sabotaging, shifting, to get us to stay on the floor of our kitchen feeling stuck. But maybe that's why the Sermon on the Mount has the reputation of being one of the most powerful talks ever given. Because it both lifts us and redirects us. It reminds us of our blessings and abilities while at the same exact time guiding us on how to navigate through our tricky seasons.

Jesus never commanded or yelled for anyone's attention to get His message to others. At the height of His popularity, He retreats "*up into a mountain*" and simply sat down and "*he opened his mouth, and taught.*" Any who followed Him, any who found Him, went to Him themselves, are the ones that heard. Isn't that a beautiful reminder? The ones who went to Him, received more. We could even maybe sum up these three chapters in Matthew as *receiving more.* He pulled His disciples closer and spoke with profound intention. We now have 111 verses to help us better understand the blessings God has in store for us and what it means to be a follower of Jesus.

There are eight beatitudes within this sermon, beatitude meaning supreme blessedness or *exalted* happiness. They are promises of comfort and help as well as righteous traits to develop; it's a call to a higher living as well as a promise to receiving lasting things. "*Blessed are the poor in spirit,*" "*blessed are they that mourn,*" those that are *meek, merciful, pure, peacemakers,* those that forgive, those that are persecuted, those that *hunger and thirst,* His message it to "*rejoice, and be exceedingly glad,*" because this sermon is rich in blessings as we grow into these traits of a righteous disciple. *Rejoice* because He's bound by promises that we *will* be comforted. We *will* be filled. And our sacrifices, our efforts, and our pain will not be in vain, there is so much more coming as we continue to grow into being *children of God.* We are told that we are to be the "*salt of the earth*" and a "*light to the world*"—this is about becoming *more,* becoming a fuller version of you, becoming even as God is. Truly, *blessed are* we!

"*Theirs is the kingdom of heaven.*" "*Great is your reward in heaven.*" They shall "*inherit the earth,*" the earth which becomes the Celestial Kingdom! "*They shall see God,*" seeing God is living with Him *exalted*. Everything in this sermon is directing us to celestial glory, exaltation, eternal, endless magnifications! Everything is reminding us to refocus on "*treasures in heaven, where neither moth nor rust doth corrupt.*" Treasures that are never ending, never to be taken away. This sermon was when Jesus was living His earthly ministry and He spoke saying, be "*perfect, even as your Father which is in heaven is perfect.*" Christ, who was obviously perfect, did not Himself claim to be until *after* He was resurrected. His sermon in Bountiful, given after His resurrection, is when He then adds to say, "*Therefore I would that ye should be perfect even as I, or your Father who is in heaven is perfect.*"[1] After resurrection! Perfection was never taught by Jesus to be attainable *here* on earth. We don't need to be perfect here, that's not what He was teaching. He was teaching that we *can't* be perfect here! He who was perfect, wasn't even perfect here, only hereafter, after following in God's ways. Perfection was meaning exalted, exalted meaning living with our God as a god. Perfection here in this estate is an illusion that the adversary uses to get us to lose sight of our *eternal* promises and goals. Resurrection, exaltation, everything that is asked of us here is meant to bring us to something much greater. Everything we have been taught, everything we have been given as a guide, even Christ's entire purpose of coming to earth, has always been about us *receiving more* and *becoming more*. God's entire purpose for us has always meant to bring us back to Him and to be as He is.

One of my favorite realities is that when we read of all our promised blessings, everything we are trying to attain, in scripture, they are all written in past tense: *prepared*. They're already there. God who is your father, has already spent the time, the work, the effort into preparing the best that has ever been created and it was all set to be before the world even was. Which means

---

1. 3 Nephi 12:48

saving *you,* getting you back, giving you everything, was always part of it all.

Let's recommit to act. Let's recommit to read. Let's refocus on the principles of the gospel. Let's recommit to study, really study. To learn. To turn to Him. To talk to Him. To preach. To participate. To always exercise our change of heart muscle. To be the ones to find and follow Him to receive more. Let's recommit to Him. To trusting Him, His teachings, and His path for us. Because every single bit of it is worth the sacrifice, the time, the trust, the loss . . . Because sacrifice, suffering, loss, etc., doesn't even come close to what we receive in return. Because His promises are real. And He will show us. Refocusing and living how Christ has taught absolutely takes effort, but our efforts are not in vain. But can we think of anything more important than endless life and eternal bliss?

We may be in a long or unwanted season right now and the adversary may have a grasp on us with his skewed illusions meant to keep us down, but we have blessings and guidance to refocus us and lift us higher. Regardless of how real and hard and subtle the adversary's pathetic attempts are, the reality is, they're still pathetic. Because regardless of his pathetic yet dangerously subtle attempts that absolutely slow us down, that can't take away from the reality that we are part of something so much greater than the here and the now. The refocus we may need is available with the blessings to lift and redirect us anytime we may need. The adversary may tell us we are lacking, we are falling, and we are failing, but how God sees us is the only thing that matters, and He sees us as someone capable of becoming like Him. So "r*ejoice, and be exceedingly glad* "! *Blessed are they who shall believe on Him* . . . "*great is your reward.*" You *will* be *led.* You *will* be comforted. You *will* be *filled.* God already has treasures that are endless waiting for you to receive. Celestial glory, exaltation, eternal and endless magnifications are intended for you. Because saving you, getting you back, giving you everything, was always part of it all.

Blessed are you.

Finding Yourself in . . .

Consider the Lilies

Matthew 6 & Luke 12

While living in Arizona, God told my husband and I to move back to New York, where I am from. Having already done a cross-country move *to* Arizona just the year previous, another one so soon was not an easy pack-up for our family of five. But we did because it was God's idea. We were seamlessly and spiritually brought to a specific house by God to buy over the internet, packed up for our eighth time in our, at the time, eight years of marriage, and we sacrificed to complete my seventh cross-country drive. We planned our entire cross-country move around our closing date. We thought it best to drive straight through so we could get huge chunks of mileage done while our three very young kids were sleeping. So, all five of us, plus our incredibly large dog, drove 2,300 miles through 10 states, for the duration of 44 hours straight with *no hotel*.

And because of God's promptings, there we all were, on moving day, in New York, in front of the house He led to us to buy. Except after we'd already arrived, we are told we couldn't move in. It was a continuously growing list of unexpected and unwanted and unraveling that led to us not having a home to live in. *We found ourselves houseless.* And it was all out of our hands. We were all crammed into a single room hotel room. It was an extremely tight space, the five of us in a single room with our giant dog. I'm not much of a crier, I don't do it often, but during this season of struggle, I could not look at my children without tears streaming. My youngest at the time wasn't even a year old and I would watch her sleep and be consumed with indescribable anguish wondering how life led to me not having a home for my children. How many times would God allow my heart to break from the repetitive question from my four-year-old wondering why we don't have a home. All of their toys, their clothes, our belongings, packed up and out of sight, all of us only having what could fit in a single suitcase that fit in our car. We had nothing with us. *And the weeks kept passing.*

Deep sacrifice is not foreign to me. I was baptized after I finished college which came at the cost of sacrificing my family. *It was them or God.* And could you choose? Could you choose a God you just met—over those you've always had? Raised by? Loved by? It took *everything* out of me to move forward in a new way of living completely alone. And just when I thought God could not require *even more* from me, He prompted me to move across the country, leave behind the only way of living that I knew of, trying to cope with the idea that maybe I will never see my dad ever again.

While Jesus was still giving His sermon on the mount, He then turns to speak to His apostles directly. "*Take no thought for your life,*" He says. But *take no thoughts for your life* has seemed so impossible, so illogical and reckless so many times. How could I not? I collapsed on the floor of the hotel room while we were houseless, yelling at God with pleadings I have said to Him many times. My body was aching from being stretched so thin, aching from carrying a weight for too long. Aching then collapsing. I told God from the floor, collapsed under that weight I could no longer hold, "*I'm done.* I got nothin' left." I have never felt so thin. My faith, my strength, my optimism, it's just done. I felt like I was left out to dry. And I'm telling Him that. *And He responded.*

"Why won't you let me bless you? Why won't you let me take you somewhere better? That's why I exist!"

Do you believe that? He said that to me at a time when we didn't have a home to live in. He said that to me at a time when I didn't have a family to turn to. He said that to me during an entire year of unemployment. He said that to me during a high-risk pregnancy when the odds were against me. He said that to me every time I have wondered where He was and every time I have collapsed on the ground with my pleadings with the weight I could no longer carry.

When God watched His Only Begotten Son be betrayed, falsely judged, abused, and killed, it's said, *"it pleased the Lord to bruise him."*[1] Why? Because there was, in fact, something so much more to come. *Something greater.*

As I tally up my losses, I am told that, *"your Father knoweth that ye have need of these things."* With humility and desperation, I ask myself if I'm allowing God to be God. Am I giving Him the opportunity to show me how great He really is?

"Consider the lilies, how they grow." They grow! They blossom! They live, they continue, they become something more, something greater. God is good even when our situation is not, because He knows something we don't. So what if we got it all backward? What if every step is the miracle? When I allow God to be God, when I allow Him to take me somewhere better, when I see my seasons through, *wow*, does life blossom. Never is it what I am wanting or asking for, but truly, profoundly better than I ever could have imagined.

When it's out of our hands, it's in His. Through the unwanted and unexpected, He is not overlooking or ignoring or punishing, but in fact, working hard with every little detail to be sure things will be even better than what we had in mind. All of it part of the plan to begin with.

If I am being honest, I wouldn't have a single thing I have now if it weren't for God and *His* ways. I wouldn't have a single

---

1. Isaiah 53:10

thing I have now if it weren't for the times I was yelling at Him wondering where He was. It was every single moment I was yelling at Him wondering where He was, thinking I couldn't make it any longer, that has brought me everything I have now—the best things. *My favorite things.* And it breaks my heart to imagine my life any different.

Sometimes we don't always know the what or the why behind things, but we do always know the who. A God who solely exists to bring us to the better and to make us better. And seeing it through one hard or unexpected time, and seeing the blessings that come from that, will make it easier to trust Him the next time. And then the next. And then times will come when we will find ourselves feeling at ease even among trials, because from consistently trying to trust, we will have experienced time and time again that we are being led to the greater things. Times will come when the scary, the hard, and the unexpected turn into exciting, thrilling new adventures that come with peace, with our knowledge that we are in motion to the best-fit blessings.

And we'll be profoundly grateful things didn't go our own way because we will find ourselves living our best self in our best life, living and experiencing things we didn't even know were available to us, with new knowledge and talents we wouldn't have wanted to go any further in life without. Because we chose to trust the most powerful being to ever exist. And we will one day pause and look around, and we'll see where we are, what we've gained along the way, the something different and the something greater. And we'll wonder why we hadn't done better all along. Because *my,* how we've *grown!*

"*All these things shall be added unto you.*" *Added.* Losses *will* be made up. Blessings will be magnified. The "*Holy Ghost will teach you.*" You will *grow.* Blessings will blossom. He will take you somewhere better. So, "*take ye no thought.*" Embrace the unexpected knowing Who is guiding you. "*Fear not, little flock; for it is your Father's good pleasure to give you the kingdom.*" Every step *is* the miracle. And you will stand all amazed.

Finding Yourself in . . .

The Lord's Prayer

Matthew 6 & Luke 11

My first prayer I had ever said was in the Sacred Grove. Which may seem super cool, but not knowing what the sacred grove was, it was more like, *why did we drive thirty minutes to stand in the middle of the woods?* I had never said a prayer before this. I grew up in another religion where prayer was recited by word the same each time, or it was repeated after someone else. I had never felt more uncomfortable in my entire life than when I was asked to pray by the missionaries. I just felt like I was talking to myself: how does one even pray? Like, I didn't know how, I didn't know what to say, I didn't know what to do with my hands or even if I should close my eyes. For the first little while, I would pray with one eye opened while glancing at a church pamphlet of bullet points as a guide.

The Lord's prayer is one of the prayers that I had memorized *very* early in age from my previous religion and is found in different places in the New Testament. Mark 6 is during the Sermon of the Mount, and Luke 11 is in the last months of His life. But it isn't as literal and exact as I grew up thinking it was, it blossoms in deep ways to show us how real and personal our connection to our actual Father should and can be. Culturally, in the day of Jesus, priests were specifically set apart and commissioned to pray on behalf of the people in a sacred location, like church, the Sabbath, tabernacles, and temples. So back then, personal prayers weren't taught or encouraged or shown. The Lord's Prayer and the few verses before it, first and foremost show us that we can, and we should be saying our own prayers, something I personally wasn't even aware of in my own upbringing.

"Our Father which art in heaven, Hallowed be thy name." *Hallowed,* Holy. My Father. He is my *Father.* Immediately addressing our relationship to whom we speak, for who He is to us. The adversary absolutely exploits our mistakes and short-comings and one of the ways the adversary wins is getting us to feel like we are unworthy or unqualified to pray. Remembering our relationship to God will help remind us that we are always deserving of His help and attention because He is our *father.* We are His. Nothing can change that.

"Thy kingdom come;" eternity is reality. *"Thy will be done;"* He is leading, and He is perfect. *"Give us this day,"* acknowledging Him as the giver and our reliance on Him, *"our daily bread,"* expressing and asking Him for our needs. Expressing to Him and asking for what we need to help us, sustain us, strengthen us. *"And forgive us our sins,"* our faults, our wrongdoings, because He can and will forgive us when we go to Him. Praying with intention, with purpose, with faith, with sincerity. *"As we forgive our debtors,"* forgiving others which is important for us attaining our own forgiveness. *"And lead us not into temptation,"* He leads and guides and participates in our life in a fallen world. Him leading and guiding us is Him participating in our personal lives. *"But deliver us from evil,"* Jesus Christ has the title of *deliverer,* remembering the reality we have to be saved. Saves us from *evil,* from sin, from hurt, from pain, and even from this world. *"Amen,"* an agreement and acceptance of so be it.

"When thou prayest, enter into thy closet, and when thou hast shut thy door, pray to thy Father which is in secret." Not limiting

to a *place* to only speak to God who is your Father, but that our prayers should be intimate; they should be personal. Things that would require privacy are honest things of our heart. Not physical location.

When Christ prayed, it was an actual communion with His God, it was an actual tangible relationship. And although I say I didn't know what I was doing when I first got started, just talking openly absolutely cultivated a real relationship with my God. Even with my awkward efforts, life started to blossom in new ways. Even with my awkward, uncomfortable, and worst-God-has-ever-seen kind of efforts, beautiful fruits came. And perhaps the best fruit that came was God became real to me. Not knowing *how* to pray was the greatest gift given to me.

I'd picture Him standing right in front of me and speak to Him as I would a conversation with anyone in person. When I was mad, confused, scared, tired, I would tell Him. When I didn't understand something, when I didn't want to do something, I told Him. If I was really excited about something, I told Him. I told Him everything. And He became real to me. I guessed, I experimented, I explored, and our relationship blossomed. My honesty brought productivity with my struggles and my wonders. I'm most productive with life and moving forward when I'm specific and don't tip toe around my feelings, but am completely transparent with my doubts, questions, concerns, and trials. Specific prayers receive specific answers. I have found that holding back in prayers not only prevents answers, productivity, new perspective, and relief, but also prevents an intimate, trustworthy, and real relationship with our *Father*. I have spent a lot of time on the ground yelling because of how hard things were and how much I didn't understand, but it was in those honest prayers that I received more detailed comfort and counsel.

Having three kids, there are prayers my kids fight with each other to be able to say, and then there are times where no one wants to say it at all. Between parenthood and teaching in callings, I have found even with myself, that there is a wildly different response when *let's say a prayer,* is rephrased to, *let's talk to*

God. We get in the car, *alright, time to talk to God*. Blessing the food, before bedtime, *let's talk to God, God is excited to hear from you, what do you want to say to Him?* Has that rephrase shifted with how we view and approach Him and made a difference in what we are then saying? Night and day difference. There's absolutely more thought and meaning in them just from a perspective tweak. We aren't just *saying* a prayer, words are not equivalent to feelings and meaning. We're not just talking for the sake of speaking; we literally are talking directly to the creator of the universe. We can talk to Him directly, no middleman or putting in a request for a time slot. Can I even fully wrap my brain around that? Probably not.

"Use not vain repetitions, as the heathen do: for they think that they shall be heard for their much speaking." Failing to express what we really want to actually say, little meaning or thought behind them hold little power. Never have I ever said nourish and strengthen to bless food because I just don't talk like that. Even just asking ourselves, *wait, is that really what I wanted to say,* can be a solution and self-check to speaking just to speak. To reword repetition into what I actually want and need; I'll ask that it will be good for my body, give my body what it needs, what it lacks, that it won't make me sick (especially if I cooked it), or that I won't overeat, *ha*. Showers and driving in the car allow me to take my time to open up to Him, ramble even, not feel rushed, and break down some barriers of repetition or empty words. Those help me to take more time to think and listen, to speak out loud.

Are we sometimes talking to Him like a butler, or like we are making a food order and leaving? *"Ask, and it shall be given you; seek, and ye shall find; knock, and it shall be opened unto you."* But how can that be when we all know very well we don't get everything we ask for? We are taught that we will receive according to His will, but what if we don't know what His will is? What if I am talking, and pleading, and not receiving? Sometimes when I don't know what to ask for, I ask for His help. I've learned that He is not playing some weird, losing, guessing game with us. When I address Him and ask, "Please help me with this prayer," so far, it's been one hundred percent of the time I've find myself asking or saying new things I never thought of until then. And sometimes when I don't know what to say, maybe because everything I had been asking for hasn't come, my productive prayers have also come from the ones I say, "Heavenly Father . . . you go first." What ideas come to mind in the listening? What reoccurring thoughts are there?

It's true that God does not always tell us what's right. *But* He does always tell us what's wrong. It's a promise to us that He will not lead us astray. The adversary can exploit our yes or no questions by getting us to stand still in our wondering and in our planning and problem solving. We go in circles if it is us or if it is the Spirit speaking. Sometimes the worst thing we can do is simply stay in the same spot making no progress—that's Satan's way. I've found its faster if I just pick an option and move forward with it and see what falls in or out of our lives and pay attention to my reoccurring thoughts and how I'm feeling. Feeling "off" when moving forward is usually my faster way to understanding right decision making. If it is good, it is God, including feelings. If it is *not* good, it is not God, including feelings.

Like the popular video with Elder Holland about the wrong roads,[1] where he and his son both felt they should go one way when they reached a fork in the road, only to find out it was a dead end—so then they corrected course and knew they were steadily going in the right direction. Where would they have gotten if they stayed at the fork in the road waiting? Even if we do choose a wrong path, He will always tell us, and then we can more quickly correct course and move forward, onward and upward. I think of the analogy of the man on the side of the road with a busted car. Who will God help faster? Someone who is praying and pleading for help? Or someone who says a prayer and then opens the hood and starts tinkering? Probably the second one. Because the second one is moving and working and making

---

1. "Wrong Roads," YouTube, 5 Nov. 2013, The Church of Jesus Christ of Latter-day Saints

it easier for God to help him. Can He move us in the right direction if we aren't in motion? Absolutely. But that version is often the longer version.

Shortly after baptism, I wanted to serve a mission. I was certain God would say yes because that is a righteous, good thing to want to do; why wouldn't He? But my answer was "move to Utah." I was mad because that wasn't what I asked for. I wanted to help people, not move across the country. My answer came as a reoccurring thought. I figured to take a chance on my reoccurring thoughts to see where it would lead as part of my ongoing experimenting. Although it seemed incredibly irrelevant to what I wanted and also painful to not get what was important to me, I did it. I moved from New York to Utah just a few months after my baptism. But it was in Utah that I started writing. It was in Utah I started public speaking. Two things which both overfill me with overwhelming passion and purpose. It took me a few years to realize God gave me exactly what I was asking for, it was just packaged differently.

Sometimes I inaccurately think that God is not listening because I'm not getting what I want. As Elder Richard G. Scott said, "Sometimes answers to prayer are not recognized because we are too intent on wanting confirmation of our own desires."[2] Could God be trying to give us what we are asking for, but we aren't heeding because it's packaged differently? What reoccurring thoughts have we been putting off? I like picturing our whisperings and our recurring thoughts as second chances. Just in case the first time it came we might have dismissed it as a fleeting or weird thought. Or maybe we didn't pay attention because it was a new or different thought that would lead us in a different direction than our intended desire? What if the unexpected is God intervening? I don't know; I've always just liked to picture our whisperings and our recurring thoughts as our souls directing and guiding and pulling us to what we were meant to do all

2. Richard G. Scott, "Learning to Recognize Answers to Prayer," Oct. 1989 General Conference

along. As if our souls remember more than we do. Because my absolute favorite things have come from the times I was wondering why God wasn't listening. My favorite things have come from when things were going differently than I had in mind.

"If ye then, being evil, know how to give good gifts unto your children: how much more shall your heavenly Father give the Holy Spirit to them that ask him?" Knowing that our prayers are direct and personal and intimate conversations with our *Father,* then how come we feel sometimes we aren't recognizing Him from it? I remind myself that His entire existence is to bring us to better things, even if on our way to them it's on a path longer than anticipated or packaged differently. When I was engaged to a boy that I didn't end up marrying, I was more spiritually confused than I was upset over the breakup. Because I wondered, "I thought this is what I was supposed to do because after my prayers, this is what I was led to." I just couldn't make sense of feeling prompted to do something that was going to fail. It took me a while to realize that it not working out, was it working out. Because it put me on a different path that was filled with lessons, knowledge, opportunities and so much more that I wouldn't have otherwise received.

Through my wrestle and my experimenting due to my desperation, I had learned so many more adjectives of the Spirit and of God. What I had known and learned about Them thus far was actually limiting me from allowing Him to show me what else. I had unconsciously put a box around Him and His Spirit and what They were capable of doing and how things were *supposed* to be, that I was accidentally dismissing myself from experiencing and recognizing His vastness of blessings and miracles. I figured if God brings us to something that it should "work out," or if we experience answers to prayers in certain ways that we assume those are the only ways: "I know how to get answers to my prayers, and they come in this box because every answer He's given me so far has come this way." So when we don't notice it in that way, wonder and doubt could take over. But what if He was answering me outside of that box that I ignorantly put there to begin with? When I tried to take away these limits that I unconsciously put on Them, I was learning and noticing different ways They were showing me They were there and They were answering me and trying to guide me and teach me and bring me to better things, and it had just gone over my head. What seemed like unanswered prayers and rejection, was actually just me being led to better things than I had in mind.

Sometimes I can't help but think how much easier it would be if things had gone the way we wanted them to go. But little do we know what's right around the corner for us when we choose to remember God—opportunities that await, the people, the growth, and the blessings. Because, truly, the best things come from Him, the giver of good gifts. And where we don't find an ending to a trial quite yet, we find ease and added strength. Where we can't find answers to prayers quite yet, we find comfort and reassurance. Where we don't see promised blessings quite yet, we find love and help and continued guidance.

You are always worthy to talk to your God; He always wants to hear from you, because you are His. And He will never look at you like a waste of time. He leads and guides and participates in your personal life. Embrace the unexpected knowing who is guiding you. Your prayers have been heard, and greater is what He has in store for you.

Finding Yourself in . . .

Healing the Leper

Matthew 8 & Luke 5

Iwanted to serve a mission after I got baptized. My answer, however, was to move across the country. I hated that answer because that's not what I wanted, not even close to what I was even asking for. After my baptism, I lost everyone. Every single one of my friends wanted nothing to do with me and what I was now a part of. I had, and what would turn into, years of silence from my family; my dad looking me in the eye saying he didn't want me as a daughter anymore, because I got baptized. If I wasn't at work, it was just me. Just church pamphlets. Just missionaries sometimes. I wanted to serve a mission because I really wanted to, but what else was I going to do when nothing was there for me except loneliness and silence and continued sacrifice? Just when I thought God couldn't possibly ask me to give up anything else, my answered prayer was to now give up my home, leave behind the only way of living that I knew of, go to a state I had never been before where I didn't know a single person, and cope with the idea I could never see my dad ever again.

As much as I didn't want this, a part of me saw this as my silver lining. Things had been so painfully and unbearably hard, maybe this move was when things would thing comes together and get a little bit easier? So, I leave. I leave behind my New York upbringing. I leave behind all my belongings. I leave behind my family. I drive all the way across the country in my two-door Allero Oldsmobile by myself, only then to see things get so much worse.

I am an outgoing, confident person that is bursting at the seams with self-love and drive. I have always been that way, sure of myself, you can't help but notice it in my countenance. Yet for the first time in my life, I was having to navigate something so completely foreign to me—feeling uncomfortable with myself. I was almost immobile from all the stares. After having just given up quite literally everything and everyone, the very first day I arrived, holding a church book in my arms, I was approached with such an ugly tone, on how ironic it was to be holding that book *looking the way that I do.*

My heart sank. And then shattered. How could they? Although I didn't, I wanted to yell, *"Do you know what I just went through? Do you know what, and who, I had to give up to be here and I didn't even know why?"*

There were a lot of reactions to me. Walk the other direction, pull their kids in closer, dirty looks, scared looks, rude comments, silence. Many took me personal; one look at me and they would assume that I hate the God that they love. And they reacted that way, mad and defensive without me even doing anything. Guys my age were looking for temple-worthy girls, but I don't exactly look temple worthy, so not only did no one want to date me, they didn't even speak to me, avoided it all together. The hurt, confusion, and loneliness were indescribable. It was in this season that I discovered my calling and passion for writing and speaking. But even that just opened more avenues for people to tell me, literally, *God could never love someone like me.*

Do you know how hard it is to move forward continually through pain and judgment from others? Do you know how hard it is to move forward and navigate continuously through feeling unfit, unwanted, unworthy? Being looked down upon, being told you don't belong and being treated as less than? The shame people place upon you for not fitting *their* mold.

Do you know how easy it would have been to quit when everything and everyone is telling you that you should? And why wouldn't I? How could I stay when no one wanted me to? What energy did I have left to continue in that community anyways? Family, friends, strangers, turning away, disapproving, and disappearing. *God could never love someone like you.* How long could you continue in that before it strips you of your energy, drive, confidence, self-love, and faith? *Years?*

Leprosy was the worst sickness among them all; it's a painfully long process of someone's entire body becoming disfigured and deteriorating. In scripture, lepers are considered living dead, you just . . .slowly rot. Their bodies smelled, their sores were increasing, and their entirety was decomposing. Hands would be without fingers, and feet without toes; some victims have had rats eat part of them while sleeping and they didn't even know because of the lack of pain receptors. It was a chronic, incurable disease, what was there to look forward to? Could hope even be found with something so impossible? Every one that had fallen victim would be completely outcast and abandoned by family, friends, and society. If they somehow *did* come across anyone, they would have to literally and verbally declare that they were *unclean.* Touching a leper would then cause them to be unclean. These poor souls cut off completely from everything and everyone they've ever loved over something they could not control. No support system. No hope. And early Israelites believed that this was punishment for sin and now they were paying for their actions. They deserved this; this is what they get. So, it wasn't just fear that lepers would feel from others, it was also shame.

When suffering with this, where is their head space? Is there even any sign of morale? Passing time is continuously beating him down but somehow this man *full of leprosy* was able to dig deep to find whatever little bit of anything that was left in him to show up still. To venture away from his banishment, put his deteriorated body in the public eye, live through the embarrassment and shame of verbally declaring his disgusting state to others. He did that somehow. I don't know how he did that. He falls at the feet of the Savior, hiding his face, and his request was humbly worded with pain and hesitance. *"Lord if thou wilt,"* if you are willing, *"thou canst make me clean."* Not, *can* He heal me . . .but *will* He?

"I will."

Laying His hands upon his head, *"moving with compassion,"* touching the untouchable, *"Be thou clean."* And *immediately* the leprosy departed from him. Sores were closed, deformities removed, missing limbs restored, smell of rotting flesh disappeared, and skin made smooth. He touched the untouchable, and He cured the incurable. Our impossibilities are not a struggle for Jesus. He will not "meet His match" with our suffering. And you know, I don't doubt that Jesus's compassion is what really healed this broken man. How long had he been stripped of someone's time? Attention? How long had this man been deprived of touch? Of compassion? Of love? I don't doubt how Jesus treated him is what really made him feel whole in this experience of healing.

Jesus tells him to *"tell no man,"* but he does; how could he not? And *"great multitudes came."* I wonder if it was because people will, and do, come seeking just a healer and miracle maker, rather than a Messiah. Are we coming to Him mostly to get what we want? Or are we going to Him to listen, to hear, and to follow Him? To dedicate ourselves to Him, rather than take what we want and leave to go our own way with it. Jesus tells this man to *"go thy way"* and show himself *"to a priest and offer for thy cleansing those things that Moses commanded."* To be pronounced clean from leprosy by a priest is a whole eight-day process before they are allowed back into society. Leviticus 14 brings us through the process of not just being examined, but a sacrificial offering with two birds. One will be sacrificed and the blood of that one will be mixed with running, living water, because it's considered pure. The mixture of blood and pure, living water would then be put on the other bird who would be released in an *open field* and fly away free. The lepers shave all their hair, even down to the eyebrows, and then wash themselves and their clothes also in pure, living water. On the eighth day of this process, a one-year-old blemish-free lamb would then be sacrificed. The blood would be placed on the right earlobe, thumb, and big toe of the one being cleansed, followed by *oil*. Sacrifice, living water, lamb, oil, and blood to be cleansed and made free. Profound, right?

The adversary will tell us we are too far gone, we are incapable of change, we are the exception, and there is no hope left. The pain, judgment, lack of compassion and shame from others will make it so hard to stay. Not fitting the mold, the world tells us we are unfit, unwanted, unworthy, and that God could never love someone like you. But when we wonder what is there to look forward to, we remember the sacrifice and blood of our Messiah, our *living* water. He will not meet His match with our suffering, and our impossibilities are not a struggle, nor an inconvenience, for Jesus. When everything and everyone says no, Jesus says, *I will*. While others may fail us, He comes with healing in His wings and compassion that knows no bounds. And we can be whole.

Finding Yourself in . . .

Calming the Storm

Matthew 8, Mark 4 & Luke 8

Well known is the raging storm on the Sea of Galilee that caused the apostles to yell, *"Carest thou not that we perish?"* But perhaps we can more see ourselves in our personal storms and our pleadings of, "carest thou not that I'm struggling?! Carest thou not that this is so hard? Carest thou not that I'm sinking? Carest thou not . . . about *me?*" I have been in too many raging storms, wondering too many times if I will be able to make it, losing my voice too many times because of how loud my pleadings have been, physically aching from wondering if He is sleeping.

"Jesus entered into a ship" and *"his disciples followed Him."* The Sea of Galilee is the largest freshwater lake in Israel and is the lowest freshwater lake on Earth; it's about eight miles by thirteen miles for context of size. And *"as they sailed* [Jesus] *fell asleep: and there came down a storm of wind on the lake."* The storm's intensity was no exaggeration; it wasn't that they were just afraid that they would sink, they *were* sinking. The *"ship was covered with*

the waves," it *filled with water, "it was now full," and they were in jeopardy.* And what was Christ doing? Sleeping *"on a pillow."*

Like the Apostles waking up Christ, who was sleeping during what seemed to be a life-threatening storm, we too sometimes find ourselves wondering if He is sleeping through the times when we feel we so desperately need Him the most. We wonder where relief is, we plead for Him to calm our storm because it's as though we may not make it. Or at the very least, we plead for to Him to wake up—to be conscious, to be mindful, to be present—for our raging storms we're in the midst of.

I wonder what the disciples may have done before waking up Jesus. Some of the disciples were skilled fishermen that spent a good part of their lives on boats. I feel it's safe to assume that, as the storm was coming and as it began to rage, they applied their years of experience and expertise in an attempt to save their boat and their lives. But it proved impossible to overcome such a storm of that caliber even with their best trained and seasoned efforts. But Christ can do more for us than we can do for ourselves, no matter how skilled we may be. *"With men this is impossible; but with God all things are possible."[1]*

His disciples came to him and *"he arose, and rebuked the wind, and said unto the sea, Peace, be still. And the wind ceased, and there was a great calm."* Normally, after a storm it takes a while before waters can settle. But when Christ spoke *peace*, not only did the storm cease, but all the effects of it died away into that immediate *great calm*. The storm strong enough to sink was not a struggle for Jesus. And they *marveled* in fear wondering, *"what manner of man is this, that even the winds and the sea obey him!"* Their wonder and fear partly justified because this is a new element the apostles are introduced to, *weather*. Christ may have been known for healing people, but now we see He has rule and power and dominion even over the forces of nature! Ruler over all, truly the God of this world. Because Jesus has power over all the elements, means for you that Christ *will* continue to show

---

1. Matthew 19:26

us something *new* that He can do for us. He will not meet His match, there is nothing more powerful than He. Jesus has power and control over our storms. And His power is readily available when we call out, *"Master."*

Although not dismissing rebuke, I am overflowing with an outpouring of remembrances of His love and dedication to us reading His response. *"Why are ye fearful, O ye of little faith?"* Why would you be afraid when I'm right here? Why would you be afraid when I have power over all? *Why are ye fearful* when I am still at the helm? I like His response because it's as if He is saying, of course I won't let you drown, of course I will save you, of course I am mindful. How could you doubt that? Did you really think I was going to let the storm win? I like thinking it wasn't just for the storm, but sending *peace* was meant for us, too. *Peace*, to calm and *still* our soul.

One time at church, as I was sitting in my sinking boat, *All is Well* was being sung and it got me thinking. I don't think *all is well* is referring to times when the waves are calm, perhaps it is referring to times when our soul is content, and we feel at peace even among our struggles. Because despite my storms I was dealing with in that exact moment, I felt that all actually was well because I felt that Christ was there with me and He was at the helm. And I think that's what I love most about the gospel. Not that it prevents us from dark clouds and choppy water, but that we can feel *peace* right in the middle of it when we turn to Him. *"Thou rulest the raging sea, when the waves thereof arise, thou stillest them."*[2]

I know how easy it is to wonder and to doubt during our emotional, physical, and spiritual storms. I know the panic that sets in when our boat is filling with water. I know how easy it is to feel like we are sinking from our persecutions, trials, doubts, temptations, and monetary woes. I know how easy it is for the adversary to exploit our struggles to skew our perspective when the waves are taller than we and the land to safety seems distant.

---

2. Psalm 89:9

He tells us Jesus is sleeping because He doesn't care or that our problems are not deserving of His time or that we are not worthy to save. *Oh,* how important it is to remind ourselves the adversary's entire purpose is to stop us from sailing, to stop us from ever getting on a boat again, to stop us from turning to Christ. I think of Adam and Eve when they were in the garden, the adversary was behind getting them to hide from the only ones that could help them. Anything that is trying to stop us from trying, to stop crying unto Him, to jump ship—anything to pull us away from Him, it's clear who it is coming from.

I know how easy it is to wonder if Jesus really *does* care because if He did, then the storms wouldn't be happening. If He really were conscious, if He really were awake, why wouldn't Jesus prevent it from happening? What's worth noting is in Matthew's account, *"Jesus entered into a ship* [and] *his disciples followed Him."* In Luke's narration, Jesus *"said unto them, let us go over unto the other side of the lake. And they launched forth."* The idea and invitation and prompting to set sail in the first place came from Jesus. A year later when Peter took steps on water during another vigorous storm, they were only on a boat to begin with because Jesus told them to be. When Ether was buried under the depths of the sea because the tempest was so extreme, we read it was the Lord God who caused the winds and the waves.[3] Christ, not only is He aware, but He is at the helm as our Captain through it all. Choppy waters don't alter Jesus at the head of our ship leading us to eternal safety.

Christ sleeping on the boat was not because He was not mindful, or that He didn't care. It's just He knew that all would be well, regardless of the storm. Like with Peter, even when the waves were still high, Jesus says, *"Come."* Like in Ether, when we continue through raging waters, *light* will always be with us.[4] When we turn to Jesus, we really can continue without panic knowing He is quite literally with us. Because the storm did not

---

3. Ether 6:5–11
4. Ether 6:10

last, our storms will not last. Because Jesus calmed the seas, He will still our soul. Because Jesus was sleeping, we can remember all will be well regardless of the storm. Because Jesus is our captain, we are led with safe sailing through winds and the waves. Our hope and our safety are in turning to Him, letting Him do more for us than we could ever do on our own. And when we plead and wonder, He will lovingly correct us *of little faith*, because He's never left. All really is well. He who even the winds and the waves obey has power readily available for us when we call out *master*. *Peace* is meant for you, too.

Finding Yourself in . . .

Those with Palsy

Matthew 9, Mark 2 & Luke 5

I've spent a lot of time on the floor. There have been too many times where my situation and trials have me collapsed on the ground. Sometimes on the ground I'd be yelling out to God, or sometimes I'd be too tired to yell at Him. Most times on the ground my body would just ache, physically ache because the burden I was asked to bear was too big, too heavy, too impossible, too unwanted, too long. On the ground is where I realize I've become just debilitated and crippled by not knowing how to move forward, not knowing if I could move forward. My time on the ground is when I feel stretched thin. I feel stuck. I feel stagnant. I feel completely immobile. Heavy burdens drain you of your energy and sometimes your optimism and faith. On the ground I realize I have been the man with palsy so many times.

We know the man with palsy obviously could not get to Jesus himself, and we all know he had a group of four choice friends who were so determined for him to get closer to the Savior that they carried him themselves. And what a night they chose! Jesus was at Peter's house that day, and it was the place to be.

There were so many people there they couldn't all fit inside so they gathered all around the outside as well. There was little room for movement among this multitude filled with those anxious to listen, and even with scribes, religious teachers, Pharisees, and doctors of the law. With their efforts to make it to Jesus, "*they could not come near unto him.*" As we know, the four men pulled this man up to the roof and they "*[broke] it up.*" They peeled off clay tiles to make a hole big enough that a grown man in a stretcher could fit through, and they lowered him down. The amount of work and effort that went into this entire thing is wild. How's that for a visual of love and support! An immediate lesson we can all clearly see is one of having a good support system with those determined to see you heal and succeed and move closer to Christ. Ones that know where you want to go and help push through things that get in our way to help get us closer. Even if it feels as though we are dead weight on a stretcher, they carry us. They are determined to see us be healed and become better and make steps closer to the Savior at those times when we feel we cannot do it ourselves. Oh, how important it is to seek and cultivate those relationships that can literally lift us up. An obvious refocus lesson of the importance of bringing people to Jesus and not letting anything get in the way. And when we do, we find ourselves *elevated* in the process.

Although, there is much to learn from their actions and example, there's more than just a good friends lesson in the experience of the man with palsy. There have been back-to-back, verse-to-verse miracles and healing thus far in the New Testament, how many times did we just read "*be thou healed*"? A direct miracle to a physical ailment. But this experience of palsy is different, Jesus didn't say be *healed* from this physical handicap, it was removed from forgiving sin. "*Son, thy sins be forgiven thee*" and he immediately arose and took up his bed. His palsy was removed from a *spiritual* change. If He were to say, *be healed*, Jesus would have been limited as a physical healer. And up until this point, many only knew of His ability to heal physically. But here He is, publicly showing His power to heal *spiritually*, both body *and* soul.

"*Who can forgive sins but God only?*" The exact question on the minds of the doctors of law, the scribes, and the Pharisees. It would have been easier to say rise up and walk, as a miracle healer. But to *forgive*? How could anyone? "*Ye may know that the Son of man hath power on earth to forgive sins.*" Power! Is it surprising to make the connection that when this man's sins were forgiven, he then had mobility? Probably not. Debilitated, paralyzed, stuck, the difficulty moving to, or moving away from, are all effects of sin. And I hope it's not surprising to see that forgiveness brings both internal and external healing. When we are immobile from sin or situation here in this life, right now, we have *power* from and because of Jesus. I love the visual connection to the fruits of forgiveness to this man's immediate contrast. I know back in these times, illness like this was thought to be punishment for sin, a direct result of bad decisions they chose to make. We now have more knowledge that everything unwanted is definitely not punishment, challenges will and do come to us all regardless, and even for good reason. I'd hate to assume the worst in this man because he received forgiveness, inaccurately thinking forgiveness only is needed when we have done something terribly wrong. I love instead thinking less of the man with palsy as a wicked man and more of a Savior who is anxious to freely give all of us at any moment He has with us, the power and gift of renewal. I instead like to focus more on Jesus's immediate desire to use on us the gift and power He saw worth dying for. Why *wouldn't* Jesus come with lifting and renewing our souls at every possible chance we have with Him, no matter what we have or have not done? Who is not in need of the fruits of renewal, revival, relief, and of lifted weight? That gift and power is there's for us at any moment, because of Jesus's ability and calling to heal inward and outward, both body and soul. And "*how is it done? . . . Because of thy faith in Christ.*"[1]

"*Son, be of good cheer.*" I think a lot of us would feel burdened with all that we cannot do ourselves. I wonder if we were the man

---

1. Enos 1:7–8

with palsy, how many of us would feel guilt or be ashamed if we saw Jesus knowing we couldn't get to Him on our own? I think a lot of us, to some extent, are hard on ourselves in our times of outreach, of struggle, in our times we feel we don't measure up, in our crippling times that may lead us to the ground. How many of us would feel, to some extent, ashamed of what we are lacking? Bothered by seeing others do that which we cannot? I have no idea what this man with palsy was feeling when he arrived at the Savior. But I do know that whatever it was, Jesus speaks first by calling him *son.* Jesus first, immediately expresses His compassion towards this man regardless of what he could not and did not do. *Son,* to first show the man with palsy Jesus's relationship, love, and dedication to him, to us, regardless of our afflictions.

Not everyone will be physically healed of handicaps in this life, but the man with palsy, among many others to follow this one, shows a surety of spiritual healing and lifted weight that can come to all of us, one that can come from within. "*Be of good cheer,*" He says. Good cheer because regardless of what we can or cannot do, He is there for us. Good cheer because regardless of our difficulty moving forward, He will change us. Good cheer because regardless of our crippling times on the ground, He will make it so we can *arise* yet again. Good cheer because whatever weight is holding us down and holding us back, we have access to *power.* We have access to renewal, revival, relief. Access to progress, to change, to forgiveness. To Jesus.

Jesus comes to lift and renew our souls at every possible chance we have with Him, no matter what we have or have not done. It doesn't matter what tiles need to be taken off, what plaster needs to be dug up, or what boards are to be torn away, turning to Him allows us access to His immediate desire to use His gift and power He saw worth dying for. So *be of good cheer.* Healing both body and soul are here for us because you are His.

Finding Yourself in . . .

Publicans and Sinners

Calling Matthew

Matthew 9, Mark 2 & Luke 5

During the summer when my husband and I were engaged, I was speaking at stake conferences and girl's camps and so on, several times a week. One of my firesides I had given happened to be the stake my husband was in. After I spoke, the stake president got up and he apologized to my husband over the pulpit. He admitted that when he saw my husband with me when he got off his mission, he was concerned for him thinking, *Oh no, what's he getting into with that girl?* Worried he would leave good habits and faith with his inaccurate perceptions, he publicly apologized for his wrong assumptions.

Moving to the west, others made it very obvious their confusion, their disgust, and their judgments towards me. I don't fit the mold for anything. I don't fit the mold of how I look in my religion, my community, and what I'm trying to tackle and talk about and pursue. How can someone succeed when everything about them in their demographic implies that they shouldn't?

It's like I was failing before I could even start. And you know, I've been speaking and writing since 2010 and still I receive frequent comments from members of the church I belong to, of how "disgusting" I am. And they're not even referencing my tattoos anymore—they've mentioned specifically my weight, the color of my hair, the type of pants I was wearing one day, everything, the weirdest things. Continuously receiving comments, and yes, even podcasts episodes over me literally saying, "*Nothing about this woman is Mormon anymore.*" Comments on events I'll be speaking at saying, "*No, anyone but her!*" I have been told for every reason you can think of, and I'm sure even more of ones you wouldn't believe, that no matter what I'm doing or working on, how I dress or look, or what I write, that *I'm doing it wrong.* I'm told I'm too much of something or not enough of something. Many people have been extremely creative over the years to find the most bizarre reasons to tell me that I do not belong, that I shouldn't be doing what I'm doing. My integrity and intentions are assumed and exploited by people I'll never meet. My entire character and soul are destroyed by people who I thought were in this together with me, because there will always be someone waiting to get bothered by something because they hold the world to their own personal expectations. I wish I could say I'm unique in this, but I'm not. I wish I was the only one that was told those things, but the hundreds of emails I receive on how others feel, or stories of things that have been said—they do not belong, that they're doing it wrong, a little too much or not enough of something, hurtful faultfinding, scrutinizing from others. Oof, too many of those emails.

Other than the Samaritans, the most hated people back in the New Testament were arguably the publicans, those who worked for the Roman government to collect taxes from Jewish citizens. They caused so much grief to the Jews and making their profits from the excess taxes they collected increased hatred against them even more. They were outcasts in the community, shamed, judged, detested, ostracized, but since publicans were native Jews, they were excommunicated in their religion as well. Then comes Jesus to Matthew, a publican. *"Follow me."* So, Matthew *"left his place and followed him"*. And because he did, Matthew was among the first apostles. Jesus pulled from a group of hated outcasts, excommunicated in their community, and saw great worth and great purpose and great need of him. Matthew hosted a dinner for Him with other publicans and *"sinners"* which shocked and outraged religious leaders. *"Why eateth your master with publicans and sinners?"* The Pharisees are titled for their religious teaching, leading, and dedication to the law, but blindingly so, as they are known for the most hurt and damage to others. Their knowledge and dedication blinding their fault-finding, caustic criticism, setting an example of how looking beyond the mark can be justifiably and dangerously subtle sometimes. Potentially and painfully, *"they that be whole need not a physician,"* denying themselves a better self and better things that come from Christ.

And is not the place for a physician, among the afflicted? Jesus goes to the hated, the forgotten, the different, *the sinners,* and spends time with them, befriends them, *calls* them, blesses them, loves them. Jesus does things differently and Jesus sees things differently, always has. And luckily so. How many views, actions, and thoughts do we have that we justify as well intentioned as we profess to be well committed to teaching our beliefs, that are actually incredibly damaging to others? How much are actually our personal interpretations that limit and prevent other's growth, potential, and their right to access all that God has for them because, like you, they also have Him as their Father?

Going back to my days as an investigator, several elders later confessed to me that they wrote in their journals after my first time going to church that they do not expect to see me there again, (there were a few companionships there for ASL needs). But honestly, I was right there with them; I was *not* going back, I was adamant. Nothing in me wanted to go back for any reason, it just wasn't *my thing*—God, or religion. To them and to myself, I was absolutely the *last* person that would ever get baptized, the last person to expect to find and *follow* Christ. But without even realizing what I was doing, I was already dressed in the same exact black dress, driving back to church the following Sunday. Which wasn't even a real dress, it was a strapless black covering you wear over bathing suits, but it was all I had!

In twelve years, I have lived in thirteen different wards and branches. I have had the most beautiful and the most disturbing experiences within them. My very first branch however, used to be a tiny post office. We didn't even have pews; we'd grab a fold-out chair for sacrament as we walked in. That little building was the start of *everything*. I have never felt more welcomed anywhere in my entire life than in that building. I am what happens when we love someone without judgment. I am what happens when we live how Christ has taught us to. I am what happens when different doesn't get in the way of compassion. I have a soul that can never die and it's inside of me and it's saved, and it's fed and it's thriving, and that's a result of others putting aside pride, assumptions, "culture," and fears. I am here because when I first walked into my teeny tiny branch in upstate New York, I felt 100% welcomed. No one cared what I smelled like. No one cared that I didn't want to get baptized. No one cared what I was wearing (or not wearing) or what I looked like; it wasn't even a thought. They still sat by me, they still included me. I am here because the "all are welcome" on the church sign really was practiced. I am here because people saw me the way God does—which is His. Where would I be if they didn't? What would I be doing? I'm disgusted at the possibilities; it robs me of everything I have and everything I am now. I feel profoundly grateful that it's not up to us to choose who is "ready" or not. Who are we to decide who is "ready" for *their* Father in heaven? Who is anyone of us to deny or get in the way of someone else and Jesus?

Everyone is welcome and deserving to partake of the love and blessings of Christ. Everyone is welcome in the gospel, in Christ's circle. It doesn't matter if you're an excommunicated tax collector, it doesn't matter if you were caught in the act of adultery, it doesn't matter if you're covered in tattoos, or what age or race or gender you are, it doesn't matter if you grew up and stayed in the Church, if you grew up and left the Church, or if you never heard of any church until now—everyone is welcome and invited to partake of forgiveness. Every single person is welcome and invited to partake of salvation, of change, of real happiness, of the indescribable feeling of Christ's love, of His Atonement, of a chance at a better life.

Your only qualifying factor to everything beautiful and blossoming, you already have, and you cannot get rid of or change: *You are His.* That's it. You are deserving of everything beautiful and blossoming simply because you are His and that cannot change. You belong here. Whatever you've been through, whatever you are or are not doing, whatever mistakes you've made, sins you've committed, you are still God's and there is so much more to come. You are loved. God's mercy will always be extended to you. A chance to change and be forgiven is extended to all. The physician of your soul has come, and Christ will never look at you like a waste of time or a waste of person.

Who is anyone to tell you God is not your Father and you are not His? Who is anyone to tell you Christ didn't die for you? Other people's perception of you should not stop you from what you are called to do. Jesus sees things differently and He does things differently. You are deserving of *everything* God, who is your Father, has to offer. He exists for you. To help you thrive and succeed and to become like Him. There is not one misfit, not one outcast, not one sinner, who Jesus is not saying to them, "*Follow me,*" and offering them something *more.* There is *not one* who Jesus does not see great worth and great purpose and great need of. Because Jesus had need of Matthew, Jesus has need of you, too.

Finding Yourself in . . .

The Woman with the Blood Disease

Matthew 9, Mark 5 & Luke 8

The pain and fatigue that comes from giving everything you have to finding progress and relief, and not finding it. The pain and fatigue that comes from putting everything in and not seeing anything come out. Trying to do everything you can only for things to get *even worse*. It is too familiar for me to feel the weight of what seems to be efforts that are in vain, unanswered prayers, unfulfilled fasts, continued passing time, and things going from bad to worse to even worse.

Our struggles cause time to slow down and feel dreadfully long, but the twelve years the woman who had a blood disease struggled for really is a terribly long time even without the skewed exaggeration. To struggle with health issues for twelve years, it likely felt like her whole existence was around this disease. She had a serious ailment involving frequent hemorrhages that could not be stopped. But it wasn't *just blood*, it overspills to so many other things. When frequent or consistent blood loss occurs, she'll have had to deal with being dizzy and lightheaded for twelve years. She would have been short of breath, pale, tired, and very weak for twelve years. Loss of blood causes rapid heart rates, weak pulses, rapid and shallow breathing, confusion, even loss of consciousness. Twelve years, likely many organs could have stopped working or been on the verge. What was her state actually in after twelve years of this? I'm betting it was severely more grim than we envision.

With fatigue and failure, whatever it is that was left in her, although probably not much, it was all invested in every option there was. She used every resource and penny she had to find relief and progress and healing with all these different doctors, but it just never happened. No progress was made. Visualizing her working through her fatigue and discomfort and pain to gather new funds to try again. Each time being hopeful it would be different than last. Just to have her hope and heart shattered time and time again. And it wasn't that her repetitive efforts didn't change, it was that her condition *worsened*. She had suffered *"many things of many physicians, and had spent all that she had, and was nothing bettered, but rather grew worse."* I don't know that I can fully understand the scope of everything her disease had brought with it. Being treated by many physicians but to no avail, she'd exhausted her funds, her resources, her options, impoverished herself seeking a medical cure and she was probably thinking, what now? What next? I got nothing. Dead ends. There are no ways, no options, no hope left that I can see.

With the physical ailments aside, like leprosy, blood was believed to make one ritually unclean, and anything she touched would have been perceived as unclean also. No contact would be made with her, touching Jesus or anyone else would have been perceived as inappropriate as it would transfer defilement to them. Which results in solitary life, for her to be alone with everything. Spiritually and physically, she was alone. Her pain and loneliness must have been unimaginable. I know she felt loss of hope, loss of strength, and loss of faith, and she probably thought often about how maybe she was the exception to life getting better here. We don't know who she is—she's not named in the scriptures—but oh how much we can relate to her. To those times, those unanswered prayers, unfulfilled fasts, passing time, unwanted and uncharted paths. Times when it seems things have gotten worse from doing what we think is right. Times when it seems we're alone, unnamed, or unimportant. "Who am I? What if I'm the exception?" we ask.

Even though she was filled with fear and fatigue and failure, she is among the masses in Capernaum trying yet again for change. *"One of the rulers of the synagogue, Jairus by name"* came to Jesus asking for Him to heal his daughter. *"And Jesus went with him; and much people followed him, and thronged him."* In a large, densely packed crowd, when this unnamed woman *"had heard of Jesus, came in the press behind, and touched his garment. For she said, If I may touch but his clothes, I shall be whole."* Her faith and desperation carried her through to act even when failed attempts and society says she shouldn't.

> Her touch of the hem of His garment
> was the cry of a believing heart.

"Straightway the fountain of her blood was dried up; and she felt in her body that she was healed of that plague." It was in the exact moment of contact with just His hem, she was immediately healed. Years of failed attempts, her lingering impossibilities disappeared, and she received permanent recovery. She experienced the thrill of health throughout her body as healing power flowed from Him to her.

Touching only a tassel of His clothes, her contact was so inconsequential and minimal, no one could have felt it, especially among the throng. But Jesus did. Christ who was walking in streets that were *so* busy, it was like sardines, shoulder-to shoulder foot traffic, and Christ stopped and asked, *"Who touched me?"* His disciples were justifiably confused; if it were me, I would have laughed at His question—*everyone* was touching them. Dozens were pressing upon them, and Jesus immediately stopped in this steady pressured stream of movement of people. He was not simply touched but touched by someone excising faith. *"Jesus, immediately knowing in himself that virtue had gone out of him."* Jesus *felt virtue*, or *power* as the Greek say, leave Him.

This is an actual giving of His own to the afflicted, it is a literal giving of Himself to others.

Jesus *"looked round about to see"* who had done this. Jesus was in motion to an errand for someone else with a crowd of expecting people following Him there, and Jesus stopped for her. And looked for her. This unnamed woman trembled with fear of rebuke and fell in the dirt, buried under the crowd. Painfully aware of her perceptions of uncleanliness by societal out-casting, I wonder if she may have felt guilt that she of anyone would dare to be deserving to touch Him. Or maybe whoever He was in route to go heal was more deserving than she. Standards taught that she would transfer her ailments and ruin Him. *Trembling* with fear, *"she fell down before him, and told him all the truth."* *"Daughter,"* He calls. *"Be of good comfort, thy faith has made the whole."* Whole? Is that not her exactly worded intentions to seek Him, that she may be *whole*? Addressing her feelings and fears and desires, He is mindful. And she is deserving. By calling her daughter, He tells her that she is His. And He literally gives us some of Himself. He is the one who transfers to *us*. Unclean can become clean, corrupted can become cured. By going to Him who is holy in faith, we too may become holy.

"Thy faith has made the whole," not your act of touching; it wasn't the shawl that healed her, it was her *faith*. Our faith is more important than the acts; faith is a principal of power. If we do acts alone with no faith behind it, they will have no power. *"Go in peace,"* He says. The Prince of Peace gave some of Himself for her to able to do so.

You know what I wonder about? How many were among the masses that were purposely and outwardly following Christ, yet never seemed to act. They observed comfortably close yet distanced, but didn't act. I wonder if we, as a curious crowd, get near but never truly touch? More than a decade this woman turned to the things of this world for healing and progress, spending untold wealth on earthly remedies that could not ease her incurable disease. But Christ did. And it was her inconsequential and minimal efforts that brought that.

Maybe you feel alone or burdened, maybe you've exhausted your resources and passing time brings you to fear, fatigue, and failure. Maybe you feel there is no way or no options left, and life has brought you to the ground, in the dirt. Maybe you feel unnamed, unclean, or undeserving. Sometimes we feel our strength has run so thin that another day doesn't seem like another chance, but another burden to bear. But although we may feel those things, the woman with the blood disease teaches us truth that your efforts are not in vain, your faith has real power. When we take to Him whatever it is that we have left, He honors and accepts even the smallest of efforts. A new season will come, one filled with blessings and prosperity.

Because of the woman who fell in the dirt means for you that He will not let you go unnoticed. Every time you reach, He will pull you up. He will ease even lingering impossibilities. This means you have a Savior that is a one-by-one Savior. One who knows you. Exactly and perfectly does He know what you're going through, know what you're feeling, knows your intentions and desires. He knows all of you because you are His. And because you are His, that means you are not the exception. You are His which means you will always be deserving. You have a one-by-one Savior who looks for you, makes time for you, and stops for you. Jesus does give part of Himself to you. And you *can* be *whole*.

So *go in peace.*

Finding Yourself in . . .

The Pharisee Simon

The Two Debtors and the Woman Who Washed Jesus's Feet with Her Tears

Luke 7

In the beginning of conversion and membership, I felt like I mostly had just myself to figure it all out. All I had was church pamphlets, occasionally the missionaries, and a hope that this supposed God was as good as He said He was. There was so much I had to change and turn away from and rewire and relearn. It was such a deep reconstruction of my entire existence, it seemed. And I had no idea what I was doing. It was a lot of guessing, a lot of experimenting. And most times I felt like all I had was God. At the time that felt pretty lonely and pathetic, and it caused deep anguish. But I would never change it. Feeling like all I had to turn to was God was exactly what led to the change there has been and relationship with Him there is today. He did for me what I couldn't do for myself. I overcame things I couldn't before Him. I conquered, I *changed*. I became new. And I never went back. A deep reconstruction of myself and my life happened only because of Christ. Turning to Him, allowing Him to change us, is how we give Him the opportunity to show us how great He really is.

Through my painful struggles and sacrifices and changes, it all led me to knowing God. As hard as things were and continue to be, I know Him. And I love Him with a real love. He has become real to me. And when He becomes a reality to you, could you trade that? Could I trade my strengthened and real relationship with my Savior for anything? There's no way. I am not willing to give up the intimate and vulnerable moments because it's those moments that caused my deep trust in Him. Because of how much He has done for me, it seems close to impossible to turn away from that, to forget that. He has done much too much to have time fade something that monumental. Because He has changed me so much, because He has forgiven me of so much, because I have overcome and conquered so much, even still, I feel anchored to Him. The contrast of before and afters because of what God has done for me; even when I struggle, I find focus and commitment to keep going. I have a humility and passion to worship Him because I want to, not because I'm expected to. He is real and He is mine.

Maybe that's one of the lessons to the two debtors and the woman who washed Christ's feet with her tears. With the reality of our trials and sins come the reality of Christ and the reality of His power, His love, His forgiveness.

A Pharisee named Simon invited Jesus over for a meal and Jesus went. It's pretty clear that the Pharisee's intentions were not pure because Simon lacked the basic common greeting that all guests receive from anyone. A common customary among all is to provide water to clean dusty feet, especially before eating, as well as greeting with a kiss, and applying oil on the hair of the head and the beard. None of which happened, which seems like an obvious hint towards trying to find things to condemn Jesus for because not even the bare minimum norm was done. It was customary to remove sandals before eating, wash your feet before every meal provided by the host, and one would always sit with their legs extending behind them, so feet were the furthest from food. And then came an uninvited guest.

She was known by many others to be a sinner, which has many scholars confident in their claims that she had been a prostitute. This woman knew how others viewed her, she would have been treated as unvirtuous, unclean, and less than. Being known for your sins by others must have caused a great deal of courage to go into a Pharisee's house uninvited. There had to of been much courage and conviction to not hold back, or be stopped, or cower in guilt or shame. She *"stood at his feet behind him weeping, and began to wash his feet with tears, and did wipe them with the hairs of her head, and kissed his feet, and anointed them with the ointment."* Although uninvited, she comes prepared and equipped with an alabaster box of expensive ointment. She comes in great conviction and humility, and she does that which the Pharisee failed to do. A known *sinner* did more for Jesus than the pride of the professed leader of religion. And she did it with deep devotion and gratitude. *"Her sins, which are many, are forgiven."* The amount of sin to reach public knowledge as hers did, did not disqualify her for forgiveness and change. She had come to Jesus repentant and forgiven for her *many* sins, all of them.

Can you imagine the amount of love she must have felt to bathe and clean His feet with tears and wipe it with her own hair? To wash and anoint with loving submission and true repentance? She sought out Jesus in belief and came with repeated fervent kissing. Her gratitude knows no bounds because His love knows no bounds. She tasted the sweetness and healing power of Christ which led to a new life of committed, deep devotion of worship. I'd like to think that's what I would do when I see Him, because with reflection, it would be the bare minimum to do for Him after all that He has done for me. As we receive the Lord's forgiveness, we are filled with greater desire to love and serve Him even more.

And on top of the Pharisee's judgmental gaze, he has unspoken protest, thoughts of disgust, and justified doubt that

Jesus is who He claims to be. The host found fault with Jesus for accepting this act of kindness from a sinner. Culture had it that those in need could come in for leftover food, so her arrival wasn't what caused a reaction out of Pharisee Simon, but allowing to be touched by her? Allowing to be touched by an unclean woman who had all this sin stacked high enough to reach the level of notoriety for it? Clearly, the Pharisee did not see the woman the way our Savior sees us. Jesus has no use, nor is there any influence of His actions, for labels that society places upon others.

"*When the Pharisee which had bidden him saw it, he spake within himself, saying, This man, if he were a prophet, would have known who and what manner of woman this is that toucheth him: for she is a sinner.*" If He really were a prophet, He would know this about her and would not allow her to act as she is to Him, are his unvocalized thoughts. Jesus debunks his thoughts immediately by acknowledging he *knows* Simon's thoughts, which would in turn imply He knows of this woman as well. (And perhaps, He knows her better because of the intimate actions she would have made with Him for repentance). How could one know unspoken thoughts with exactness unless Jesus was who He claims to be? Jesus responds to Simon's judgmental disgust with the parable of the two debtors. How does the Lord see us in His eyes when we feel we have made too many mistakes? This is a parable to remember.

"*There was a certain creditor which had two debtors: the one owed five hundred pence, and the other fifty. And when they had nothing to pay, he frankly forgave them both. Tell me therefore, which of them will love him most? Simon answered and said, I suppose that he, to whom he forgave most. And he said unto him, Thou hast rightly judged.*" The debt is not forgiven because he loved much—he loved much because much was forgiven.

Although Simon probably considered himself to be a righteous man, at least by Pharisaic standards, he was blinded by pride. Comparing Simon to the debtor who owed fifty pence, Jesus was suggesting that he also needed to be forgiven for sins, as well. *Are we not all sinners?* The parable as Jesus's response was not about the repayment of debt, but to see the woman's actions differently. The parable is not encouraging or condoning sin, but more to do with change, with gratitude for our undeserved forgiveness and empathy toward fellow sinners. Others judged and condemned Jesus for eating with sinners and publicans, yet regardless of how Simon might have judged his personal worthiness, the lesson is not directed to this woman. The lesson wasn't against the sinner, the lesson was for the one who perceived he had none. Perhaps the act which is more grievous was his, one who did little with what is offered to us by Jesus.

I wonder how Pharisee Simon's attitude toward the woman may have previously made her burden seem heavier. I wonder if we sometimes make another person's burden worse because of our reaction to their sin while we minimize or justify our own. How do we see those around us? A seasoned *sinner* did more for Jesus than the pride of the exemplar leader in religion. I wonder if we are blinded by pride more than we notice and claim to be the one who owes only fifty pence and do little in return for Jesus? Are we at times guilty of inviting the Savior into our homes but then failing to treat Him the way He deserves? Are we, like Pharisee Simon, failing to provide and neglecting the things we ought to be doing?

Simon did not see her the way Jesus saw her. He only saw her as what she had been. Jesus *"said unto Simon, Seest thou this woman?"* An invitation to lift his sights to understand and look differently. *"Thou gavest me no kiss: but this woman since the time I came in hath not ceased to kiss my feet. My head with oil thou didst not anoint: but this woman hath anointed my feet with ointment."* Luckily, the Savior does not see us the way others see us. Even with our many sins, that is not how He defines or limits us. He sees us for who we really are and what we can become. He knows our mind, He blesses us for any actions we take to Him, and He has no hesitations and no shortage of forgiveness to all, for all.

"Thy sins are forgiven. And they that sat at meat with him began to say within themselves, Who is this that forgiveth sins also?"

Another direct response to Pharisee Simon's claim that Jesus was indeed no prophet. Instead of correcting him in speech, Jesus did that which *only God could do* in front of one seeking to condemn—forgive. "*Thy faith hath saved thee; go in peace.*" He was doing exactly as what the title Savior means, *save*. This woman loved much because she had been changed and forgiven much, an expression of love that flows from the freedom of having all debts canceled. Her repentance was so sincere for receiving remission, her worship and actions knew no bounds as she lived a beautiful life of *peace*. Peace within herself, with her God, and peace to take with her as she leaves Simon's house and goes into the world.

Repentance brings forgiveness and change for all who partake in doing such. Your Savior has authority to forgive even seasoned sin stacked high against us. It's the most beautiful fruits of Jesus who is yours, removing guilt, pain, bad habits, and mistakes and leading us to a beautiful, changed life of *peace*. In the times we may wonder how our Lord may see us, remember Jesus has no use, nor is there any influence of His actions, for labels that society places upon us. Even the vilest of sinners can become holy and pure, needed and useful. No amount of sin will disqualify us for forgiveness and change and *peace*. Because the act which is most grievous is perhaps the one doing little with what is offered to us from Jesus. As we approach our Savior with humility, loving submission, and true repentance, we will conquer. We will change. We will become new. As we continue to go to Jesus and allow Him to do all that He can with us, He will become more real to us. We will know Him. And love Him with a real love. And when you know that, could you trade that?

Finding Yourself in . . .

Feeding the 5,000 and Peter on the Water

Matthew 14, Mark 6, Luke 9 & John 6

Aﬀter hearing the news of the passing of His cousin, John the Baptist, Jesus departs alone to a desert place to pray. *"When the people had heard thereof they followed him on foot out of the cities."* When He sees of the gathered multitude, *"being moved with compassion . . . they were as sheep not having a shepherd."* He heals them. Perhaps Christ found healing for Himself while mourning, as He heals those He also loves.

His disciples arrive in the evening, suggesting that the multitude depart for supper; *"send them away,"* was the counsel of His apostles. Christ didn't want to depart, not wanting to leave, but wanting a continuance of giving, of helping, of loving, of sustaining, of nourishing. And Christ performs the miracle to the 5,000 with loaves and fish to show it by action. Though the idea was to bring what little there was, the apostles addressed the task to be impossible; the little bit they had was not sufficient for them. And if there's a lesson to learn from that thought on its own, it's the reality that *He* is sufficient for them. Christ wanted to be with them even more, to give even more. Until they were *filled.* Substance increased because of our Savior. One of the largest themes of Christ is magnification, doing, giving, and making more of and for us. He sends no one away but comes and stays to *fill* that which is lacking, making us whole.

The disciples then get on a ship to leave to sea, but only doing so because *Jesus* tells them to. *"And straightway he constrained his disciples to get into the ship, and to go to the other side before unto Bethsaida,"* while Jesus goes to the *"mountain to pray."* Then the winds come, and the waves rise, and they are yet again, on the same Sea of Galilee in a storm. And they struggled in the storm for hours. There was no sight of their Master of the winds and the seas until *"the fourth watch of the night he cometh unto them."* With incredible parallels to their time in the storm the year previous, they wrestle with the storm on their own first. I can already see myself in that statement on its own, putting forth my own efforts and struggle before Jesus interjects. Is that always my own doing, or is it sometimes Jesus's?

"When the even was come, the ship was in the midst of the sea," tossed with waves. *"And about the fourth watch of the night he cometh unto them, walking on the sea."* A storm with the intensity to not let up after most of the evening, waves that have grown in great heights, rains allowing minuscule visibility, and Jesus walks on and through as though on solid ground. Peter crying out in fear, Jesus speaks peace and reassurance to them in the midst of their storms. *"Be of good cheer; it is I; be not afraid."* Peter, when recognizing his Savior, is overcome with courage and desire to go to Him.

And Christ, says, *"Come."* And so, Peter steps. *"He walked on the water, to go to Jesus."*

"But when he saw the wind boisterous, he was afraid; and beginning to sink." The adversary is perhaps most successful and destructive in skewing our perspective and our thoughts. It's a dangerously subtle game to get it all backwards and to see it all wrong during our unexpected and unwanted, our times in the storms. The adversary tells us Christ is sleeping because He does not care, that we are not worth it and why bother. He is quick to

point out our failures and focus on our slip ups, our sinkings, our shortcomings, our doubts. And we go over in our heads about what we are lacking and what we did wrong and what we could have done differently.

It's true, right? That's what we do with Peter on the water. And that's what we do to ourselves. I'm not sure I have sat in a lesson about Peter without talking about everything that could have gone differently. It's the adversary that shifts our focus off the good, off the progress, off of Christ, on to all that is around us, and tells us that *other* things are worthy of concern, of time. And He gets us to feel bad about our efforts so we will stop making them.

It's the adversary's unhealthy and inaccurate perspective to get us to slow down, to stop trying, to retreat, to give up, to stay put, to sit still, to stand still, to *stay on the boat* and to keep our distance from Christ. It's his winning game to wear the negative lens and stay stagnant in the question about Peter and about ourselves and our lives: *Look how he failed. Look what he did wrong. How could you think those efforts are worth bringing before the Lord. Don't bother.*

We focus on, and then start believing, that we failed. And our efforts are not good enough or that we are not good enough, or that the waves are too big, the thunder is too loud, or that Christ is too far, or what we are trying to do is too impossible.

But before we get trapped in the critique, please recognize: *Peter is the only one who got off the boat.* He is the only one who tried, the only one who stepped, who did *something.* He is the only one that experienced and accomplished something new and something different and something *better.* He was the only one who was doing as Christ was doing. And He was the one who made it closer to Him because of it all.

He, who even the winds obey, could have stopped the storm at any time, *but didn't,* until after Peter made it back on the boat. In fact, Peter never would have even been on the boat in the first place if it weren't for Christ Himself telling him to. So, *what if,* it's not even about walking on water. *What if,* it could be about going to Him, *during it all?*

What if, He who says *"come,"* stay longer, let me *fill* you, was not sleeping on the boat a year previous because He doesn't care, but because He just knew all *will* be well, regardless of the storm.

What if, *"O thou of little faith, wherefore didst thou doubt?"* was not in response to Peter's sinkings. *What if* it was in response to Peter's pleadings to be saved? As if saying, *of course, I will save you, rescue you. How could you doubt that? I am right here. I am out here with you. Did you really think I was going to let the storm hurt you?*

Your efforts, your small steps forward, may only seem like slip ups and failures—but you are in fact moving forward. You are in fact doing something seemingly impossible. Even the slip ups and the smallest of steps are getting you closer to Christ.

As Peter knew, safety does not come from reaching for the boat. But from Him. When I feel the weight of my storms cause me to sink, I am learning to better grab the helping hand of the Savior. A hand that is never shortened. A hand that is always extended. A loving and understanding and an always-there hand. An all-powerful, perfect hand. Ones that have *"graven thee upon the palms of [His hands]."[1]*

Regardless of outside influence, regardless of slipping and sinking, you have a Savior who does not send you away. Because He is filled with compassion towards *you.* Because your Savior is one who is not wanting to depart, not wanting to leave you. With His outstretched hand, He is there with continual healing, giving, helping, and loving. When we are in need, when we are lacking, when we are hungered, and when we are in the wilderness with the sun that is setting, He is there to sustain, to nourish, to *fill.* Though the task is impossible, He comes with blessings of magnification, doing, giving, and making more of and for us. When we are overwhelmed and afraid by the storms or the steps needed to be made, Jesus comes with peace and reassurance. Because

---

1. Isaiah 49:16

the rain and the winds and the waves stopped, that means our storms will also end. Because Jesus saved Peter, He will save us too. Because Peter was protected, means you will be protected. Because Peter succeeded and did the impossible, means you can, too.

He stands unaffected by the storms with His focus set on you, with the invitation to *come.* To *be of good cheer,* to *be not afraid.* Because, *of course, thou of little faith,* He *will* save. He is right here. He is out here with you. Get off the boat. Take the step. Do the impossible.

Finding Yourself in . . .

The Bread of Life

John 6

The most frequent question I get with all my messages, emails, and interviews, is *why do I stay?* My writings are known for, and have grown organically from, my honesty. I'm honest about my consistent trials brought my way and the things that don't work out. I write multiple books on them because there are so many of mine to write about. And you know, some of which I've had to self-check in with myself and ask that same question. *Why am I here? Do I want to be still?* Right out of the gate from baptism when I lost all my friends and family, it would have been so easy to stop. To go back. Back where twenty-one years of habits and traditions lay deep within my veins. Out of all the examples I could use, I'm currently thinking of the time I was moving across the country a few months after I was baptized because God told me to. I fit whatever bit of my life could fit into a 1990's two-door car, which was not much at all. Leaving behind the only way of living that I knew of, seeing all my belongings on the side of the road for a garbage man to pick up, and having to cope with the idea that with that move, I could maybe never see my dad ever again.

While on my way, I stopped after twelve hours to take a break in a Chicago Hotel. I looked out the window and I realized I didn't recognize a single thing. And it hit me, everything hit me. It hit me that I was alone, that I was doing something new, something scary, something life changing, something I didn't want to do, something I didn't understand, something that required way too much of myself. And I collapsed on the ground in the middle of this hotel room, and I fell apart. The temptation to turn around, to quit, to go back to where things were comfortable and where things made sense, was through the roof. My body physically ached, and I was yelling at God because I didn't know if I could keep going, I didn't know in that moment if I wanted to keep going.

Ye seek me, not because ye saw the miracles, but because ye did eat of the loaves, and were filled. The Bread of Life sermon was the day after Jesus's miracle with the loaves and the fishes and He knew that the multitude had only come back because they wanted Him to feed them again. Like murmuring with Moses's experience in Exodus, Jesus's audience was expecting and wanting fulfillment on the temporal level. Which is where we can see a lot of disconnect even with us, others, and God. Sometimes we focus—and justifiably so sometimes—on immediate needs, immediate wants, personal desires, and we lose sight of, or become disappointed in, the greater things He offers.

"What shall we do, that we might work the works of God?" Provoking Christ to show them how to multiply loaves and fishes, they request Him to show them a sign and benefit even more to fill their personal wants. Using Moses as their ticket to reap their desires, they respond with, *"Our fathers did eat manna in the desert . . . He gave them bread from heaven to eat."* Jesus teaches in excessive repetition, *"My Father giveth you the true bread of heaven . . . I am the bread of life."* And how many times did He say it? *I am the bread of life . . . the true bread . . . I am that bread of life . . . I am the living bread . . . eat of this bread . . . this is that bread . . . the bread of God . . .* Well, a lot. And they weren't

understanding there was another bread that they should seek, one that would fill and sustain much longer than a moment.

Moses led the children of Israel to Mount Sinai after their deliverance, during which the Israelites *murmured* because of a lack of food. "*I will rain bread from heaven for you,*"[1] manna from heaven to gather every morning except on the Sabbath. Murmuring also because of thirst, the Lord commanded Moses to strike a rock and water came forth. Taking a quick bird's eye view of Exodus, a multitude was led with Moses by God through the wilderness and through the Red Sea. Moses went to the *mountain of God*, he foretold a coming of a deliverer, Jehovah declared His name *I Am,* the Passover was instituted by the Lord, Israel was fed from manna from heaven, and Israel murmured against the Lord. The parallels of this to Jesus and to John 6 are obvious. Multitudes follow Jesus across the Sea of Galilee, Jesus goes to a mountain, it was during the time of Passover, five thousand were fed from five loaves of bread, it was said that Jesus was "*that prophet that should come.*"

"*Except ye eat the flesh of the Son of man, and drink his blood, ye have no life in you.*" As important as food is, He was teaching the real nourishment is so much more than just sustenance for just a moment. Christ being the real bread "*giveth life unto the world.*" Isn't that a beautiful visual? He gives us *life.* He gives us a better life here, and an everlasting life of blossoming blessings hereafter, never to end. When we eat and partake of His bread, of His body, He fills us, and it's lasting. "*Your fathers did eat manna in the wilderness, and are dead.*" The difference is monumental, temporary versus lasting, "*a man may eat thereof, and not die,*" everlasting. How do we get *that* bread, Christ, the real manna from heaven?

He sacrifices His life for them, for us, and if we would "*cometh to [Him],*" and "*believeth on [Him],*" He will receive us and we will receive from Him. His invitation to partake is to come and believe! And He that goes to Him, he "*will in no wise cast out.*" He

---

1. Exodus 16:4

turns no one away. He simply says, "Just come to me and believe in me. I will give you something much better than what you had in mind." "*This is the will of Him that sent me.*" It is God's will to save us, to keep us forever, and give us something better than we had in mind, something that will last forever.

Similar to the woman at the well who wondered if He was "*greater than our father Jacob, which gave us the well,*"[2] they also wondered who on earth Jesus was that he be better than what Moses offered? "*Is not this Jesus, the son of Joseph, whose father and mother we know? how is it then that he saith, I came down from heaven? . . . How can this man give us his flesh to eat?*" Just as He taught to that Samaritan woman that He was the living water where "*whosoever drinketh of the water that I shall give him shall never thirst*"[3] because the water the He gives is from a well of *everlasting life; "If any man thirst, let him come unto me, and drink."*[4] He also taught this multitude to come, to eat of *His flesh,* be filled, be sustained, and be nourished forever.

And how many times did He have to articulate that? *He that cometh to me shall never hunger; and he that believeth on me shall never thirst . . . but should raise it up again . . . have everlasting life: and I will raise him up at the last day . . . He that believeth on me hath everlasting life . . . a man may eat thereof, and not die . . . if any man eat of this bread, he shall live forever . . . the bread that I will give is my flesh, which I will give for the life of the world . . . my flesh is meat indeed, and my blood is drink indeed. He that eateth my flesh, and drinketh my blood, dwelleth in me, and I in him.* So, a lot. They didn't understand that what He was offering was *greater* than what they were asking.

Is your mind spinning with all of the connections to the sacrament and the last supper? It should be. "*Eateth my flesh, and drinketh my blood . . . dwelleth in me, and I in him.*" It makes me think also of when Jesus healed the woman with the blood disease, when she touched His hem and He *immediately* felt "*virtue*

2. John 4:12
3. John 4:14
4. John 7:37

had gone out of him."[5] Jesus *felt virtue*, or *power* as the Greek say, leave Him. Both are a literal giving of Himself to us. To help us and be closer to us. And Moses being referenced was not just because of the manna miracle, or the parallels in the order of experiences, but also because both were during the season of Passover. Passover is when, traditionally, stories of Moses and Pharaoh, and of the plagues, and the escape through the Red Sea are told. Not only honoring through story, but the Passover meal is *bread*. The last meal Christ ate was Passover *bread*. The Bread of Life sermon absolutely has deep symbolism and connections to *bread*, the Last Supper, Passover, and our sacrament. There is incredible history and context I'm excited to add to have that blossom even more for you. All of which will be in the Last Supper chapter because it is deserving of a section of its own.

Jesus Christ was the very sign for which they were asking. But like their ancestors in the wilderness of the Exodus, these people were less interested in obeying the commandments than in eating. Jesus Christ was offering words of eternal life, and the people were hoping for a handout of immediate personal desires. The multitude murmured *and* His disciples murmured, they were *offended*, is the word Jesus uses. I don't love that word, and I've learned that word is a bit of a trigger word to a lot of people, because I can see myself in them. And in the moments that I have been them, it wasn't annoyed or prideful, like a lot of definitions imply, I was hurt. I was struggling. And sometimes that blinded me from the bigger picture.

"From that time many of his disciples went back, and walked no more with him." We go to Him for our immediate needs, we want immediate relief, immediate blessings, immediate change. We want what we have in mind for ourselves. We want Him to take our hunger away now, take this struggle away now. And when that doesn't happen, when an immediate need isn't filled, when we aren't getting what we want, especially if it really seems needed, it would be easy to become disappointed, angry, or hurt

---

5. Mark 5:30

enough to turn around, even if momentarily. The question I get asked, and maybe you too, is if we aren't getting what we want, then why stay. *"Then said Jesus unto the twelve, Will ye also go away?"* Will I also go away?

"Lord, to whom shall we go? thou hast the words of eternal life."

Collapsed on the floor in the middle of a hotel room in Chicago, screaming out to God, physically aching, not knowing if I could keep going, not knowing if I wanted to keep going. My eyes were closed out of exhaustion and then . . .I saw Jesus. I saw Him. I could picture Him standing right in front of me. And He smiled. He smiled at me. That was it. That was all I needed. I knew that no matter how hard things were, no matter how much I didn't understand, I knew that what I was doing and working towards, He was happy with. And that it was right. I felt this jolt of energy run through my body, but it wasn't energy; He jolted my soul within me, and fatigue was far, far away. And in that moment, I felt alive and sure and unstoppable and whole. And He reminded me of the bigger picture I wish I didn't lose sight of as often as I do. Absolutely worthy of repetition to remind us and to better understand what's really being offered. That there is another *bread,* another blessing, another *One* that we should seek. When we focus too much on immediate needs, immediate wants, personal desires, we become disappointed or lose sight of that bigger picture. Refocusing to Jesus reminded me that what He is offering is *greater* than what I had in mind, the best things. The lasting things. The eternal things. We are in fact, meant for something so much greater than this—so much greater than the here and now, greater than the fleeting things of this world. And it is God's will to give it to us, if we choose.

I know I don't have to stay. I know there have been times that it would have been easier to leave. I lived a good life before I was baptized; I was happy and did things that gave me purpose. I know I can have a good decent life outside of it all, but like with Moses's manna, and like Jacob's well, and like my twenty-one years pre-baptism, blessings do come still, but without Jesus, there is an end with them. The difference is monumental; temporary versus lasting. And there is so much more to come. In the times that we hunger, that we thirst—in the times when we are lacking, when we are needing, when we are weakening—He fills us, strengthens, and sustains. Unlike everything else, He does not fail, fall short, or run out.

When we take a step back and look around with a refocus, and all of a sudden, a wave of gratitude consumes us, and we are just overwhelmed for where we are and what we have with us. And somehow, we feel new. And just from that step back and a refocus comes a perspective shift. A better perspective. And somehow, we feel a contentment that electrifies us, and humility that jolts our soul within us, and a resolve that changes us. And we smile. A real smile. And even the hard and the unexpected will seem exciting to us. And the overlooked and the mundane will seem vibrant again. Because this amazingly beautiful, messy, indescribable thing we're living is something to never take for granted. And we'll wonder why we don't see it like this more often.

I want to stay. I choose to stay. I choose Him over my narrow-mindedness. I choose Him outside of just wanting Him to fulfill my personal wants. I don't want to turn to Him because I want Him as my butler. He is my friend, my brother, my advocate. One who gives us true *life.* He gives us a better life here, and an everlasting life hereafter. You have life in you and part of you. *He* is your Savior. He literally gives of Himself to us to have *Him* in you and part of you. *This is the will of Him that sent me.* It is God's will to save us, to keep us forever, and give us something to satisfy once and for all.

So . . . *to whom shall* I *go?*

Finding Yourself in . . .

Jesus's Unwashed Hands

Mark 7

Looking beyond the mark is a warning in scriptures and a warning over pulpits. But, *gah*, how hard that is in actuality. Looking beyond the mark is such a subconscious thing, getting caught up in the weeds with things that seem like they matter but aren't actually important. Slowly causing confusion, distraction, and haze. Smoke and mirrors to intellectually and blindly fall victim to the adversary, causing us to shift our focus, get it all backwards, standstill, or fall away.

The first thing I think of with unwashed hands is looking beyond the mark. Spending so much time and effort on things that don't actually matter, pursuing with so much dedication that which is not from God, that which is purely cultural, purely man-made tradition. The apostles in Mark 7, and Jesus in Luke 11, did not wash their hands when they were among Pharisees and scribes. Clearly, this was not a matter of sanitation, but once again, critiquing their actions for worthiness and law breaking. Following the Traditions of Elders, it had everything to do with ceremonial uncleanliness. They believed if you do not wash your hands, you do not eat.

There were a ton of different things added that the Pharisees ritually did with exactness, another which was mentioned in this particular experience, was *"as the washing of cups, and pots, brasen vessels, and of tables."* Tradition of the elders, although I'm sure you can guess by what it's called, is not the law of God.

Original purpose had been lost with their interpretation and added laws; the Pharisees added thousands of regulations and rules themselves, most of which were not in harmony with the law of Moses. One of them being that Jews were not bound to deliver non-Jews from death, for such a person was *not* a neighbor, (more on this in the Good Samaritan). To a Jew, none were neighbors but Jews. Plucking a blade of grass was considered harvesting, dipping a radish in salt too long and they'd be guilty of pickling, spitting on the ground and rubbing it with your foot, you're guilty of farming—the list goes on. And compliance with the Traditions of the Elders was more important than observance of the law itself, penalties for violating carried out by the scribes. Those that did not wash their hands were deemed defiled, ritually impure, and *not Jews.* And to no surprise, the Pharisees *"found fault"* and accused Jesus of behaving in a way that would make Him unclean with respect to their traditions.

And how does Jesus respond? He calls them *hypocrites,* just like Isaiah prophesied of them. *"Full well ye reject the commandment of God, that ye may keep your own tradition." "Laying aside the commandment of God." "Teaching for doctrines the commandments of men."* Their traditions, their focus, their actions, their judgments are of men alone, and are holding more weight and importance than building up God. Well intentioned or not, looking beyond the mark. *"Making the word of God of none effect through your tradition, which ye have delivered: and many such like things do ye."*

This is bringing up a self-reflective, discerning look on culture versus doctrine. We too, can sometimes value the traditions of men more than we should. Who knew how easy it would be to be influenced by the confusion and the hurt of the world? How dictating the worldly trends could be with our time? Who knew how damaging the distractions of good things are to keep us from the best things? Who knew just how easy it would be to overcomplicate enduring? Who knew the subtleties of the adversary could be so damaging, and yet so hard to pick up on sometimes? Who knew how easy it would be to get distracted? How easy it is to lose focus. How easy it is to lose sight of those simple truths of the gospel. We too, are sometimes tempted to elevate man-made rules above compassion and love. Holding other people to our own personal standard as a rule of judging righteousness. The amount of pain caused from this same stamp of Pharisee view and actions, judging someone else's righteousness based on what they wear, what they watch, what they look like. I have been on the receiving end of so much judgment and pain from people's personal reactions to how I look and how I act. Too many people have been hurt from the judgments of others based on cultural things that have no relevance to who they really are and their relationship with God.

"This people honoureth me with their lips, but their heart is far from me." Cultural views holding more weight than the commandments of God, we all have been affected by this. Thinking teaching right and wrong to *others* is more important than the command to love all and leave it to Jesus. Talking more about this is the woman caught in adultery chapter— fault finding, finger pointing, even when against commandments, is not tolerated nor is it our responsibility. When we worry what others are doing and define their righteousness by it, Jesus calls that *hypocrisy.* And *"in vain do they worship me."* Passing *"over judgment and the love of God: these ought ye to have done."*[1]

How do we navigate that? Jesus told them that their inwards are *"full of ravening and wickedness."* Ravening, meaning a wild animal that's hungry and hunting. Which is not great for them to hear but freeing for us. That solidifies to us that He knows us. He

---

1. Luke 11:42

knows everything about us; He knows our motives, our efforts, *our insides.* Freeing because that pain and judgment from others holds no weight. What do we do with people like that? What Jesus did. *"Let them alone: they be blind leaders of the blind. If the blind lead the blind, both shall fall into a ditch."*[2] We keep going. We keep living. We set boundaries with others. We keep praying. We keep turning to God. We let go of any hurt or weight caused by someone who is oh so human. Because other people's perceptions of us is the adversary's game and ain't none of our business. Who is anyone to tell us that God is not our Father and we are not His? Absolutely nothing is worth turning away from the most powerful being to ever exist.

I know there's a whole lot going on right now, a ton of different viewpoints, a lot of passion, confusion, and so on. And it's challenging, right? Trying our best to figure out what to do and what to say and what to stand up for amidst the confusion and the hurt and the passion and the conflicting, or tiring or hurtful or exhausting. Trying our best to navigate which things are worth our efforts. And with it all, I find weighted confusion, deep self-reflection and soul searching and reevaluating and refocusing. Where I've landed is . . .more Jesus. I want and need more Jesus—it needs to be more about Him. I want Jesus. After a lot of dead-end attempts to navigate through so much coming in our direction, my pursuits to learning more of Him, becoming closer to Him, have been what climbs me out of ditches, clears the air, and reprioritizes my view. When I turn to Him more fully, I receive a freeing fire of redirection to trim down, to cut back, to let go, turn cheek, and to *run* with better simplification to Him. Because it really is about Him.

More Jesus.

---

2. Matthew 15:14

Finding Yourself in . . .

The Transfiguration of Christ

Matthew 17, Mark 9 & Luke 9

I was not seeking out any kind of personal fulfillment with talking to the missionaries; I felt fulfilled enough to enjoy life on my own in my own ways. But after a few weeks into meeting with missionaries, I vividly remember coming home from work late into the night, late enough that the nightlife was already settling down around my apartment and it was becoming a strange kind of quiet. And I remember I was just standing there, looking up at the sky, and I remember thinking, *Is there really more than just this? Is there more to me? Are there really answers to the most gut-wrenching questions of the soul? Are there really solid answers to the biggest questions of the universe?*

I remember life extremely well not knowing the answers I do now. I remember the unrest that came from not knowing; this pit that was in my stomach every time I started to wonder the meaning, if there was one, of why we are here. And I remember extremely well the sweaty palms I got just by driving by a cemetery because of the lack of answers I had about what was going to happen to me. I found myself consumed with these questions of the soul, the meaning to this all, what some people dedicate their whole life looking for and never find.

And then I read something, and in the thirty seconds it took to read it, I realized, I had it. In thirty seconds, I had the answers to the questions of the universe. *"And it came to pass that as I was thus racked with torment, while I was harrowed up by the memory of my many sins, behold, I remembered also to have heard my father prophesy unto the people concerning the coming of one Jesus Christ, a Son of God, to atone for the sins of the world. Now, as my mind caught hold upon this thought, I cried within my heart: O Jesus, thou Son of God, have mercy on me, who am in the gall of bitterness, and am encircled about by the everlasting chains of death. And now, behold, when I thought this, I could remember my pains no more; yea, I was harrowed up by the memory of my sins no more. And oh, what joy, and what marvelous light I did behold."*[1]

Whoa, *the coming of one Jesus Christ?* Meaning all of that happened when Christ wasn't even born yet. All that forgiveness and renewal and healing happened before Christ came to earth. Because Christ could heal and forgive Alma before Christ even came to earth, that means Christ was preordained to be Christ. That means that pre-earth really existed. And that means I existed before I came to this earth and the entire plan of salvation really is real. That means God is real and I am His. Confirming where I am to go next after this life and that eternity was a reality, which means why I am here has meaning and purpose. And that would mean I had the answers to the questions of the universe.

Christ being transfigured has everything to do with us. It has everything to do with what we are doing here and what that means for here after. Having gone up a mountain, Peter, James, and John witness Jesus in a way no one else would until after resurrection. A week previous, Jesus foretold of His coming death, all of which His disciples responded in total confusion and disbelief. He told them that He *"must go,"* and *"suffer many things,"* be *"rejected,"* and *"be killed,"* but that He will *"be raised again*

---

1. Alma 36:17–20

the third day." Peter trying to *rebuke* His words, professing that would not happen—*"this shall not be"*—Peter would make sure it wouldn't. Jesus always knowing what He came to earth to do, responds to Peter, *"Get thee behind me, Satan."* Although well intentioned and said with love, *Satan* was used to imply that anything that would prevent Jesus from doing what needs to be done to save us, is the soul drive of the adversary, and He will not heed. This is when the famous invitation from Christ comes, to *"take up his cross daily, and follow* [Him] *. . . For what shall it profit a man, if he shall gain the whole world, and lose his own soul?"* What does it profit us to gain what the world has to offer when we can't take it with us? What good will it do to neglect and deprive our soul that can never die?

Taking up our cross, our struggles, our suffering, and following Him until the end doesn't mean follow Him just until we die, follow Him to our death. This is another invitation to follow Him to where He went after, following Him to what's next. Inaccurate to what the Pharisees thoughts, death is not a destination, and it is not an end to Him or to us; we shall *"not taste of death."* Continuing His original point of resurrection, we are to continue to move forward through our sorrows and struggles, on His path that continues through a doorway to another life of magnification. Our pain and our path have purpose. Everything Christ has ever done has been for a much bigger picture than just what's *here*. It's always been about receiving more *hereafter*. Taking our cross and following Him leads us to exaltation, receiving all that He has, becoming as He is.

His kingdom is not of this world, and neither is ours. But how could Peter, James, and John fully know what He meant at this time? A week after, the mount of transfiguration is like Jesus saying, *Let me show you.*

Jesus takes the three of them *"up into a high mountain."* Just as the three of them will in Gethsemane, while Jesus was praying, they fell asleep. They awoke and *"saw His glory, and the two men that stood with him."* They did not witness the beginning of the transfiguration, so we are unsure how long they were together already, but Peter, James, and John awoke to Moses and Elias (Elijah) and Jesus in full glory that fell upon Him from heaven. *"His countenance was altered, and his raiment was white and glistering,"* His *"face did shine as the sun."* No longer relying on His word alone, they saw with their eyes that He was in fact, more than just a rabbi, more than just a man of flesh and bones. Illuminated with light, elevated, His whole presence reflected a divine radiance that showed them who He is really is. They became eyewitnesses to the Lord in a glorified and transfigured state; *"We beheld his glory, the glory as of the only begotten of the Father,"* they became witnesses that He is in fact, king of kings, and the Son to our God. A glimpse of where all of this leads to, for Him, for them, for us.

Moses and Elijah spoke of the Savior's *"decease which he should accomplish at Jerusalem,"* the atonement. His sacrifice was planned before the creation of the world, prearranged, always intended to happen, Christ always having been willing. Saving us always was part of it before the world ever came to be. What happened on this mount was preparing for His coming death in six months, as well as completion of the Law of Moses and the fulfillment of the prophecies in the Old Testament. Great significance lies with the two visitors being Moses and Elias. Because Moses came, it marked the end of the Jewish Law, the Law of Moses would be done away, and we are to now look to Jesus. God gave laws through Moses for moral, ethical, spiritual commands, performances, and sacrifices. *"And in me is the law of Moses fulfilled;"* a profound connection as He prepares for His death, as sacrificing by shedding blood will be done away, with the one great and last sacrifice of Himself. Precisely why Pharisees felt so threatened by Him. Not just because they thought He was blasphemous, but because without the laws of Moses to uphold, what use would there be for them? New laws, new ways, new leaders, would take away everything they were.

Elias is Elijah, representative of the Jewish Prophets, the one who had not died, and who was the last prophet of the Old Testament that held the keys of the sealing power. A week previous,

Jesus said to Peter, *"I will give unto thee the keys of the kingdom of heaven."*[2] And in this moment on this mount, the transfer of keys of authority is carried out and Elijah, *"who was to restore all things,"* gave a fullness of divine priesthood authority, the promised keys of the priesthood to Peter, James, and John. Because this happened, these apostles can now carry the work of the kingdom on the earth forward even after the departure of Jesus.

Jesus is preparing for His death by distributing keys because His entire passion and purpose is to save *all* mankind. These same three apostles who had just received the keys, will be the same ones to appear in great glory themselves to Joseph Smith and Oliver Cowdery in the temple at Kirtland, Ohio. Granting them authority and essential keys that we still have today, never to be taken away. These promised keys of the priesthood include the saving ordinances to bring us all back; this is how we *all* can be saved, how we *all* can return to Him. When we think about all the work in the temple, even death cannot limit the power of these keys to bringing us back to Him. Everything that happened on this mount and everything that Christ has ever done, has been driven by passion and purpose to get us back to Him. He exists for you. He lived for you, He died for you, He wants you back. And He has done everything to make sure that that's possible.

"It is good for us to be here." To be there, with Christ, with the vision of eternal realities shining in front of them. Peter was anxious to delay the departure of the heavenly visitors, that he offered a spot for them to stay in from the annual Feast of the Tabernacles that was there for each individual worshiper to use. While speaking of his suggestion, Peter was interrupted by the climax of this experience. *"A bright cloud overshadowed them,"* and they heard the voice of Elohim Himself, the God of all, speaking directly to them, *"This is my beloved Son; hear ye him."* A witness from the creator of the universe Himself, giving His stamp of approval that this is right, this is the right way, this is from Him. Not only is this a witness that God and Christ as

---

2. Matthew 16:19

different Beings, but because God spoke to them, we know that God speaks, and that means He speaks to us, too. Because God directed them, we know God directs us, too. Because God gave approval, we know that God is very much involved in our lives. That all of this matters to Him; *we* matter to Him.

The three apostles "*fell on their face*" in fear. And when they raised their eyes, it was all over, and they were alone with Jesus. Having become a personal witness and received spiritual enlightenment, they were "*charged*" by Him "*that they should tell no man what things they had seen, till the Son of man were risen from the dead.*" It would be this inner circle of understanding they would have, and continue to be, as the three of them would soon be the three witnesses in Gethsemane for His suffering as Jesus takes upon Himself the sins of the world. No doubt that as they were taught and shown in great beaming glory of His coming death and also His resurrection, that it would prepare and strengthen each of them in the eventful and painful days ahead.

And after Jesus had risen, Peter and John would both finally be able to testify of the things that they had seen firsthand, so powerfully. John, being a witness *of light,* tells that He was not of blood, or of flesh, or the will of man, *but of God.* That *true light* and *grace and truth* comes from Him. And "*many as received him, to them gave the power to become the sons of God.*" And my personal favorite, is Peter's words, "*We have not followed cunningly devised fables, when we made known unto you the power and coming of our Lord Jesus Christ, but were eyewitnesses of his majesty.*" Meaning, this is not some fable, some fairy tale, not some mythological folklore only there to make us feel good as we drag on to inevitable death. It's real. All of it is real. Everything we have been taught, everything we are working towards, it's all real. He's real. This really did happen. *They saw it,* they were there. Which means our faith and our efforts are not in vain. Why we are here has real meaning and purpose. And that would mean we have the answers to the questions of the universe. "*Take heed, as unto a light that shineth in a dark place, until the day dawn, and the day star arise in your hearts."*[3]

Because of the Mount of Transfiguration, they were able to move forward through their suffering and sorrows knowing there is more to come. Because of who Christ really is, we are able to move forward through our pain, through our suffering, through our sorrows, as we take up our cross, and follow Him. Life on earth is like a tiny little in the middle of this bead on this never-ending string. Following Him will take us well past this life and into blossoming, glorified magnifications to become as He is. *Lord, it is good for us to be here.* With him. Having what we have. With all that we need. Driven by passion and purpose to get us back to Him, He has done everything to make sure that that's possible. Because it has always been about giving us more, even before the world even was.[4]

---

3. 2 Peter 1:19
4. Note: In Joseph Smith's translation of Mark's record, we learn that John the Baptist was also present on the Mount of Transfiguration. We are unsure of His role because our New Testament account is incomplete, but others believe that we could potentially learn several others were there and much more was said and done than we currently know about. Joseph does reveal that on the Mount of Transfiguration, Peter, James, and John were also transfigured. They saw a vision of the future transfiguration of earth as it will appear in its glorified condition.

Finding Yourself in . . .

The Good Samaritan

Luke 10

*A*h, the Good Samaritan, a famous and misinterpreted parable that is far from a simple lesson on doing good deeds or a discouraging and damaging lesson on always going the extra mile for others. There is deep culture and history around this to give different meaning. Most parables fit into two categories: given for instruction, or given to entrap or rebuke. After the return of the seventy, Jesus was teaching a group of disciples when we are taught this parable that fits into the second category.

Along comes *"a certain lawyer stood up and tempted him saying, Master, what shall I do to inherit eternal life?"* A man who knows his scriptures very well, is attempting to trick, to test, to ensnare the knowledge of Jesus, the infamous teacher, by asking Him how to get to heaven. What the real question was, what would Jesus say is most important, following the Law of Moses, or Jesus's own teachings, hoping His answer would prove that Jesus did not honor the law.

Jesus responds with a counter question, *"What is written in the law? How readest thou?"* The law, referring to the Torah, include the books of Moses, Genesis, Exodus, Leviticus, Numbers, and Deuteronomy, and this *certain lawyer* is a man who knows his scripture. Knowing by heart the law and perfectly reciting the commandments, that we are "*to love the Lord thy God with all thy heart, and with all why soul, and with all thy strength, and with all thy mind; and thy neighbor as thyself,*" Jesus responds his answer is *right*. But perhaps the lesson this lawyer needed was what Jesus said next, "*This do, and thou shalt live.*" Differentiating contrast between knowing and doing, teaching him directly where he is lacking. The lawyer must have picked up on that lesson because he responds "*willing to justify himself.*"

"*Who is my neighbor?*"

It's an interesting question, which again, points to following the laws and seeing how Jesus falls within those laws. The Pharisees had added hundreds of laws to the law of Moses, one of them being that Jews were not bound to deliver non-Jews or those of unknown ethnicity from death, for such a person was not a neighbor. *Not a neighbor.* To a Jew, none but Jews were neighbors. But even outside of trying to entrap Jesus, the lawyer doesn't really want to know who his neighbor is, but rather who his neighbor *isn't*, to narrow the field so he can claim that he is fulfilling the law at bare minimum. Laws were being used as excuses and man-made bounds against those that were different from them, anyone who was not them. Is your mind racing with history of wrong actions against those that are different?

Jesus's response is the famous Good Samaritan parable, so well-known that it's left a positive, common name and term even outside religion and believers to imply someone or something who shows love and care for people. And you know what's interesting? Jesus chose a Samaritan as an example for the Pharisees, *a Samaritan!* What a plot twist, what a sting. To the Jews, Samaritans were anything but good, literally the very last culturally to be praised as an exemplary neighbor, or really, praised for anything at all.

After centuries of increase, the time of Christ is at the peak of some of the most intense hatred in history. They claim a title of half-breed mongrels because they intermarried when the ten tribes of Israel were taken into captivity, marrying outside of covenant, and breaking the Law of Moses. They're impure, covenant-breaking heathens, that were avoided and shunned at all costs. And Jesus uses the most hated and unclean above any other gentile as the hero to the parable. Jesus's parable has a Samaritan being the only one who acted correctly and the one who truly kept God's commandments. If this was just about doing a good deed, there would be no need to make the *good* man in the story a Samaritan, any ordinary, decent Jewish man would have done just as well.

"A certain man went down from Jerusalem to Jericho, and fell among thieves, which stripped him of his raiment, and wounded him, and departed, leaving him half dead." With Jerusalem being high on a hill, the road itself winds down about 3,200 feet, the stretch being about eighteen miles. The victim is believed by most scholars to be a Jew, traveling down a road that is so infested with crime, it's called the Red Path or Bloody Way because of the known and frequent atrocities. He was robbed, beaten, abused, and stripped naked. Being left *half dead* was worse than being killed, he was left to feel, to struggle, to suffer with unquenchable pain. Disgusting.

Then comes a priest. Then comes someone who should have, out of respect to his office, been more than willing to act with service, love, and mercy. But *"when he saw him, he passed by on the other side."* But he *did* see him there. Then comes a Levite, a Jewish male who has patrilineal descent from the Tribe of Levi, and who is an educated and devotee of God who serves. Second-ranking figures to the priest, Levites had an obligation and specific charge to help travelers both economically and in other ways, and *"we see that he came and looked on him, and passed by on the other side."* Showing a little more interest, yet ultimately, did not act. There is one who gave it close to no thought and we have one who examines and contemplates the pros and cons, but both come up fruitless, because regardless of little or great thought, no action was made. With those that were obligated to help those in need, did they only act when it would be seen by men? Did they think they were too important, high in title, to help? Justified in the man-made tradition alone, the wounded was not in their circle of community, thus, he was *not* their neighbor and not worthy, not deserving of help.

The lawyer tried to *justify* himself, and the same could be said with the priest and the Levite. We sure are a people of justifications. The list of excuses in this parable is long and seem worthy to defend. They could have been in a hurry. What if the thieves were still there? Surely, someone else would come along, right? What does it have to do with them to get involved? They had their own duties, their own spiritual well-being to look out for. The priest would become unclean by touching a corpse or blood, which would make him have to undergo an elaborate seven-day ritual cleansing. This would make him virtually useless for an entire week, not being able to serve in the temple, leaving his community short staffed. It must not have been worth the hassle.

But both men were travelling *away* from Jerusalem where the temple was, not towards it. So, who is to say where their justifications land? Whatever it may have been, both were totally off the hook when it came to the man-made traditions of rabbis—those added laws by the Pharisees to not have to serve non-Jews—they were, after all, not their neighbor. They certainly weren't obeying the law of Moses—but those man-made single-community culture.

I can't really blame them because we do the same thing, don't we? I have been them so many times. And a lot of those times, I have felt comfortable in passing up helping. I tell myself all the reasons why I can't, and feel content within my own reasoning. Within my community, don't I do enough as it is to qualify for the blessings I'm wanting? If I were the priest and was asked about this on judgment day, just like I will be in all my many passed opportunities to help, I will say, *I know, I wanted to, but I was busy! I almost did, but I was scared. I couldn't because it would have affected all these other things.* We look for the loophole so we can do what we want to do and still get the rewards.

Perhaps not knowing why they didn't stop, not knowing their reasoning, is a lesson for us in of itself. Potentially it could be implying, yes, there are many excuses, there will always be excuses; that's the point. There are always pros and cons to weigh, always effort, always sacrifice. The Samaritan may have had an even longer list of reasoning to pass by as well, it is, after all, a coming together and clash of the most hated and despised sect of *dogs*.

"*A certain Samaritan, as he journeyed, came where he was: and when he saw him, he had compassion on him.*" He bound up his wounds, administered emergency care with "*oil and wine,*" both having medicinal qualities, to sooth and to disinfect. "*He put him on his own beast, and brought him to an inn, and took care of him.*" He made arrangements for further care, paid two days' worth of wages to the innkeeper, "*and whatsoever thou spendest more, when I come again, I will repay thee.*" The last suspected to be a hero, did what he could do, and he did what no one else would do. I love that. But it's more than being compassionate towards the less fortunate.

"*Which now of these three, thinkest thou, was neighbour unto him that fell among the thieves? And he said, He that shewed mercy on him. Then said Jesus unto him, Go, and do thou likewise.*"

The emphasis in the story is on the doer, the Samaritan, not on the good deed. And the adversary exploits this hero Samaritan to use against us. Maybe you have fallen victim to it too, like I have on some occasions. Have you sat in lessons where the emphasis point is on going the extra mile? He gave everything to this man and went above and beyond—that's an exhausting lesson that can drain us, discourage us, guilt us into thinking we are never doing enough, not measuring up, and even more is always required. The adversary distorts this parable by shifting our focus and gets us to feel bad about our efforts so that we stop making them, to stop us from making healthy boundaries and take care of ourselves so we can thrive. What is the balance of losing yourself in service of God and finding yourself, versus just losing yourself?

I find I am more productive and filled when I remember the strategic choice of characters that Jesus uses. As important as what he did was, there's even more to learn from what the Samaritan did *not* do. It's so easy to love those that love us, but he did not limit his service and compassion though the wounded was a stranger and an enemy. He was not stopped by prejudices and fears and differences. He was not concerned of others' perceptions or blurring the lines of class, titles, and cultural expectations. He was not persuaded with loopholes, nor was he influenced with prideful justifications. He did not follow man-made traditions and barriers that separate. He was no respecter of persons, nor did he believe his community was above others. A Jew's neighbor were only Jews—restricted to only their community, within their same way of thinking, within their same beliefs, actions, and standards. But nowhere does it say, comfort those in need only if they deserve it, bear only when convenient, serve to only those who make good choices, love only those who think, act and belong to the same church as you. This Samaritan's love knew no bounds and lived outside of inaccurate and fictitious boxes. Putting the words *neighbor* and *Samaritan* in the same sentence seems, to Jesus's audience, like a contradiction in terms. But this certain Samaritan also did not let history, past, and community define him in negative ways, or hold him back. The first (the Priest and the Levite) will be last, and the last (the Samaritan) will be first, I suppose?

"He had compassion on him," and it was his compassionate heart that made him different and made *the* difference. I like to think that this hated and despised half-breed was so full of compassion because he knew a thing or two about being judged, mistreated, left behind, and hurt. I don't doubt this healed and saved victim went off to do likewise because of the impact it had on himself. Is his view of Samaritans and those different than him a little altered now? Absolutely. Will he be looking at others differently, perhaps a little more the way Christ really sees? Absolutely. Will it be more likely that he will *"go and do likewise?"* Absolutely. Change happens with change. A beautiful fruit of the pure love of

Christ is a ripple effect of softening hearts, changed perspectives, peeled back layers of tradition, and man-made barriers that may have taken hold. Breaking patterns, breaking prejudices, learning and teaching and changing from example. Then the term brothers and sisters will blossom far beyond the walls of our church membership. Because truly, we all are in this together. Are we in such a hurry on the covenant path that we are passing those on the other side without stopping?

This was Christlike love, a love that knows no bounds, no restrictions, no outside influences. Loving as Christ does is a love that sits with sinners, calls the publicans, touches the unclean and impure, forgives in the act, reaches for those sinking, stops for those buried in the crowd or alone in the heat of the day. To the original listeners of this parable, when it was first told, such a concept would have turned their world upside down. But loving as Christ loves with no bounds; the heroes—the called, the forgiven, the changed, the humble—are always the "plot twist" in every one of his stories.

This was a reoccurring lesson Jesus had with the Pharisees; they kept the smaller commandments while ignoring the spirit of the law of God, which was loving as He did. If we are honest with ourselves, is there someone we would be hesitant to help? Why is that? We likely will be confronted with our own prejudices and cultures. That is the challenge for us, to allow Jesus to change us, to strip away man-made layers and influences to *His* ways of seeing and being. Christlike love knows that no bounds is not for us to feel, but also to grow in and to attain to have towards others.

But the perspective I love most in this parable, is the symbolic one of Christ's role in our life. When all those who may fail us in this fallen world of skewed perception and excuses, we may feel like we keep getting passed by. Look to this parable in a bird's eye view of the reality of pure Christlike love, from the source Himself.

This man who fell could be us on this journey in this fallen world, or the Fall of Man. If we are traveling to higher and holier places, symbolic of this road to Jerusalem which was on a highly elevated hill, or whether we are for any reason making a descent away from it, Christ *will* come. When others pass us by, we are to remember the half-Jew, half-Gentile Samaritan who came, is symbolic of our half-mortal, half-immortal Messiah. And He *does* come. He does stop for us. And He stops with *compassion*. Jesus is no stranger to dark, dangerous paths and the roads less traveled. He does what no one else can do. He comes with oil and wine, symbolic of oil and blood, His Atonement, which is able to bind up our wounds. Like the Samaritan who set the man on his donkey, Christ carries us. He carries our burdens and bears our griefs and our sorrows. He holds us up when we are weak. When others fall short, and when we fall short, our Savior has already paid the price of what is needed for us to recover, for us to be better, for us to become different.

You are always deserving of help and healing. Your Savior's love knows no bounds. The unfailing pure love of Christ *endureth forever,* and comes from the source Himself straight to you, His *neighbor.*

Finding Yourself In . . .

The Adulterous Woman

The Barren Fig Tree and the Woman Healed on the Sabbath

Luke 13 & John 8

What we think is a clean-cut lesson on forgiveness to sin, is actually deeply layered and interwoven thick with way more ties to us than just *sin,* but trauma and pain caused by others. Knowing what happens right before this *adulterous women* was caught in *the act* is just the start of the unraveling of these numerous deep scenarios and connections to us.

THE ADULTEROUS WOMAN

If you're reading this book in order, then perhaps one of the most apparent things you've picked up on is the relentless efforts to accuse and arrest Jesus. Almost all the encounters of inviting Jesus to dinner and seeking His responses has been a strategy to get Him to condemn Himself and then get rid of Him. This encounter with the woman caught in adultery was a product of exactly that. This was not some organic offense that someone stumbled in upon. It was a prearranged, deliberate attempt to put an end to the Savior of our souls. How any of this happened has nothing to do with justice for this woman and *adulterous* actions, which may not have been what we even think it was, but a lash out of built-up anger from a series of conversations at a feast.

This happens the day after the Feast of Tabernacles, which is a seven-day festival of thanksgiving and praise, while ending on the eighth day with a holy convocation. This is happening in the fall, and Jesus will be crucified in the upcoming spring. During the span of this week-long festival, Jesus had taught in the temple multiple times. Why does He teach often in the temple? The city of Jerusalem was overcrowded and busy, which leaves little wonder why Jesus retreated to mountains and seas for more to gather and hear Him. To preach in Jerusalem, the only place to gather a crowd would be in the temple, an incredible thirty-six acres, the size of twenty-six football fields. *Twenty-six.*

Large crowds of people gather to listen to Jesus as He teaches in the courtyard of the temple on the third or fourth day of this feast. Jewish teachers marveled in confusion, *"How knoweth this man letters, having never learned?"* He was no graduate of their schools, never sat at the feet of their rabbis, nor had He received official accredited or license to teach by them. Many professed with conviction that it was because Jesus *"is a good man,"* Jesus is the Son of God, while others were committed to prove He was a deceiver, a coworker to the devil, possessed with a demon. And many of the Jews actively sought Him out among the masses to tell Jesus exactly that. They approach Him with anger and hatred as they professed to His face that He has *a devil.* John even tells us that even Christ's own close relatives did not believe that He is the Messiah.

As Jesus teaches of who He is and who sent Him, *"they sought to take him, but no man laid hands on him, because his hour was not yet come."* The Pharisees heard others speak of other miracles

He will continue to do, so they sent for *"officers to take him,"* to arrest Him. *"Yet a little while am I with you, and then I go unto him that sent me. Ye shall seek me, and shall not find me: and where I am, thither ye cannot come."* And here we have a group of the most educated in scriptures and in the letter of the law, but cannot comprehend the simple plan of salvation, *"what manner of saying is this that he said"?* His hour was not yet come; knowing His entire purpose to even come on earth, to save us, hadn't happened yet. Their anger and hate had been bubbling up over time, and after He had taught a second time in the temple on the last day of the feast, they were driven to action to finally put an end to Him once and for all.

The timing of Jesus's words could not have been more precise. Visualize at this week-long event at the temple, the ending service is at the Pool of Siloam, (a lot of great historical context on this pool is found in the Healing the Blind chapter). And here is where a priest fills a golden jug that someone could wash with, being carried to an alter to pour out symbolic water from the well of salvation upon it. And *this* is when Jesus teaches the beautiful truth that *He* is the living water to draw upon. *"Jesus stood and cried, saying, if any man thirst, let him come unto me, and drink."* I'm assuming the Pharisees took the timing of this truth as a turn of the knife in their blasphemous wound against Him. This is also when Nicodemus, a member of the Sanhedrin, infamously defends Jesus by asking, *"Doth our law judge any man, before it hear him, and know what he doeth?"* Which was received as insulting and maddening for some of his colleagues to respond, *"Art thou also of galilee?"* Meaning, are you also a disciple of this devil-possessed Galilean?

The priests, teachers, and Pharisees were more enraged because, despite repeated attempts to discredit Jesus and get Him arrested, they continued to fail. They were determined to take Him by force but could not lay their hands upon Him because His hour was not yet. So, what did they do?

The woman we know as the one caught in an adulterous act. This woman was a result of a prearranged and deliberate attempt to finally get Him. "*The scribes and Pharisees brought unto him a woman taken in adultery; and when they had set her in the midst, They say unto him, Master, this woman was taken in adultery, in the very act.*" I am sick thinking in what circumstance had they *taken* her. Absolutely, death by stoning was the penalty for *both* involved in an adulterous act. But because this woman was brought to Jesus alone was more evidence of a specific plan, and the other man involved, was likely one of their own. This is speculation around facts, but I personally cannot help but leave the option on the table that this woman could have been lured, coerced, or even forced by a man in position of power for the sake of their planned attacked against Christ. The Jewish leaders cared nothing for true justice, evidenced by the fact they only brought the adulterous woman when law required both to be punished.

As they drag this woman in front of a crowd, I'm mortified what kind of state she was in as they forcefully took her. They ask what is to be done to her, in hopes to get him to say something in opposition to the law of Moses concerning punishment for adultery. Had Jesus said she should be stoned according to law, the accusers might have said that Jesus was defying the existing authorities. Had He said that the woman should go unpunished or suffer only minor infliction, Jesus could have been charged with disrespect for the law of Moses. This whole situation was designed to be a lose-lose ploy against Him.

Could this not also be a painful reminder of the too-many-to-list reasons why it is unnecessary and severely damaging to judge others not knowing anyone's full story? Judgment was never meant for the Pharisees, but for God only. The responsibility to point out and condemn what other people are—or are not—doing, was not theirs and it is not ours, even if we may think we do have the full story. And before I move on to what I love so deeply, a quick thought on how ironically sad it would be if we were to treat others as we have been mistreated. Fault finding, finger pointing, even when against commandments, is not tolerated nor is it our responsibility. Pharisees, who were so set on "teaching" above anything else, caused the most pain and damage, because damage is a sure fruit of any kind of judgment. Is our focus on the actions of others? Can some comments and actions of ours be blocking another's route to their Savior who is ready to forgive, just as He is with us? Let's allow people to repent. Let's focus on the reality of mercy and forgiveness in our own life, and on the reality that we can be better and do better. *Moving on.*

Whether it's pain, damage, and trauma caused from others, or caused from herself, Christ comes to us. In our dark times, our hard times, our messy times, He comes. Not only does He forgive sin, but He heals that trauma and hurt and pain from others and ourselves. The power of Christ blossoms beautifully even more in this story, teaching us that He comes with healing from all.

I imagine how quiet the crowd got as they watched and listened to what Jesus would choose. I imagine how she was feeling as the Lord saw her and who she was. I imagine the woman scared to death to hear the fate of her life. The life of this woman depended on Jesus. How true that rings for even us. At the risk of danger to Himself, Jesus responds, *"He that is without sin among you, let him first cast a stone at her."* Jesus silenced His critics while graciously addressing a sinner in need of mercy and understanding. He delivers a healing balm to her and anyone with a heart weighed down with guilt, shame, trauma, and pain. Convicted *"by their own conscience,"* the silence was now filled with the noise of dropped stones hitting the dirt and slow shuffles as *"one by one"* the accusers walked away. Jesus exalted Himself above the Law of Moses, reestablished righteousness, and skillfully illustrated the harmony of justice and mercy in Christ's salvation.

"Jesus was left alone, and the woman standing in the midst. When Jesus had lifted up himself, and saw none but the woman, he said unto her, Woman," which was a term of high respect in those days, using the exact term Jesus used for His own mother, *"where are those thine accusers? hath no man condemned thee? She said, No man, Lord."*

The only one who was qualified to throw a stone, didn't.

We know very well God does not condone, overlook, or deny sin; I'm sure that's the main lesson you've always had around this experience. We know the Savior came to earth to save us *from* our sins and not *in* our sins. God pronounces judgment on sin, but He also provides a way to escape condemnation.

Maybe those moments Jesus took to pause while drawing in the dirt were because He was upset from injustice that may have happened to her. Maybe the silence was a result of someone— *Him*—who loves her without judgment. She is not named, we do not know her, and unfortunately, the only thing we do know has branded her by this one little blip in her life. But He knows her. He knows her heart. He knows exactly her mistakes. Her sins. Her trauma, her pain, her embarrassment, her fears, everything. And at the worst moment of her life, Jesus is with her. Contrast to how the Pharisees and scribes handled her, Jesus treated her with dignity, care, and mercy as He spoke and listened to her, and called her by the same respected term He used for His own mom. Her fear immediately being swallowed in Christ's compassion. *"Neither do I condemn thee: go, and sin no more."*

She is not condemned. Jesus does not ask for explanation, nor does He begin a sermon on self-improvement. Not because He doesn't care about wrongdoings, but because of His immense love that is so eager to forgive so He can, like He did with her, present us with an opportunity at new chances, at new life. Even a crime worthy of death, and He raised not His voice, nor hesitated with forgiveness. *"As often as my people repent will I forgive them."*[1] As often as we need, He *does* quickly and fully forgive. Why would that be so readily available though? Because that's precisely why He purposely died. He lived and He died just for us to have the ability and privilege for us to change, to be better, to do better, to do it again, to start again, to try again. If He found

---

1. Mosiah 26:30

that much importance to allow Himself to be murdered, then absolutely He stands ready with open arms and more chances.

Shortly after baptism I received a priesthood blessing that said, "God does not see your tattoos, you are clean in front of Him." And to me, this is the best visual I can use to describe His forgiveness. He's not forgiving my tattoos, those being representative of this entire life I lived before Him and out of line with Him. Forgiven means forgotten. God does not choose to look past, or just promise not to bring up again, it's that our wrongdoings are completely erased. Non-existent. It never even happened, wiped completely clean, off the record, kind of forgiveness.

I just really hate the title I was given of *Tattooed Mormon*. I fought hard to not have it in the title of my first book but settled on a compromise and a lengthy explanation on the inside contents. The reason why is because it has nothing to do with me and who I am and what I'm doing. It's completely irrelevant. I hate that Thomas has the title of *Doubting Thomas,* because he has a reputable legacy of faith and bravery as an apostle. It was him that said with conviction, *"Let us also go, that we may die with him."*[2] And yet, the one time he had a doubt defines his whole character to us of who *not* to be. I just hate so much that this woman is known for this one terrible moment. Embarrassed and humiliated publicly in that one moment, that may or may not have even been her fault, and she carries the title of the *adulterous woman*. She did not speak her side; we don't know anything outside of this one moment that was orchestrated by the ones who killed our Savior.

She just had so much life that she lived after this story, this was not the end of her. She kept on living! She enjoyed new seasons and unfolding blessings and prosperity. I wish we could hear about this amazing life she led after. I don't doubt that for a second that it was blossoming, and it was vibrant, and it was beautiful, and it was noteworthy. I believe that because, like me and doubting Thomas and even the seven demons out of Mary Magdalene, when the Savior becomes a reality to you, your life and your entire

---

2. John 11:16

being is just undoubtably changed. "*The woman glorified God from the hour, and believed on his name.*"

Sometimes we condemn and punish ourselves by defining ourselves for our mistakes and the worst moments we've ever had. Maybe your real self is buried under your own mislabeling. Sometimes we clench our grip tight on our imperfections rather than seeking to be cleansed or moving past forgiveness freely given. We wear the stains of our sins like scarlet letters before God thinking we deserve to stay stuck in the shame and guilt. Anything that is pulling us away from Him and getting us to stand still is the adversary, and it's the adversary winning. He gets into our heads and into our hearts, telling us we aren't good enough, we aren't worthy to pray, we aren't worthy to come back, or all is lost. It is the adversary that tells that we are too far gone, what we did was too big, or maybe we deserve the stones. *Do not heed.* I hope we can forgive ourselves as quickly as God forgives us; forgive ourselves quickly and move on because He has, that's part of it all. Not that He chooses to overlook, but it is completely non-existent. "*Will ye not now return unto me, and repent . . .that I may heal you?*"[3]

Christ will always choose to spend His time and stay *with us.* Because to Him, connecting with us, loving us, listening, understanding, and forgiving pain, trauma, sin, all of it, is most important to Him. Seeing us heal and move on from the hurt is most important to Him.

The laborer in the vineyard asked if they should cut down the branches that didn't seem to be doing well, but the Lord responds the same way He did with this woman and the same way He does with us, "*I will spare it a little longer, for it grieveth me that I should lose the trees of my vineyard.*"[4] So, there they stay, and the Lord continues to stay there with it. The Lord saying, "I don't want to get rid of it, I don't want it to go, I want it here still, I want those more chances there for them still, because all is not lost, time has

---

3. 3 Nephi 9:13
4. Jacob 5:51

not run out yet." Now is not the time to judge us but to love, and revive to restore, and forgive to forget, and correct to change to blossom. Now is the time for Him to fight for us to be there with us, and stay with us, and nurture and nourish us as much as He can to give us more chances. Because He doesn't want to lose you.

THE BARREN FIG TREE AND THE WOMAN HEALED ON THE SABBATH

The same thing is taught with the barren fig tree and the woman that was healed on the Sabbath in Luke 13. After having articulated to spare the barren fig tree, to give it more time and chances to bring forth fruit, a woman who has suffered for eighteen years with *a spirit* came to Jesus and was healed. Eighteen years is a terribly long time, but even still, change. Blossoms.

We don't have to be who we used to be. What is and what was isn't what will always be. We are not stuck, not stagnant, not living linear. Things *can* change—*we* can change. We have a God of commas, not periods. Because of Him, every passing second is a chance to turn it all around. Please do not give up on the person you are becoming. Because like me, and Thomas, and this woman, we have so much vibrant and blossoming life left to live because of Him.

Your Savior is there knowing that good can always come with His help, even if it is coming from, like the olive tree, the *"poorest spot in all the land."*[5] The *poorest* sin, the *poorest* habits, the *poorest* past. In scripture, those that came from there are the ones that brought forth the most fruit. No matter what we are overcoming, where we are coming from, and no matter what season we're in, whether withered in the vineyard or shamed in the courtyard, we really *can* grow into something different and really blossom. No matter how long you have traveled in the wrong direction, you can always turn around.

---

5. Jacob 5:21

You are loved. You are not alone. You are not a bad person. The world will not be better off without you. All is not lost. "You have *not* traveled beyond the reach of divine love. It is not possible for you to sink lower than the infinite light of Christ's Atonement shines."[6] Listen. Life is worth living, *really* living. You are needed. You are wanted. You are noticed. Let's hang on, okay? Help and healing and change and forgiveness are always there because Christ is always there. And He will never look at you like a waste of time. He will always choose to spend His time with you. Because to Him, connecting with us, loving us, listening, understanding, and forgiving pain, trauma, sin, all of it, is most important to Him. Seeing us heal and move on from the hurt is most important to Him. We have an endless God, with endless chances, endless help, endless hope, endless comfort. And we do not need to be any more of anything to feel, to receive, and to be loved endlessly by Him.

There *is* a love that satisfies. His love will heal you. His love *does* heal you. I have given too many reasons for God not to love me and none of them has changed His mind. Jesus sees the real you, and He chooses to stay. *"If the Son therefore shall make you free, ye shall be free indeed."*[7] Drop the stones. You won't ever need them.

6. Jeffrey R. Holland, "The Laborers in the Vineyard," April 2012 General Conference
7. John 8:36

Finding Yourself in . . .

Healing the Blind:
The Light of the World

Matthew 20, Mark 8, Luke 18 & John 9

After the full healing of a man who had been blind since birth, he was rigorously questioned multiple times before then being excommunicated. He was excommunicated and pushed out of his community all because he was healed. Before we get into the history and context, first and foremost, let me just say, there will be others who will try and dim your light. They will try to get you to doubt it, to be ashamed of it, and they will try to distinguish it and push you out. But that light is yours. It belongs to you, it's part of you, it's *in* your soul since before the world even was. And *darkness cannot overrule the light*. Shine on

Jesus was in hiding from an angry crowd that wanted to kill him. And as He passed through the midst of those after Him, it's then He sees the man that has been blind since birth. When He was under intense circumstances for His own life, He stopped for a lowly beggar, a beggar who has spent the entirety of his life consumed with people continuing past him. But Jesus noticed

Him and stopped for Him. He stops to save someone who was in the valley of darkness, dark both situational and literal. A known beggar, where many in the community have spent a lot of their lives seeing and passing this man, finally someone has stopped for them. Fleeing for His own life, Jesus stops to reteach and correct inaccurate views and beliefs and dispel stigmas.

Bodily afflictions have always been believed to be the result of personal sin. If this man had been blind since birth, who sinned, *"this man, or his parents?"* Jesus responds that neither have, *"but that the works of God should be made manifest in him."* His blindness will be used as an opportunity for God's divine power to be manifested in his life in big and beautiful ways. How many times have we seen this in the scriptures and in our own lives? When our dark times and our times that have brought us to the ground, like this man, have been times where God has shown us beautiful miracles where He has then become more real to us? I can't count how many times in the scriptures or in my own life. Because our God is a God of greater magnifications.

"I must work the works of him that sent me, while it is day: the night cometh, when no man can work. As long as I am in the world, I am the light of the world." Because Jesus is the light of the world, we will never be fully consumed in darkness. Darkness cannot win because Jesus is here and He is light, a *"light that is endless, that can never be darkened."* We are naturally drawn to light, because we are light. And like a plant, with light, we flourish. Like the two blind men who *followed him* walking in the streets and down into a *house,* they were able to recognize and follow that light, even without sight. That is the power and pull of the light of Christ that He has and that we have inside of us. *"Believe that I am able to do this? yea lord."*

What comfort that is when the darkness seems to be closing in on us, that it can't consume us fully. And that it has power to dispel as we get closer and closer to Jesus, actual light. Like in Ether with the Jaredites, sometimes we feel we are crossing great storms buried in the sea in darkness, but the light we do have, even if it may seem as small as a stone, will be what we need to make it through. And it's just not making it through this lifetime, because it's not ever about just making it to the end and hoping for a better go at it in the next round, the hereafter. Because like in Ether, life didn't end for them when they reached land. It wasn't the end to the story or to them. They continued living and they enjoyed new seasons with blessings and prosperity. So no, it's not just about trying to get by until we die. It's about holding on to the light we do have, knowing a new season will come in this life, one filled with blessings and prosperity. *"I am the light of this world, He that followeth me shall not walk in darkness, but shall have the light of life."*

"Light is come into the world," but *"men loved darkness rather than light."* The irony of the Pharisees in this experience is unbearable to me when I read of this experience. Because it is so obvious that it was the Pharisees who were the ones who were so destructively blind. Blind from their own ways—blind from their own laws, their own cultures and views—that they could not see. Even with working sight, they could not see the awaited Messiah standing right in front of them working miracle after miracle. Seeing is not believing, even all of these blind men knew that. They could see Jesus for who He really is, even before their eyes were healed. And this poor man who could now see after a lifetime in the streets, was then ridiculed and excommunicated and driven out. All because the Pharisees were the ones with eyes that were not opened.

Christ *"spat on the ground, and made clay of the spittle, and he anointed the eyes of the blind man with the clay."* To anoint is to consecrate and make sacred. Jesus made this disabled beggar sacred with His touch. And Jesus didn't *need* to touch him to heal him; He could have performed any miracle of healing from any power of His own and God's. But He chose to. He wanted to. Like the way we touch those we love to connect, to offer comfort and compassion, companionship, and love. He touched them because He wanted to, to convey compassion, connection, companionship, and love to us intimately and personally.

The clay over his eyes has connections to Enoch who was also anointed on his eyes with clay, and when *he* washed, he came away seeing a grand vision of God's creation. Healing this blind man with clay is symbolic of seeing as God sees. *"And said unto him, Go, wash in the pool of Siloam."* Siloam is also mentioned in the chapter with the woman caught in adultery. Jesus is currently outside the great temple with this blind man, which means, they would be surrounded by cleansing pools Jews used before entering into temple. Yet instead of utilizing one of those cleansing pools right by them, Jesus sends him still blind to the complete other side of Jerusalem to reach the specific pool of Siloam. It was first constructed back when Isaiah was around, more than 700 years *before* Jesus, in a time of war. Although safe within the walls of Jerusalem, water was *outside* those walls. They built a tunnel under the city through limestone to create a water channel that connects to the pool of Siloam. It was the literal lifeblood of Jerusalem. Even after 2,700 years, that tunnel is still around and still constantly running without pause pure and clean water.

During the time of Jesus, it was a major and needful stopping point for Jewish pilgrims on their way to the temple. Bathing in the pool wearing white was obedience to the cleansing preparation required for temple worship. *"He went his way therefore, and washed, and came seeing."* And he did. He didn't even question what Jesus asked of him. Jesus created a situation that allowed him to act for himself. Instead of making the healing instant, it was a journey. This journey across the entire city is a significant downward hike that all people need great finesse to do even *with* their sight. Many travelers who have done this walk even now, as it's available even as part of tours, most do not do it at night because they wouldn't be able to because the long, downward intricateness requires skill and awareness. But with clay covering his eyes, this blind man was humble and happy to do it because he knew it was worth it. Even without his sight, he was able to make and succeed in his journey in the darkness because Christ was part of it.

And he was healed. Who once was blind now can see. *"I went and washed, and I received sight,"* a literal fulfillment of Isaiah that *"the eyes of the blind shall be opened."*[1] Light versus dark, blind versus sight. Because this blind beggar who had become a recognized staple to the people who lived there, *"the neighbours therefore, and they which before had seen him that he was blind, said, Is not this he that sat and begged?"* Having heard of his miracle, this man was brought to the Pharisees and was questioned rigorously multiple times. *"This man is not of God, because he keepeth not the sabbath day."* But how *"can a man who that is a sinner do such miracles?"* After questioning the beggar but staying in disbelief, they sought after his parents to question if he really were ever blind to begin with.

It was a tricky thing to answer their interrogations because *"if any man did confess that he was Christ, he should be put out of the synagogue."* So directing them back to their son, this poor man who could hardly celebrate in his new life, was tracked down yet again by the Pharisees who were so blind themselves *"and said unto him, Give God the praise: we know that this man is a sinner."* Properly declining to enter the questionnaire of what constituted sin under their man-made construction of the law, *"one thing I know, that, whereas I as blind, now I see,"* was his response. With continued questioning and prodding, they tried to get him to reject, to retreat, to question, to doubt what good happened. The relentless questioning to try and get him to turn his back on the impact of Jesus. But he didn't, the impact of Him was too deep to deny. He allowed them to cast him out because he held on to the truth that happened. Knowing what would come with his words, he spoke and confessed and worshiped anyways. *"If this man were not of God, he could do nothing."*

"How were thine eyes opened?" Jesus. How did darkness dispel? Jesus. How were you able to change? Jesus. How were things able to become better? The answer will always be Jesus.

---

1. Isaiah 35:5

"And they cast him out." He lost community back when community was everything. His whole life outcast and again pushed out. I'm devastated at their dedication to rip the joy out of what was supposed to be joyful celebrating. The irony continues as blindness has a symbolic relation in Israel to spiritual decay and apostasy; and in scripture, blindness is referred to several times as *moral blindness.* Covenant Israel was in apostasy. The ones upholding this skewed perception are the ones who were the textbook definitions of it. Disowned by his parents, ignored in the streetside by his community, cast out of the synagogue and excommunicated by Pharisees, this man knew weariness and having nothing. But he went back to it knowing that choosing Jesus was having everything.

Believing that Jesus was evil, they were blind to this man's miracle and blind to their Messiah. Their blindness makes them say that his light wasn't a worthy light, not the right light; therefore they took actions to dismiss and distinguish it. After hearing what happened, Jesus sought him out *"and when he had found him"* asked, *"Dost thou believe on the Son of God? . . . Lord, I believe. And he worshipped him,"* He who gives *"light to them that sit in darkness and in the shadow of death, to guide [their] feet into the way of peace."* When surrounded by darkness, He is our light that is *endless.* If we are needing to see more clearly to be guided through unstable terrain, He will open our eyes to truth and light. When we have fallen streetside from our own blindness, Jesus does seek us out, and compassionately with touch, makes us sacred. As we move closer in proximity to Jesus, light will continuously beam brighter. We will succeed with our journey through darkness because Christ is part of it, our literal guiding light that can never be darkened, the most reliable illumination to peace and to clarity. He will use our journey towards better sight and healing as opportunities for God's divine power to be manifested in our life in big and beautiful ways. And we'll flourish.

The answer will always be Jesus.

People will try and doubt, question, and distinguish our own light. The Pharisees of this world will tell us our flame is too small or too weak and cut you down, push you out, and make you feel less than. But that brilliance of illumination from the Savior that has power to pull in the blind. It is part of us, put into our souls before this world even was, divine energy, power, and influence that proceeds from God through Christ and gives life and light to all things, including us in our dark times. That light belongs to you, not to be taken away, not to be overpowered.

Your light is never too small for impact. A single one-inch candle flame can be seen by the average human's eye from up to 3.6 miles away. It's true. A regular small candle flame, in complete darkness, can be seen from *that* far away. That's incredible. A light as small as a stone, has an impact with that great of depth to guide and survive even the longest and worst storms. So, try as they might, the dark doesn't stand a chance. Shine on.

Finding Yourself in . . .

The Lost Sheep and the Good Shepherd

Matthew 18, Luke 15 & John 10

I have a long list of all the times I've looked back and wondered, "How on earth did I make it through that?" My husband and I just passed an anniversary that had us looking back with everything we had been through together and it was filled with a lot of those. When we were first married, we didn't have a bed, so we slept on the floor for the first several months. We only got one because someone from the ward saw our sleeping arrangement and got one for us. Our place was so small, that we ate on the floor because we literally couldn't even fit a single chair inside, let alone a table. We couldn't even open the door all the way because that mattress we were gifted was only a few inches smaller than the size of the entire room. The next place we had lived in was a "basement apartment." But it wasn't an apartment at all, actually, it wasn't even a basement at all. It wasn't finished. But by "wasn't finished," I mean it wasn't even started. There was no bathroom. No running water. The entire floor and perimeter walls were cement. There were no walls, no rooms, just wooden beams where a wall was supposed to maybe one day go. No real ceiling, just pink insulation. No natural light, just those little rectangle windows at the very top by the ceiling. No separate door to enter. We had two very large dogs at the time and stacked furniture so the dogs—and sometimes us—would come in and out through the window. Just an open space of a cellar, during a really cold winter. Our first child was *just* born. We really did spend most nights with hand warmers in our socks and sometimes I'd fall asleep with them on my nose.

I just asked Ben what he had to say about our time in "the basement," and after a series of bad facial expressions and horizontal headshakes, he even said, "The basement was an unfortunate situation that I'm not sure looking back how we got through it." So then we moved to Arizona, and, shortly, after I lost my job and our health insurance when I became pregnant. I went my entire pregnancy not knowing if our baby was healthy, not knowing if the baby had all its limbs, not ever hearing the heartbeat. It was terrifying. We tried so hard to look for work, but it just didn't happen. Time kept passing, the pregnancy was approaching the last few weeks, and we had only thirty dollars left in our account after draining our savings during our time of unemployment. And with only thirty dollars, we made another out-of-state move and lived off of someone else's food storage. I don't know how we did any of that. After a few years with an awesome job, we followed an impression to move cross country to New York, left that job, moved across the country, and lived out another over a year of unemployment. Another cross country move, *and back*. To a third pregnancy, diagnosed high risk, and I was told I would likely myself not live through it. We spent that whole pregnancy thinking there was a chance I could not make it, and worries that the baby wasn't growing at all. To then move cross country again during a pandemic and have the house we bought not work out while being houseless in a hotel room for almost two months. I literally have no idea how we got through it. Any of it. And yet we did. And we will. It has been incredibly beautiful as I have spent my studies this week thinking of all the different ways He carries me. Can you recognize all the different ways for you?

When Jesus ate with the publicans and sinners and was met with the constant attack from the Pharisees, He responded with the parable of the lost sheep. *"What man of you, having an hundred sheep, if he lose one of them, doth not leave the ninety and nine in the wilderness, and go after that which is lost, until he find it?"*

It's actually quite easy for a sheep to get lost; they are likely to go astray on a lot of occasions. Sheep are hot-wired to follow each other and stay together. But they are simple animals who are easily distracted, easily scared, easily lose sense of direction, and even need help getting back on their feet if they were to fall over. They also have monocular vision which means they can see really well behind them, but are near sided, and can barely see in front of them.

The lost sheep is *not* a prodigal son. Sheep do not intentionally leave. They do not think, "Forget this place, forget this herd, forget this shepherd, I'm out of here." A sheep that is by itself as the one separated from the shepherd and the ninety-nine, is not separated by a purposeful action to leave. A lost sheep is a sheep that is feels alone. One that is in unwanted and unfamiliar places. That one sheep feels tired, feels scared, feels stressed, weak. Is confused, is in possible danger, is distressed, discouraged. That sheep is one who suffered loss and one who suffered. We have all spent time as *the one*, but perhaps more times than we realized. Not intentionally separated, but feeling alone, feeling tired, feeling lost, being in places we do not wish to be in.

Jesus, the great I Am. *"I am the bread of life, I am He, I am the way, I am the resurrection, I am the living water, I am the true vine, I am the light of this world."* Is also a shepherd. And He is good. And what better shepherd is there than the Lamb of God? A shepherd who is also a lamb, who knows perfectly what it is like to know perfectly how to lead and rescue. *"He calleth his own sheep by name . . . and leadeth them out . . . he goeth before them."*

He does not herd, He does not force. He leads. And He does not lead astray.

"All that ever came before me are thieves and robbers," not authorized by God to lead sheep. There is comparison between a *hireling* and Jesus, *the good shepherd.* A hireling is a paid servant who does in fact see wolves coming and flees. Sees and flees. They do not protect. They do not sacrifice. They do not stay. They do not care, they *"careth not for the sheep."* They leave the way open for the ravening beasts, *"and the wolf catcheth them"* to scatter, *"to steal, and to kill, and to destroy."* They appear in sheep's clothing, not shepherds clothing.

Our good shepherd sees what's coming and does not leave us. He stays ready to fight in defense of His own. *"I am the good shepherd: the good shepherd giveth his life for the sheep . . . I lay down my life for the sheep . . . No man taketh it from me, but I lay it down of myself. I have power to lay it down, and I have power to take it again."* On purpose. He sacrifices His own self on purpose. It is His choice. He chooses us *"that they might have life, and that they might have it more abundantly."* And His sacrifice was not limited to His death, but also His entire existence and time sacrificed to be with us still now. The phrase "His work and His glory" is perfectly applicable. It is His job, His passion, His calling to protect us, guide us, take care of us, nourish us, save us. To give us life *more abundantly.*

Why? Because we are His. He knows us. He knows our name. We are numbered. He calls, *"I am the bread of life."*[1] He is the *"living water,"*[2] He who gives everlasting nourishment. *"I am the light of this world;"*[3] He who gives light and guidance and hope in darkness. *"I am the good shepherd;"* He who goes after *"my sheep which was lost."* Ten sections previously in Matthew, *"the Son of man is come to save that which was lost,"*[4] referring to

---

1. John 6:33
2. John 4:10–14
3. John 8:12
4. Matthew 18:11

us. What He wanted to teach Zacchaeus was this exact thing as well, *"for the Son of man is come to seek and to save that which was lost."* It has always been about us. Strengthening, leading, and saving *us.*

But we are not lost to Him; God is fully aware of whereabouts. He knows our hiding places. He doesn't misplace us because He does not care or is not mindful—it is the actions of the sheep, not the shepherds. He does not lose sight of us; we lose sight of Him. And what is interesting is the wording of *"a stranger will they not follow, but will flee from him: for they know not the voice of strangers."* Alma 5:37 says, *"A shepherd hath called after you and is still calling after you, but ye will not hearken unto his voice!"* How? *The sheep did not hear them.* Why? It is hard to follow who we do not know and recognize. Can you recognize Him? Can you hear His voice? Can you hear Him calling out to you? How do we know what it sounds like? The Good Shepherd's voice is a voice that is *good*, a feeling that is *good*.

It doesn't matter how we became lost, whether intentional leaving or not, He reacts just the same—seek and save. He goes after them. The sheep is always worthy of rescue because it is His. It is loved by the shepherd, it belongs to the shepherd, named by the shepherd. He does not give up on us, He does not grow tired or weary, nor will He be in need of a break from coming and carrying us. It is what He was foreordained to do—it is His existence to do, to rescue. When thinking of His sheep, He says, *"I must bring,"* must. Like the parable of the lost coin, who lights a candle, sweeps the house, and seeks diligently, our shepherd does everything to bring us back to be reunited with Him. *"The worth of souls is great in the sight of God."*[5]

We have all experienced the pain of losing something and the joy of finding it again. When He comes, He does not yell or talk to us about disappointments and what we could have done differently. He is completely overcome with the pure joy of

---

5. Doctrine and Covenants 18:10

AL CARRAWAY

reunion for what He was missing. He rejoices so much so, that He invites others to *"rejoice with me."* Whether unintentional like the lost sheep, whether intentional like the prodigal son, and like the lost coin, *"he calleth together his friends and neighbours, saying unto them, Rejoice with me!"* How proud He is to be yours.

Isaiah tells us. *"He shall gather the lambs with his arm, and carry them in his bosom, and shall gently lead."*[6] He comes Himself and offers of Himself. We know He puts us *"on His shoulders,"* but how does that even translate to us? I have become overwhelmingly humbled as I have spent the time thinking about all the ways He carries me. Can you think of all the different ways in your life?

When I think of all the times I have wondered, "How did I do that?" Those times of poor living conditions, poor health, poor financials, *how did I get through that?* He carried me. He carries us out of those lonely places, those tired places, those unwanted places, those painful places. When we are on His shoulders, He is literally lifting us higher. To give rescue, to relieve, the rest. To carry is to do that what we cannot do on our own. When we allow ourselves to be carried back by Him, He brings us somewhere better; He brings us to new places, better *pastures*, filled with nourishment, protection, care, guidance. He gives us *"life, and that they might have it more abundantly."* Life more abundant!

We may be like a sheep who are sometimes easily distracted, easily scared, and may need help getting back on our feet, but He says, He *"must bring"* you back to Him. Your shepherd does not back down, nor does He flee. Jesus, He protects, He watches, He speaks, He sacrifices, He saves. He does not lose. He loves. He gathers. He carries. He rejoices. *"Draw near unto me and I will draw near unto you."*[7] We can always be brought back. We will never be too far gone. He leads and He does not lead astray.

---

6. Isaiah 40:11
7. Doctrine and Covenants 88:63

166

He *is good*. He is a good shepherd. He is *your* shepherd. He is your safety, He is your fighter, He is your leader, He is your protector, your rescuer. And He does not grow weary in being *yours*. Because we are His. Because we are numbered. Because *He is good*.

Finding Yourself In . . .

Forgiving Seventy Times Seven

The Wheat and Tares and
the Unforgiving Servant

Matthew 13 & 18

The parable of the Wheat and Tares is a parable that Jesus explains the meaning of Himself. *"The field is the world; the good seed are the children of the kingdom; but the tares are the children of the wicked one; The enemy that sowed them is the devil."* This parable illustrates a servant eager to pull up weeds but were told that in so doing they would root out the wheat as well. Tares are a weed that looks like wheat as it's growing, and as the roots of it grow, they grow intertwined with the wheat's roots. Both are to grow together until the *"harvest"* which is *"the end of the world."* This answers the question of why the Lord doesn't always seem to do something about the wickedness in the world. It teaches us that God is very much aware and all things are done in great purpose and reason. One of which is shown above. Another——that we've learned in other lessons and promises from God—is the chance given to all to change.

The servant in the Wheat and Tares asks if for the bad, they should *"go and gather them up? But he said, Nay."* The same response is given to the laborer in the vineyard in the Book of Mormon, *"I will spare it a little longer, for it grieveth me that I should lose the trees of my vineyard."*[1] What He offers us, He offers to everyone, the ability to be changed by Him who is always there. He will not rob anyone of the chance and the time to turn around, like in Jacob 5, as the good in people grows, the bad can gradually clear away. Like Mary with many devils was changed and deserving of distinctive honors, such as the first witness of the resurrection. Like Peter himself who led the church after his triple denial. The woman at the well who left and told all she passed and led masses to conversion. The time and chance to change is offered to all, even the wicked. *"Then came Peter to him, and said, Lord, how oft shall my brother sin against me, and I forgive him? till seven times?"* Surely, benevolence should have a limit. *"Jesus saith unto him . . . Until seventy times seven."* Obviously, the Savior was not establishing a limit of 490, but articulating the profound truth to not establish limits on forgiveness. There are no limits on repentance. We receive that chance, and so do the tares. And everyone will have that chance until the *harvest* which is *the end of the world.*

So, until then, celebrate in our gift of more time and more chances to do better and become better. Allow others to have their gift of more time and more chances. And the reason why I put this in a section of forgiveness is because in the season of wheat and tares that we are in, the tares can sometimes be the reasons we hurt, and the reason why we need the lesson from Peter to forgive seventy times seven. It is because we are in a world where we coexist with wheat and tares, but again, strategically so. How do we navigate through it all when we are to coexist with it until the *end of the world?*

---

1. Jacob 5:51

The Unforgiving Servant paints the irony for us with our forgiveness and mercy received but not extended. Falling down in desperate, humbled *worship*, this man pleads, *"Lord, have patience with me, and I will pay thee all."* Having owed ten thousand talents, the equivalent to sixty million workdays, *"the lord of that servant was moved with compassion, and loosed him, and forgave him the debt. But the same servant went out, and found one of his fellow servants, which owed him an hundred pence: and he laid hands on him, and took him by the throat, saying, Pay me that thou owest."* This other man reacted with exactness, just as the servant had just done. Humbling falling down at his feet, saying word for word the same plea the servant just had, *"have patience with me, and I will pay thee all."* But *"he would not."* Instead, cast him in prison until he can pay, which of course wouldn't be possible, because he was in prison. *"Shouldest not thou also have had compassion on thy fellow servant, even as I had pity on thee?"* When we feel we have been wronged and we continue to coexist in the hurt and pain of others, we sometimes, however, take the punishment into our own hands.

We are told to forgive but forgiving others is so hard when someone has wronged us and hurt us, and we feel they just carry on. It seems painfully unfair that they get to move on when we are stuck with all this weight they caused and left us with. There are times we wonder if their punishment will be avoided and if justice will ever be served. *"Judge not, and ye shall not be judged: condemn not, and ye shall not be condemned: forgive, and ye shall be forgiven."*[2] But sometimes we mistakenly believe that if we forgive, justice will not be served, punishments will be avoided, and they will not be held accountable. We harbor what seems like fully justified feelings of resentment, animosity, and anger toward the people who have hurt us. We almost feel we need to hold on to our hurt and pain so we can show them that what they did was so terrible. If we are still mad, still hurt, we can prove to them just how wrong what they did was. Right? We can't forgive

---

2. Luke 6:37

because we can't release the offender, forgiving is condoning or excusing and forgetting, right? But who does that end up hurting more and affecting the most? Us. Resentment or anger we have towards another person does little or no harm to them in the way we would like, but endless effects on us, even down to poor sleep, increased fear, depression, physical pain, and issues with proper cardiac function.

Dwelling can allow the resentment and hostility we hold for that person to take root in us. If we allow negative feelings to crowd out the positive ones, we might become swallowed up by bitterness, overflowing to other aspects and other relationships in our life. Holding on with unforgiveness can make it so we can't enjoy the present; we can become depressed or anxious or feel that we're at odds with our spiritual beliefs. We continue to carry a weight that is not meant for us to carry. I still remember a lifted weight I didn't know I had until I heard Neill F. Marriott say, *"Your resentment diminishes your progress and damages your ability to have healthy relationships. You can let this go."*[3] Isn't that beautiful permission backed up by God's command and role, *You can let this go.* Forgiveness isn't always for others, it's for us. To free us, to lift our weight. That pain and hurt and responsibility to take care of the actions of others, we can let that go. That isn't meant for us to carry. That's God territory.

Judgment and punishment are meant for God. Passing time on earth is not condoning, forgetting, or excusing. *"Man shall not smite, neither shall he judge; for judgment is mine, saith the Lord, and vengeance is mine also, and I will repay."*[4] The *end of the world* will come. Mercy cannot rob justice. *"For behold, and lo, vengeance cometh speedily upon the ungodly as the whirlwind . . . I will visit her according to all her works, with sore affliction, with pestilence, with plague, with sword, with vengeance, with devouring fire."*[5]

---

3. Neill F. Marriott, "Yielding Our Hearts to God," October 2015 General Conference
4. Mormon 8:20
5. Doctrine and Covenants 97:22, 26

We can take great comfort in knowing that God will compensate us for every injustice we've experienced. *"Leave judgment alone with me, for it is mine and I will repay. [But let] peace be with you."*[6] There is an enormous physical burden to being hurt and disappointed. Peace given to us is a fruit of what it means to let go, to drop weight, to allow healing to happen. Forgiveness can take away the power the other person continues to wield over us. Forgiveness in no way means tolerance. It is not a connection to be stuck in unhealthy situations or to unhealthy people.

But as we release the control and power of the offending person and situation in our life, we are able to better grip to that *peace* He promises us. We may not get the apology we deserve, but forgiveness can come even without reconciliation. In those times, choose to validate your own feelings and give yourself permission to close that chapter and set up boundaries.

Forgiving others is a gift He gives us and we give ourselves. It frees us. It allows us to take our power back. It brings *peace* to help us go on with life, healing and thriving in our emotional, psychological, spiritual, and physical health. The energy and emotion we had invested in certain people or situations is now free to be moved to something that makes us feel filled and move forward on our spiritual path. As we allow forgiveness into our souls, we are partnering to bring the Savior's power into our lives. By embracing forgiveness, we are embracing peace, hope, gratitude, and growth.

"[God] will console you in your afflictions, and he will plead your cause, and send down justice upon those who seek your destruction."[7] We can celebrate and use our gift of more time and more chances to do better and become better. Knowing that our God is a God of endless forgiveness and endless repentance until the world ends, that also means we have endless healing offered to us as we coexist with tares, and even have seasons with our own personal tares as well. *"The Lord compensates the faithful for every loss. . . . [E]*

---

6. Doctrine and Covenants 82:23
7. Jacob 3:1

very tear today will eventually be returned a hundredfold with tears of rejoicing and gratitude."⁸ We have beautiful permission backed up by God's command and role to let go, to drop the weight, to be free, to move on and allow His peace to heal and lead and lift.

"Peace I leave with you, my peace I give unto you: not as the world giveth, give I unto you. Let not your heart be troubled, neither let it be afraid."⁹

8. Joseph B. Wirthlin, "Come What May, and Love it," October 2008 General Conference
9. John 14:27

Finding Yourself in . . .

Mary, Martha, and Raising Lazarus

John 11

Waiting is the worst. Waiting for answers, waiting for relief, waiting for a new season, for blessings, for change. I feel like I can look at most trials I've been given with determination, optimism, and faith. But when time keeps passing with little or no change, all of those things start to thin. I have been asked to wait for a lot of things I desired or even desperately needed. The passing years of being single, waiting to find someone. The passing years of silence from my family because of my decision to get baptized, that was painfully long and lonely. The passing years of unemployment while pregnant with no health insurance. How I couldn't bare another moment to not know if our child was healthy or not because we couldn't see a doctor until birth. The passing time when God told us to move across the country for our house we were prompted to buy, for it to not work out, and for us to find ourselves houseless living in a hotel as a family of five. Passing time has been my hardest reoccurring trial that causes me to wonder, "Why aren't mountains moving anymore? I thought He was in this with us. This was His idea." Oh, the feelings of exhaustion are indescribable, to have nothing to show for our efforts. It was devastating and complicated and long. Leaving me to physically ache—stretched too thin.

Isn't it wild all the questions that run through our mind when we feel things should have worked out by now? *Is God punishing me? Why did it have to happen to me and not them? Or why them and not me? Did I do something wrong? Why would God bring me to this just for it not to work out? What am I supposed to be learning? What is the hidden blessing from this? What tragic thing could I be avoiding from this falling through? Is there even divine meaning behind this, or is this just life being life? How much more am I going to go through? Is this the adversary trying to stop me, or is it God? Maybe my efforts aren't good enough. Maybe I'm not good enough. It isn't fair. It wasn't supposed to be this way. God must not be with me. If He were really here, this wouldn't be happening, this could have been avoided.* And we think, and we cry, and we wonder, and we plead, and we pray.

"Jesus loved Martha, and her sister [Mary], and Lazarus"— one could argue that Lazarus and his two sisters were even His closest friends. When near Jerusalem, Jesus would actually spend nights sleeping at their house in Bethany and stay with the three of them. Jesus even chose to be there the last week of His mortal existence. When Lazarus fell sick, Jesus heard about it; *"his sisters sent unto him, saying, Lord, behold, he whom thou lovest is sick."* But He didn't go. *"He abode two days still in the same place where he was."* You can imagine how confused and hurt the three of them were by this, two-fold. They knew that, as the Savior, if He came, He could heal him, He could take this away. And secondly, they were so close—as a friend, why wouldn't He come to be with them at a time like that? Didn't He care about them?

When Lazarus died, Jesus heard about it but still didn't go. And then a day passed. And then another day passed. And then a third day passed. Why? I can really visualize the heightened feelings of Martha and Mary. I can't imagine their grief and the swirling thoughts they must have had during this passing time. Surely, they too must have thought, "This didn't have to happen, if He were here, this could have been prevented. Where is He? Why has He not come by now? Why is He not here with us? I thought He loved us?"

Like Mary and Martha, I have found myself wondering at times, "Where is He? Why hasn't He arrived yet? If He truly were here with me, then why is this happening? Why wasn't this prevented?"

I thought He loved me.

When I was pregnant with my third, I was diagnosed as complicated high-risk and there was a "good chance" I wouldn't survive. I went my whole pregnancy with fear as it continually unfolded in unexpected and unwanted ways. Talk about slowly passing time. Low and behold, before a planned procedure to deliver the baby early, everything was gone. All the complications just went away. My doctor said he'd never seen that happen before. Obviously, I left the appointment saying vocally to myself, "God is good!" But I hated that I thought that because what did that imply? What, was God just not good the rest of my pregnancy? Was God just not good during all of my hard and unexpected? Is God only good when we get what we want? Is avoidance and prevention our goal? Is avoidance and prevention a measurement on the Lord's love? How are we to navigate our Mary and Martha times?

If our goal is avoidance and prevention and getting what we want, then what does that imply for Lazarus, Jesus's close friend whom *He loved*. If our goal and happiness and worth is measured around avoidance and prevention, what does that even imply for Christ's life, and His life of betrayal, abuse, and death? Was His life of being mocked and spit on and falsely judged and murdered, was it because angels were not there? Was it because God was not mindful of Him? Was it because Christ was not deserving of that prevention? Was it because God is not always good?

Despite being ill-advised and questioned on His decision because *"Jews of late sought to stone thee,"* Jesus did eventually arrive in Bethany. He arrives *four* days after Lazarus had passed. Jesus was well aware and *"said plainly, Lazarus is dead."* And He finally goes, but why four days after if He knew? Why didn't He go sooner? Why did He have them wait? Why didn't He prevent it from happening? *"Could not this man, which opened the eyes of the blind, have caused that even this man should not have died?"*

Christ first saw Martha, and she said to Him, *"Lord, if thou hadst been here, my brother had not died."* Jesus assured her that He would rise again and that all would be well. And Martha, assuming He was referring to resurrection, agreed. *"Yea, Lord: I believe."* But Christ corrected her with one of my favorite responses, *"I am the resurrection, and the life."* Then *"her sister secretly, saying, The Master is come, and calleth for thee."* Mary, who was deep in despair, just collapsed at His feet when she saw Jesus and through her tears also muttered, *"Lord, if thou hadst been here, my brother had not died,"* not knowing those were the exact words of Martha. She wept. And Jesus wept with her. Jesus knew He would raise Lazarus, yet He still spends time with her, weeps with her. He sits with her, feels with her, understands her. Loves her. Knowing what He can do for us, He still first comes to us with compassion and understanding.

"Lazarus, come forth."

"I am glad for your sakes that I was not there, to the intent ye may believe."

In the days of Jesus, culture believed that the spirit lingered around a deceased body three days after passing. On day four, the deceased were officially *dead*, dead. Day *four*. The exact time when Jesus came. Had Christ come any sooner after his death, many would doubt His miracle to raise Lazarus from the grave, or even struggle to call it a miracle at all. Had Christ come sooner and prevented the death of Lazarus, many would not have been converted and they would have been shielded from the bigger miracle. A miracle so big that all the chief priests and the Pharisees held a council and said, *"What do we? for this man doeth many miracles. If we let him thus alone, all men will believe on him: and the Romans shall come and take away both our place and nation."* A miracle so big, they knew in time, none could not believe in Christ. *"The chief priests and the Pharisees had given a commandment, that, if any man knew where he were, he should shew it, that they might take him."* It was exactly this miracle that put into motion their planning to *"put him to death."*

The waiting was intentional, and it was strategic. For *"the intent ye may believe."* For the intent of greater magnifications! Our waiting can be intentional, strategic, for the intent of things greater than what we had in mind.

If we aren't seeing what we are asking for, we feel God is not listening, He is not there, or He does not care. But that's the adversary's voice. God is *not* only good when we get what we want, and miracles are not defined as avoidance and prevention. If Christ would have prevented Lazarus from dying—mass conversion would have never happened. If Old Testament Joseph never went into a hole, to slavery, to prison—he never would have saved an entire civilization and become a leader over all of Egypt. If Lehi never suffered his passing years in the wilderness—there would have been destruction, and death. If Christ was never killed—we would not have . . . sheesh, where do I begin the list? If I never went through everything I have gone through, I wouldn't have a single thing I have now. My favorite things, the best things, have come from my unwanted passing time. The unexpected can be God intervening. The unwanted can be the path to things greater than we knew was available.

Surely, avoidance and prevention is not the goal. Surely, God is good even if our situation is not. He is good even during unwanted circumstances, in missed opportunities and passing time. Because through it all, He is not overlooking, ignoring, or punishing, but in fact, acting strategically and intentionally. And He does not play favorites. God is good because He keeps His promises, good because we are a part of something so much bigger than our narrow-mindedness. So much bigger than what's *here*. Not abandoning or overlooking, but intricately and profoundly involved in bringing us to what's next. God is good because whatever that may be, He is there. He is in charge, He is leading, and He is perfect. God is good even when our situation is not, because He knows something we don't, because there is, in fact, something so much more to come. Something greater.

Although He doesn't always take away or lead us to what we want, it does always lead to magnification. Things may not go the way we want and pray for them to, but they will always be profoundly better than what we even knew was available for ourselves. Sometimes we can't help but think how much easier it would be if things had gone the way we wanted them to go. But little do we know what's right around the corner for us—opportunities that await, the people, the growth, and the blessings.

What I have learned from waiting is, first, that He cares. Both as a Savior and a friend. When I continue to turn to Him with my questions, like Christ did with Mary, He comes to me, and He has wept with me. Although He doesn't always take away, He is always there with deep love. And sits with us, feels with us, understands us. Because like with Lazarus, "*behold how he loved him,*" He loves us. When I am open and honest with Him, I have felt His understanding. I have felt and been reminded that He is driven with love and compassion. That although we are on a longer than anticipated path, we are not abandoned. And He can be felt in the darkest and most confusing of times if we continue to turn to Him. I have seen that all that He does is fueled by that *love* and compassion for us. And that love and dedication to us does not situationally fluctuate. Every time I push myself to trust, I am shown that He is strategically working on our behalf and that everything we are asked to do is for a something greater, and nothing is in vain. With passing time, I have seen that everything is in its own season. Like in the story of Martha and Mary, another day may be passing, but seasons don't last forever.

During passing time in trials, I grow tired of wondering and doubting and time counting—what kind of living is that? That's not living. I love Mary and Martha who were able to say with meaning, "*Yea, Lord: I believe*" even before they knew. Lazarus would be raised from the dead. We may have faith to be healed or for things to change in that moment, but do we have faith like

Mary, when it's not? To turn to the Lord still with conviction when unwanted things continue with little or no change?

Not to digress to a different experience in a different book of scripture, but I think of Joseph Smith in Liberty Jail, but not for the well-quoted verse that things *"shall be but a small moment"*[1] to bring perspective but seeing *how* Joseph had spent his time *while* locked up. While the Saints are suffering, the Prophet is pleading with the Lord for things to be over and things to be different. And what happened? Months passed, and he was still in jail. But just because time seems to be standing still doesn't mean God is. And just because we may be waiting doesn't mean that we are to be idle. I think of all the revelation Joseph Smith received while captured, the many chapters in Doctrine and Covenants that we wouldn't have if Joseph decided to shut down from his situation, if Joseph had allowed the adversary in his mind any longer with those negative thoughts that keep us standing still or moving back. That maybe it's not just about making it out alive and dragging ourselves to the end, but what if, like it was with Joseph Smith, it's about what we get during it all? Like the passing time with Lazarus, He knows something we don't. If we but keep going and not pray for trials to be prevented but pray to hold out for the bigger miracles. Because blessings do not dim with passing time.

When I am reminded of that, that's when life starts to unravel and blossom in ways I never would have imagined. In the times I am like Mary, and continue in faith during the unwanted, I have learned lessons I couldn't imagine living life without, and I grow beyond what I thought I could in such a short time. Truth is, I'm not sure what kind of person I'd be without the qualities I gained, lessons I learned, and talents I developed while I was "waiting," because I am such a better person because of them. It "not working out" was actually it working out perfectly how God had in mind the whole time! Because it led me to a wrestle, which led me to learning vital lessons I couldn't imagine living

---

1. Doctrine and Covenants 121:7

life without—lessons I would be lost without knowing. Because it "not working out," led me to a new path I wouldn't have gotten to otherwise, a new path filled with those greater magnifications.

If we are trying and a trial hasn't ended yet, is there room to be more productive with our time and better actively seek out lessons and opportunities? Move forward with the things you know you should be doing and what God wants you to do. There will always be something to overcome, something hard to handle, or something new to figure out. How unproductive it is to long for the trial to be over, to crave a fast-forward button, to hang on to that make-believe mortal vision we create in our minds. That's not living.

I have learned in the times I wonder why mountains weren't moving, weren't disappearing, and I was still struggling on the trail, God shows me my view. My steps, my efforts, whether walking, hiking, or even crawling around my mountains, were not in vain. As I have taken time to look around in the unwanted, the mountains seemed to have move. Though it still may be there, step by step, parts of it were eventually behind me. I'd be on a different place of the path, the mountain seemed to move because *I* moved. Because those small steps added up.

Maybe that's a way that faith like Mary can move mountains—because faith moves *us*.

So, what if we got it all backwards? What if every step is the miracle?

Jesus has come to you *"and calleth for thee."* Let's go to Him and allow the unexpected to blossom into greater magnifications.

Finding Yourself in . . .

The Ten Virgins
and the Ten Lepers

Matthew 25 & Luke 17

We've already peeled back a lot of layers of leprosy in a previous chapter, so we know that with the ten lepers, when Jesus said to *"go shew yourselves unto the priests,"* it's because that's who then is the one to pronounce them clean in this whole eight-day process. *"And it came to pass, that, as they went, they were cleansed."* They found their healing and progress in actions of faith. And as we know, only one healed leper returned. I know this Sunday school lesson will often go in the direction of gratitude, but what I love most is that this one leper went to Jesus when he didn't need anything. He was healed, had no immediate needs, and yet he chose to go to Jesus still because he wanted to. *"And with a loud voice glorified God,"* recognizing to whom all good comes from, and allowed himself to be changed by it, converted by it, driven by it. *"And Jesus answering said, Were there not ten cleansed? but where are the nine?"* How often do we go to Him when we don't need anything? When we are enjoying a season of contentment, are we still just as diligent in turning to Him, as we are in our desperate times of great needs? Are we allowing what He does for us change, convert, and deepen our dedication to Him in daily ways? Exactly the questions I think of with the ten virgins.

All ten virgins had lamps with oil in them. All ten were willing, and waiting, and wanting for the bridegroom. They all were dedicated and looking forward to the same thing. So where was the disconnect?

This parable is based on local marriage customs. Celebrations leading up to a marriage ceremony lasted, not a few hours of a reception like we often do, but several *days*. It's filled with family and gatherings so large it could often be moved into tents if they couldn't all fit inside the home. A party would start at the bridegroom's house, and a separate party at the bride's house, and eventually the two parties would set out walking towards to meet up and then together make their way to where the ceremony would be held. As the wedding party progressed, others would join in little groups who had waited at convenient places along the route. No one knew when it was time for the actual ceremony to start because it was dependent on someone at the groom's house, usually the father, who simply decided in the moment when *they* wanted it to be time, just based on their own feelings. Unpredictable and different from across each and any wedding.

"While the bridegroom tarried, they all slumbered and slept." Tarried meaning, this party took their time, and it took longer than anyone thought it would. And with passing time came lowering guard, and the feeling of settling and fatigue to cozy in. *"And at midnight there was a cry made, Behold, the bridegroom cometh; go ye out to meet him."* Wake up, the time has come, we gotta' go! These ceremonies were always in the evening and night hours, and obviously, there is not electricity, no headlights, no bright lights, it was just darkness. All ten virgins had oil in their lamps, they were all invested in the invitation to attend as they all committed to wait. *"But five of them were wise, and five were*

foolish." Not wicked, not rebellious, not undesiring, but *foolish.* As they had enough oil to currently be there, not having oil was a natural result of unpreparedness to extended beyond that moment. So they left in quest to *"buy for"* themselves, and when they came back, the *"door was shut."* They had missed out. Their waiting had been in vain because they did not do anything with what was given them.

Elder Oaks calls this parable "chilling."[1] These virgins are to be seen as believing members with testimonies. They all have a belief and a hope and a longing in Christ and His coming. There is no difference between the five wise and five foolish as far as what they were told to expect—same counsel, same lamps, same coming of the same bridegroom, same wait time. The arrival of the bridegroom did not require unusual or elaborate preparation. No virgin was given a disadvantage. The only difference was what they chose to do with what was given. The lamp is an outward profession of their belief and practice and the oil is their inner, private spirituality. Did they become distracted? Or busy? Did they think they were *safe* because they simply had lamps and the invitation extended? There are those who feel protected or better off than others simply because they are members of this church. But are they doing what they should with it, or does membership feel like a safe card to coast? Maybe. Maybe they were content. Currently, right now, in the middle of a trial I am in, I caught myself viewing coasting as a luxury. I would love to ease up a little on my desperate pleadings that are a result of the thick unwanted season I'm in, but I feel I can't afford to right now because we are in need of so much. How much I crave contentment, but I also know the adversary preys in there, too. The ease that comes with feeling like we have all this time is dangerous. I laugh at the small-scale example of all the Sunday's we as a whole family had everything ready to go for church, gathering by the door ready to leave, only to then realize we still had time left. So, we all just sort

---

1. Dallin H. Oaks, "Preparation for the Second Coming," April 2004 General Conference

of aimlessly filled our time and became too careless in the ease of waiting, and the next thing we know, we were late.

The five foolish virgins had oil in their lamps; it's just that the five inspired virgins had *extra* oil. They replenished, they prepared in advance for whatever was to come. That oil was a result of one drop at a time, daily efforts, patiently, consistently, "*line upon line, precept upon precept.*"[2] No shortcuts, no last-minute frenzied search, no coasting. It couldn't be shared because it is made up of individual, internal consistency with their souls— consistent choices, consistent efforts, consistent focus, consistent turning to Him, even when in no immediate need.

Like the nine lepers who went their own way, when we ease up on our efforts, the adversary proactively attempts to turn us away from our daily efforts of going to Him, telling us that we're doing fine on our own, we don't need to do that right now, we're not in immediate need. But with the adversary, contentment can lead to complacency, and complacency can lead to procrastination. The truth in President Kimball's words, "One of the most serious human defects in all ages is procrastination, an unwillingness to accept personal responsibilities *now*,"[3] absolutely rings true to human tendency to delay anything unwanted, anything that seems too big for the moment, and push it for a different future time.

When we are complacent, we are no longer striving to do our best, we're not pushing ourselves, not growing, not seeking out new opportunities, failing to meet our potential. We are not adding to our spiritual experiences, but resharing in the old, because we are not taking a chance on our faith and in His path. The adversary is most effective with me by not getting me to do anything bad, but by not getting me to do anything, to stay put. He gets me to linger longer in the problem solving and planning, to stay in my current phase, to put off blossoming self-discovery and new seasons with new fruits. Contentment and

2. 2 Nephi 28:30
3. *Teachings of Presidents of the Church—Spencer W. Kimball,* (The Church of Jesus Christ of Latter-day Saints, 2006), 4

procrastination are a comfortable snare the adversary uses to put off the better which is to come and slow our efforts of preparedness and turning to God. The adversary uses comfortable contentment to alter our focus and priorities until we slowly burn our oil out and we fall short and come up empty in our waiting. When we dangerously believe we have enough to get by, we are dismissing the truth that we aren't here just to *get by*, but to prepare and receive the greater things intended for us.

Why I think the one leper who returned to Jesus after his healing is so relevant to the parable of the virgins, is the articulation of proactive versus reactive. Reactive are the five foolish virgins who are in search to buy oil when they realize their lamps are now empty. Reactive are the nine lepers who went to Jesus only in need. They are reacting to a need, a problem that presented itself, in search for a solution, a blessing, a miracle. Proactive is the leper who went back without the immediate need. Proactive are the five wise virgins who realized that to keep their lamps full beyond immediate circumstances was a simple, everyday task.

So how can we better navigate this? How can we keep our lamps full and our priorities around the right focus? How can we be proactive and not reactive? How can we do something more with what is given us? There are a few different times in the New Testament we read *"ye never knew me"* and *"ye know me not."* One of which is the response to the virgins who stood at the closed door. How can we know Him? Like the leper, we keep going back to Jesus. We praise Him and recognize our need to become better only happens with Him. We know Him by relying on Him and not letting situations alter the effort we put in. We learn of Him but reading of Him, by serving Him, and by exercising our change-of-heart muscle. We know Him better by taking time every day to tell Him everything. By giving Him the opportunity to guide us and show us how great He really is by embracing the unexpected, knowing who's hands we're in. Like the one returned leper, we should allow what He's done for us to *change* us and deepen our love and desire and dedication to Him who is mighty, and willing, to save and heal and give even more to us. The contents of our lamps are our private spirituality, what we do in our personal life, and private relationship with God. The same things to do to know Him, are the same things that refuel our exhausted lamps.

I received a priesthood blessing that said to pay close attention to the spirit living within me. What an anchor that reminder has been. I have a spirit *inside* of me. The adversary tells us to retreat in efforts if we don't immediately recognize what we *get* out of it. I read scriptures *but I didn't get anything out of it.* I went to church, *but I don't remember what was even said.* Well, guess what? I don't even remember what I had for dinner two nights ago. But I know I ate, because if I didn't, I wouldn't be doing too well. We have an actual spirit living within us, and it is crucial that we feed it. Regardless of learning something new or not when reading scriptures, regardless of receiving a specific answer or not, the act alone of reading scriptures is *feeding* your spirit living inside of you. And if we don't do those things that feed our soul, it won't be doing too well.

The adversary tempts us to retreat in our efforts in returning to Jesus, knowing our God, feeding our spirits, and filling our lamps to get us to miss out on what we're invited to receive. Any choice to delay efforts that brings us closer to God, closer to our eternal goals, and steal our happiness, is the adversary winning. When we've fallen into the mindset that things are *good enough*, we've becoming overly comfortable in staying with how things are, and we have lost sight of our dreams and ambitions and greater purpose. And we will come up empty and our waiting and longing will be in vain. Looking inward can help notice if adjustment needs to be made. If we heard our bridegroom was coming tomorrow, what would we need to do today? Have we fallen victim to procrastination and contentment? Are we doing anything with what is given us? Are we being reactive or proactive? What is in my control? What good am I putting off? What prompting are we ignoring because it seems too much effort? Am I moving forward? What does my next step look like, even if that step is small? As we are mindful of our efforts and continuously go to the Lord, we will close the gap of disconnect.

Just like the lepers, we will find healing and progress in actions of faith. Just like the wise virgins, we will thrive and receive by deliberate acts every day to add, drop by drop, our fuel of faith to carry us through what is to come. *"Be faithful, praying always, having your lamps trimmed and burning, and oil with you, that you may be ready at the coming of the Bridegroom."*[4] As Elder Wirthlin has said, "The days of our probation are numbered, but none of us knows the number of those days. Each day of preparation is precious."[5] Each effort matters to our spirits and to our lamps. We have everything we need. The invite is ours.

---

4. Doctrine and Covenants 33:17
5. Joseph B. Wirthlin, "The Time to Prepare," April 1998 General Conference

Finding Yourself in . . .

Anointing by Mary
and Palm Sunday

Matthew 21 & 26, Mark 11 & 14,
Luke 19 & John 12

Preparing for Passover, floods of people flock to the city to participate in the rituals of remembrance and worship from the deliverance of the children of Israel from 400 years of bondage. After suffering plagues of frogs, lice, flies, the death of cattle, boils, blains, hail and fire, locusts, and thick darkness, the firstborns were threatened with death. With the blood of an unblemished firstling lamb on their doors, the angel of death passed by the marked houses. That pass over represents Jesus Christ ultimately overcoming death and saving us.

Six days before Passover, Jesus was in Bethany with His close friends Mary, Martha, and, newly risen from the dead, Lazarus. Bethany is actually a Hebrew word that means *house of the poor,* which is a fitting name for who Jesus devoted His ministry to. They were in the house of Simon the Leper, but there is no other mention of him in the Bible outside of this story. We can only assume he was healed by Jesus of his leprosy because he was accepted back into society and among people again, and because leprosy was incurable without Jesus. Because Martha was cooking there, some believe that he was related to, and potentially the father of, Lazarus and his sisters, but no one knows for certain. We do know that Jesus knew this Sabbath was His last in mortality. After the Friday Sabbath, Simon the leper held a dinner for Jesus and the twelve in his home. There were many other that were in the home for this meal *"not for Jesus's sake only,"* but the news was still spreading on Lazarus's miracle, and they wanted to come and see.

Martha took charge of cooking, while Jesus sat at the table with Lazarus, when Mary came to the feet of Jesus with a *pound* of extremely expensive spikenard ointment. Abundant amounts were poured on His head and feet as she anointed Him and wiped His feet with her hair. Anointing the head of a guest was to do them an honor, but to also anoint feet was rarely done even to kings. We know Jesus often spent time with Mary, Martha, and Lazarus, they were close. And still very soon after the raising of her brother, I can only imagine Mary's overwhelming adoration and indebted gratitude towards Him as she gave such an outpouring of worship and affection in this act. After all He has done for them, nothing to be given back to the Lord is too much.

With the onlookers of many other guests at this dinner, of course someone had to say something about what was done. *"To what purpose is this waste?"* Even today, there will always be onlookers to critique our efforts of worship and serving Him. *"Why was not this ointment sold for three hundred pence, and given to the poor?"* Jesus responds, *"let her alone,"* in certain declaration of the unfolding events of the next few days, *"for the poor always ye have with you; but me ye have not always."* Jesus commended Mary for what she had done, *"for she hath wrought a good work upon me . . . for in that she hath poured this ointment on my body, she did it for my burial."*

We don't know if she knew His death was to come this same week; that could have been gathered from His many remarks yet not understood, not even by His apostles. Or if perhaps she was just inspired to do so regardless, or if she was moved upon by that overwhelming gratitude and devotion to Him. But her actions are in line with ancient Israel where it was common to anoint bodies as part of burial rituals, like Jesus made mark of. In earlier periods, the Israelites also anointed living people that were to serve either as rightful kings or as high priests. And we can't forget that Jesus the Christ literally means *Jesus the anointed.* Her act was one that both recognized Him as a rightful king, as well as prepared Him for His infinite sacrifice that would be made for her. And for you.

The following morning, Jesus directs two disciples to retrieve a colt that was tied. Returning with it for Him, they laid their coats on its back for Jesus to sit and ride into one of the few times Jesus will be received and treated like the king that He is. Masses of Jewish pilgrims from all over flocked to Jerusalem many days before Passover to prepare. Arriving early to get themselves in order for retrieving a lamb, goat, or dove for sacrifice, as well as the time they needed for themselves for personal purification. Precisely the reason why there were money changers in the temple the following day when Jesus flipped the tables. It was for all these Jewish Pilgrims coming in from all over in need of currency change to purchase their required sacrificial animals. At the time, with such high demand and strict worship laws and traditions, it made sense to have the central place be a one-stop shop to get everyone from all over situated and taken care of. I'm sure most travelers were so grateful for the convenience after a long journey to have money changers and sacrificial animals readily there for them in the place of where they needed to be.

Unsure if Jesus would arrive publicly in Jerusalem at all because of the well-known plans to take Him into custody, word would spread when Jesus started His journey on a donkey, and crowds lined up to greet Him. The prophet Zechariah had specifically foretold that the messianic king would come in this fashion.[1] Old Testament kings, especially David, commonly rode donkeys. The donkey in Hebrew symbolism is for humility, and whereas horses were symbols of war, donkeys were symbols of peace. *"Thy king cometh,"* the prince of peace. Shouts of *hosanna!* Hebrew for *save us*! What I love about the hosannas is the symbolism of a two-word prayer, *save me.* In our depths of need, sometimes all we have is two-words; but our Savior comes willingly, helps willingly, and perfectly, even in response to our two-word pleas, *save me.* Save me from this, save me from this loneliness, from this pain, from this illness, this addiction, this mess, this heart break. Save us from it all, *hosanna,* save me. And what I love so much is Jesus's name is a variant of Hebrew names which mean *salvation.* They were shouting variants of His name. As they shout to be saved, Jesus is the literal meaning and response and answer of salvation.

"Jesus was glorified." Many of those who traveled in had heard of the miracles of Jesus and were excited to greet Him. Others were hopeful that He would be the answer to political or military change and triumph. Making space for Him, the crowds place palms and cloth for Jesus's path, a customary act worthy of the highest honor. Hails with palms has deep significance in several different angles. In the Ancient Middle East, palms represented peace, victory, and eternal life. For Jews in particular, it reminded them of God's victory over Egyptians and deliverance from bondage. Palms were seen as a gift from God because of its many uses in their lives. Within Jewish symbolism, the palm was often depicted on coins and important buildings, like their temple, for God's triumph and victory. Their waves of palms were an enthusiastic act of recognizing and celebrating Jesus for peace, deliverance, victory. Those who believed Jesus was the Messiah waved their palms for spiritual declaration, recognizing Him as a gift from God; others waved to show their declaration and hope for military and political triumph over Roman enemies, waving their palms in belief that He was their answer to freedom from

---

1. Zechariah 9:9

political oppression. And although they were partly right—He would be their answer for freedom and victory over the enemy—it would be so much bigger than they had in mind. And then there were those who asked my favorite question to ask myself, especially as I worship and prepare during the Easter season, *"who is this?"*

This is Jesus.

This is Jesus who even as a boy, underage and unfit, elders were *hearing Him* and asking *Him* questions as He taught in the temple. This is Jesus who filled and started sinking two ships of fish in great abundance. This is Jesus who supplied a luxury for His friends at a wedding because of His deep love and dedication for us. This is Jesus who even evil spirits confessed Him to be *the holy one of God.* This is Him who cleansed the temple because He has the ability to cleanse us.

He who sleeps during the storm, not because He doesn't care, but because He knows perfectly that all *will* in fact be well regardless of the storm. He who is aware, conscious, mindful, active. He who is perfect regardless of our narrow-mindedness because He does not turn His back, neglect, abandon, or play favorites. There is not one misfit, not one outcast, not one sinner, who Jesus is not saying to them, *"Follow me,"* and offering them something more. There is not one who Jesus does not see great worth and great purpose and great need of.

This is Jesus, who gives us access to *power* to change, to renewal, revival, relief. This is He who goes to the hated, the forgotten, the different, the outcasts, *the sinners,* the excommunicated, and befriends them, *calls* them to great things, blesses and loves them. He who goes to the shamed, the judged, the detested, ostracized, and sees great worth and great purpose and great need of them. He who sits with sinners, calls the publicans, touches the unclean and impure, forgives in the act, reaches for those sinking, stops for those buried in the crowd or alone in the heat of the day.

This is Jesus who, even among mass multitudes, blesses us one-by-one, personally and individually. He who purposely travels where others don't to help, to teach, to connect, to love, to forgive. He who comes to us when we are facing emptiness, and weeps *with* us. He who stops in the middle of a moving masses because He notices us on the ground, in the dirt, buried under the crowd, to heal even lingering impossibilities. He who meets us where we are and comforts and lifts us. He comes to us because He doesn't lose sight of us. He who *only* exists to bring us to be better and make us better. He who is yours.

This is Jesus, who will not meet His match with our suffering; our impossibilities are not a struggle, nor an inconvenience, for Him. When everything and everyone says no, Jesus says, *"I will."* While others may fail us, He comes with healing in His wings and compassion that knows no bounds. This is Jesus who stays until we are filled, and we can be whole. There *is* a love that satisfies.

That is this Jesus. That is your Jesus.

Finding Yourself in . . .

The Rejection of Jesus

Cleansing the Temple, Cursing the Fig Tree, and the Wicked Husbandmen

Matthew 21, Mark 11 & 12, Luke 19 & John 12

Although His entrance into Jerusalem was *triumphant* and was surrounded by praise, Jesus wept. *"Now is my soul troubled."* Troubled and weeping, over wickedness, over destruction of both temple and city, over refusal of acceptance of Him, and of what He knows are the last few days of His mortal life. That path so lovingly lined will soon lead to Calvary. Troubled and weeping knowing those who watched and cheered at His entrance will, only days later, watch and spit on Him to His death.

Among the multitudes coming to Jerusalem for Passover are people of many nations, some of which are converts to Judaism. There were even *"certain Greeks"* who sought Him out directly after His arrival on what we call Palm Sunday. *"Sir, we would like to see Jesus."* The Pharisees *"therefore said among themselves, perceive ye how ye prevail nothing? Behold, the world is gone after him.*" In other words, we haven't been able to do anything about Jesus and now everybody, even those from other nations, are seeking and following Him. Almost the same words they have been saying for a bit now, like when Lazarus was raised from the dead, they held a council and said, *"What do we? for this man doeth many miracles. If we let him thus alone, all men will believe on him: and the Romans shall come and take away both our place and nation."* They knew in time *"none could not believe in Christ."* The Pharisees have lost every public debate, and every snare to catch Jesus in His words, and now they are losing the people to Him, too. They *"could not find what they might do: for all the people were very attentive to hear him."*

The parable of the Wicked Husbandmen is an obvious parable against the Pharisees. A *"householder,"* Heavenly Father, planted a vineyard, did all the work to cultivate and nurture and nourish it, and then *"went into a far country"* and *"let it out to"* a steward who was supposed to take good care of it. But, one servant was *"beat,"* another *"killed,"* and the other, *"stoned." "But last of all he sent unto them his son."* And when they saw the husbandmen's son, they said *"among themselves, This is the heir; come, let us kill him . . . And they caught him, and cast him out of the vineyard, and slew him."* When Christ spoke of the Wicked Husbandmen, the Pharisees were not ignorant, they knew exactly that parable was about them, *"they perceived that he spoke of them,"* but in their repeated efforts to *"lay hands on him, they feared the multitude"* because Jesus was winning the people on His side.

This parable was not the only thing against them in this small time frame of His last days. As Jesus was again coming from Bethany to Jerusalem, like He did every day coming into Jerusalem for Passover, and leading to His arrest, He was hungry. Seeing a fig tree in the distance and knowing they produce fruit, He approached it, but it had none. An obvious parallel of the Pharisees; how they take pride in their actions to the law, but do not produce fruit. *"Let no fruit grow on thee henceforward for ever . . . and when the disciples saw it, they marveled, saying, How soon is the fig tree withered away!"* Just like that, it was dried from the roots up, just like in Job when describing the wicked. *"His roots shall be dried up beneath, and above shall his branch be cut off. His remembrance shall perish from the earth, and he shall have no name in the street. He shall be driven from light into darkness."*[1]

The laws and actions of these Jewish religious leaders, in their hypocrisy to protect only themselves and their position, held no root or nourishment. Directly after speaking of the fig tree, and with continued ridicule and questioning from chief priests and elders, He gives the parable of the Two Sons. Teaching that the *"publicans,"* hated Jewish tax collectors, and the *"harlots,"* prostitutes, *"go into the kingdom of God before you."*

Cleansing Monday is the second day of Holy Week, when Jesus returns to Jerusalem and goes to the temple. As we previously read about people flocking from different nations to celebrate and worship, they would arrive early to retrieve a lamb, goat, or dove for sacrifice, and have the time they needed for themselves for personal purification. Jesus flipped over tables and chairs and *"cast out all them that sold and bought in the temple."* Convenience turned the blindness of purpose, completely losing sight of what mattered most. But the money changers in the temple were not just there for convenience of incoming travelers in need of strict items to participate, but they would collect taxes and gain earnings from it. Those who could not afford a lamb or goat, those who did not have much to offer, were allowed to use a dove for their sacrifice. Overthrowing *"the seats of them that sold doves,"* they were all there taking advantage of and taking from even the poor.

Just four days until the cross, this is the second time Jesus had cleansed the temple. The first time was during the beginning of His mission three years previous. Clearly, they had not learned their lesson and had not allowed Jesus's teachings lead them to change. The difference is three years previous Jesus had cleansed and defended the temple as *His father's house,* but Jesus is now, teaching it is *His house.* And *His house* is a *"house of prayer,"* not a

---

1. Job 18:16–18

"den of thieves." As popularity and praise increased in Jerusalem, and Jesus the center for gathering, with His life at risk, He openly and publicly announces He is the Christ. The anger against Jesus at this point is indescribable. After repeated failed efforts to stop Him, there He was within the very area over which they claimed supreme jurisdiction and announces He is the awaited Messiah, their Savior.

"And the blind and the lame came to him in the temple, and he healed them." Jesus didn't leave the temple after He cleansed it. After that whole scene, in front of those who threatened His life, Jesus did not leave. Even the religious leaders who were *"sore displeased"* told Him that staying was really dangerous. But He stayed. And He healed. And *"he returned daily in the temple."* These last few days, knowing what is to come, Jesus chose to spend it among His people, teaching and healing, regardless of His safety.

Despite chaos and darkness and unfairness, beautiful things happened and were taught amidst it all. Warnings, things to be aware of, things to come, guidance, and the most important focus were given. *"Love the Lord thy God with all thy heart, and with all thy soul, and with all thy mind."* To serve one another, to love one another. Blessings came, healing came, change came, truth came, light came. Jesus came. And He stayed. Even now, amidst us, He stays.

By this point, there were in fact *"chief rulers"* who *"many believed on him but because of the Pharisees they did not confess him, lest they should be put out of the synagogue"* and be excommunicated. Like the money changers in the temple, and those who lined the streets both in praise and then in condemnation, did not allow themselves to be changed by Jesus. Like the Pharisees who *"loved the praise of men more than the praise of God,"* their personal vision for their lives held more weight than the limitless possibilities with Jesus. Even as witnesses to *"so many miracles before them"* and disregard to a time when they once celebrated Him, they *"blinded their eyes and hardened their heart."* Like the cursed fig tree and the wicked, their roots were dried up and were *"driven from light into darkness."*

This is where I bring myself to some serious self-reflection. In our Nicodemus chapter we talked about the battles within us with our own Pharisee-like qualities up against deep in our hearts where we want to follow the Lord. How many times do I deny what Christ is offering me, because like the Pharisees not wanting to lose their position, I am afraid of the loss? How many times am I turning away from Jesus because I am afraid and unwilling for the unknown, for change. Like the money changers, has seeking convenience caused me to lose sight of what matters most?

As bleeding Christ is publicly struggling with His cross among onlookers that lined the streets, I think about what changed in them. As I think of all the different ways people were wanting something from Jesus as He entered in on a donkey, I can see myself in them as they find disappointment in not receiving specifically and exactly what they were looking for. They were hoping for a military leader, or for political change, and when they didn't get exactly what they wanted, they turned back to their own ways. How many times have I done that? How many times did I pray for something so specific, and when I didn't get it in that exact way, I turn back to my own ways? Am I close to Him even when I'm not getting what I want in the way that I wanted it? Because of my pride, am I completely missing the better things with real, lasting *fruit* that *withers* not away?

"While ye have light, believe in the light. . . . Whosoever believeth on me should not abide in darkness."

The first day that marks Holy Week, the countdown to His great and last sacrifice, our Father spoke. A *"voice from heaven, saying, I have both glorified it, and will glorify it again."* The voice was not only spoken to Jesus privately. The voice was real. People who were standing by *"heard it."* This voice didn't come for Jesus, but for *"our sakes."* The dedication that our Savior and our Father had to us has always been their focus and driving force to bring us to greater things than we had in mind. *When* I fight the battle within myself of convenience, fear, pride, and protection from the unknown and uncharted, a refocus comes when I answer to myself the question Jesus asked the Pharisees, *"What think ye of Christ?"* When I reminded of who He really is, His character, and His purpose, I feel a comfort and an invite to refocus to allow Jesus to change me, to take root.

Other than actual temples, our homes and our bodies are both referred to as temples. Perhaps we might want to take time to reflect on the things within our homes and ourselves that might need changing and cleansing and removing. Because Jesus cleansed the temple, He can cleanse us. Because of the cross He carried, we can change, we can turn back around. No darkness, no outside force, will chase away Christ being here with us as our Savior and awaited Messiah. When weeping during His palm and praise entrance, He spoke, *"Father, save me from this hour,"* but in the same breath answered himself immediately, that *"for this cause came I unto this hour."* He came for us. He continued for us. Amidst our chaos, and darkness, and unfairness, light is here, truth is here. Jesus is here. And He stays. And He cleanses. And He heals. And beautiful things happen.

Finding Yourself in . . .

The Last Supper and Judas

Matthew 26 & 27, Mark 14, Luke 22 & John 18

"*Then entered Satan into Judas . . . being of the number of the twelve.*" Knowing the "*chief priests and scribes sought how they might kill*" Jesus, Judas, on his own, "*went his way*" to the "*chief priests and captains*" and offered himself to help. Judas was not peer pressured or threatened to betray Jesus, nor was he even approached individually at all. Knowing that Jesus could not be killed in daylight "*on feast day*" in front of crowds, "*for fear of the multitude,*" Judas "*sought opportunity to betray him.*" Asking "*what will ye give me*" if he were to make a deal, He bargained to sell the Savior of the world for what today would only be seventeen dollars, pocket change. Judas cut down the worth of the Messiah to the lowest price to purchase a *common slave*. John says Judas is a "*thief,*" Mark says he "*turned away him*" because he *was* "*offended.*" Except Judas didn't just sell the sinless One over to the sinners for scrap blood money, he sold his soul for pocket change to the devil. Actions dictated by pride and blinded by the fleeting things of this world, Judas switched Masters. Except this master subtly and slowly *"leadeth them away carefully down to hell."*[1]

And *"they were glad."*

Jesus had taught and brought up His coming crucifixion at least twelve times—at the first Passover, to Nicodemus, while discussing the bridegroom, to the Pharisees when talking of the whale's belly for three days, during the sermon on the bread of life, following Peter's testimony, on the Mount of Transfiguration, to a disciple in Galilee, in route to Jerusalem, while teaching the good shepherd, in the parable of wicked husbandmen—and yet it was not understood by His apostles.

The Last Supper was obviously Jesus's last earthly meal before what He knew very well was to come next. *"Ye know that after two days is the feast of the passover, and the Son of man is betrayed to be crucified."* He knew with perfect detail and timing how these next days would all unfold, His death and crucifixion, as well as Judas's betrayal, down to the very second of the arrest. I wonder what thoughts were going through His mind as He ate of the sacrificial Passover lamb knowing it represented His upcoming sacrifice of Himself. *"With desire I have desired to eat this passover with you before I suffer."* His greatest desire was to be there with them, to feast one last time with *"His friends."* His greatest desire was to teach them about the greatest commandment, *love.* His greatest desire was to cleanse them both physically with washing their feet, and spiritually with the sacrament. And His greatest desire was to prepare the way for that cleansing and renewal to be available to all even after that upcoming weekend. That was His greatest *desire*—love, unity, service, and the gift of change and progression.

And as He first takes a cup symbolic of His own perfect blood and breaks the bread representing His own body which will shortly be broken, He *"gave thanks."* On the night Jesus was

---

1. 2 Nephi 28:21

betrayed by His friend, on the night which set into motion the path to His death, *He gave thanks.* If Jesus can give thanks in that situation, in that kind of heartbreak, it is possible for us to give thanks in anything. If it is possible for Him to find light in that kind of darkness, it is possible for us to find it, if we look. Jesus was moved by gratitude while His time was quickly coming to an end because He was giving us so much more. And to Him, that was worth it. To Him, we are worth it.

"He took bread, and blessed it." Because it is blessed, as we eat and internalized Him, *we* are blessed. Our weekly sacrament prayer, *"to bless and sanctify,"*[2] as we remember Him, and participate with Him, make Him part of us, we *are* sanctified! And as we drink of His perfect, sacrificial blood shed for us, we receive *"remission of sins."* Remission is cancelation. We have gone over so often already how forgiveness is not choosing to look past, but an actual clean slate of non-existence. Leaving us with these ordinances was absolutely essential to Christ coming here in the first place. All the failed attempts to lay hands on Christ would continue to fail because His work was not yet finished. The sacrament and Gethsemane needed to happen first because they were both parts of the entire purpose of us coming here to begin with. Giving us the ability to be cleansed, to change, to become better, to be better, to become sanctified, was worth dying to give us. Because of this ordinance, we can be brought to something more, something better, to return back to Him and become as God is. *"In remembrance."* We think of Him because He always thought of us. Everything He has ever done, was with us in mind.

In one of these last lessons before He leaves to His death, He finds great importance to again teach of and promise the Holy Ghost. We went over in greater detail in the baptism of Jesus chapter on how to recognize it in the times we don't—if you'd like to go back and read it. And here again, before leaving us, Jesus is speaking of His promise of guiding us, teaching us, offering constant companionship to never leave us comfortless, and

---

2. Moroni 4:3; 5:2

that which will grow our light within us. We mistakenly think that we have felt the Spirit before, but unsure if we have ever felt Him. But when we are guided by and feel the Spirit, that is Him. It is how He communicates; it is the tool He uses. The Spirit is God participating in our personal lives. United and one in purpose and great *promise,* ranked top of the list of things Jesus wanted us to really understand on His last night alive.

A piercing self-reflection question is posed when after Jesus says during dinner, *"One of you which eateth with me shall betray me."* And in the best response, the apostles did not blame or wonder about others among them, but instead looked inward. *"Lord, is it I?"* Fearing he would look suspicious from not asking like the others, Judas has the audacity to ask the same question. I wonder if he could look Jesus in the eye as He asked it. *"Thou hast said,"* Jesus responded, which in many versions of the Bible means *yes.*

The eleven were *"exceeding sorrowful"* over the thought and reality of betrayal. Perhaps their surprised and sorrowful reaction was in part thinking how could anyone? After all they have been shown, been taught, witnessed, felt, experienced, after all they had been through with Jesus, how could one of them turn away from Him? And yet Judas did. And so did the believing elders and priests, and so did those that lined up for Him on Palm Sunday, and sometimes, so do we. Even after all He has, and continues to do for us, we turn away from Him. Sometimes even wonder to the world the same question Judas asked, *"What will ye give me?"*

Sometimes people ask for fun, "Well what would you do if you knew it was going to be your last day alive?" When I was asked recently, it occurred to me—Jesus knew. And He washed feet.

As the apostles were bickering about who was greatest among the apostle group, Jesus teaches by example that the greatest among others is the one who serves. Washing the apostles' feet was symbolic of His ability to cleanse, as well as an act of humility and love to us. But more so than this, it visibly shows us the promise we read in scripture, that Jesus is not above us, but *among* us. He was showing that He is a humble servant not just to God, but to us—here to help, here to cleanse, here to serve, here to love. Washing feet of guests was often an act for slaves to perform, and Peter in protest withdraws, because how could He allow the Messiah to wash the feet of someone so unworthy in comparison. *"Depart from me; for I am a sinful man, O Lord."* Jesus answering, *"If I wash thee not, thou has no part with me,"* to which Peter responds with deep devotion to Him, *"Lord, not my feet only, but also my hands."* And teaches that because Jesus washed their feet, we should do as He has done and *"wash one another's feet."* To lay aside our garments, to take a towel, to pour, to wash—in essence, to serve.

And Judas? His feet, too. The very hands that will soon be driven through with nails are washing and serving even Judas. As Jesus teaches about change, forgiveness, and the command, *"Love one another; as I have loved you,"* Jesus is passing to, feasting with, and serving the one who He knows betrayed Him. Speaking volumes towards His love for us even with our sins. He willingly comes down to our mess. Jesus is a better Savior than we are a sinner.

John later says Jesus *"loved his own"* disciples *"unto the end."* And *his own* included Judas Iscariot. Jesus does dismiss him; *"That thou doest, do it quickly,"* in other words, I know what you are going to do, do it quickly. No one else knowing the real *intent* Jesus spoke of, but Judas did, and he *"immediately"* left. But Jesus could have done that before the Passover meal and before washing his feet if He had wanted. But He didn't. While supping and washing first, it was as if Jesus was saying, "You are still one of mine. And I still love you." Even until the end. Judas's and Jesus's. And so, Judas left to betray Him. And he did so with clean feet.

Like the apostles' initial reaction, we wonder how could Judas do what he did? But also, it's who I sometimes am, I am a betrayer to Him. After all He has done for me, how many times have I turned away because of my own selfishness? After all I have been shown, been taught, witnessed, felt, experienced, after all I have been through with Jesus, and yet, how many times have I prioritized things above Him? It was my sins that put Jesus on the cross. And yet, He serves me. He loves me. And even though Jesus knew of the times I turn away, He went to the cross for me, nonetheless. What a love. A love *unto the end.*

It's an easy game of the adversary to look elsewhere rather than inward and ask the self-reflection question, *"Lord, is it I?"* It's the adversary's lens to look at ourselves and our desires with a filter of biases, excuses, and justifications, but by doing so we turn away from Jesus. And we are *carefully* led by that different master. If we keep that lens, then we are like those described in the Book of Mormon who are living as if no redemption had been made,[3] and the redeeming power of the Savior cannot heal and change and receive that which is *prepared* already for us. By examining our lives, confronting our weaknesses, and continuously shifting our desires from the fleeting things of this world, with grace and mercy, we will receive all our Father has for us, everything that Jesus saw worth dying for to give us. The privilege to be changed, to be cleansed, to be sanctified, to be forgiven, to be better, to be loved *unto the end,* and receive everlasting life like God's. It's His greatest *desire.*

During this Last Supper, His greatest and last command is to *"love one another,"* just as He does. If Jesus can dip from the same bowl as Judas, then, in Christ, we can better share the same table, the same space, with others. Knowing how much grace we have been in need of for our own times of turning away, we can better see and offer grace to others. If Jesus can wash and serve even the feet of Judas, we can better sit and sup and serve those around us. Everyone is invited to Jesus's table. And when we sit at the table with other Judases, we'll better understand the love of Jesus.

In our times of mistakes and betrayal, Jesus all knowing, comes and sits close still. Because Jesus's last night alive He did not turn Judas away, Jesus wants you at His table, too.

---

3. See Mosiah 16:5.

Because He chose to eat with and serve Judas, Jesus is with you still offering to serve and to cleanse you. He chooses to come down to our mess. As Jesus passes the bread also to Judas, He offers and passes His body to you, too. To be unified and one with Him. He sends Judas away to carry out the act of arrest and death because His greatest *desire*, even knowing our mistakes, is to give us so much more. And to Him, that was worth it. To Him, we are worth it.

Finding Yourself in . . .

The Intercessory Prayer and Gethsemane

Matthew 26, Mark 14, Luke 22 & John 17

After Judas leaves to lead the enemies back, Jesus continues to teach the eleven and sing together a hymn. Their sacred time together in that upper room was coming to an end, just as Jesus's time in mortality was coming to an end. And when Judas had departed, Jesus was *"glorified, and God is glorified in him,"* in other words, now is the time for His Atonement. Calling His eleven apostles *"little children,"* the command to love, the promise that He *"will not leave [us] comfortless,"* and His commitment of His return are His last words before making His way to the garden.

Peter asks why He cannot follow Him where He is going, saying, *"I will lay down my life for thy sake."* A week previous, Peter, James, and John were with Christ on the mount of transfiguration when Jesus foretold of His coming suffering, rejection, and death. Peter tried to *"rebuke"* His words, professing that would not happen; *"This shall not be."* Peter would make sure it wouldn't. Just as we see his same conviction here to defend and follow now, Jesus always knew what He came to earth to do, and Jesus is driven by passion and purpose to save *all* mankind. Peter was as confused then as he is now; here they are a week after the Mount of Transfiguration, and as they make their way into Gethsemane, it is like Jesus saying, "Let me show you."

The promises Jesus gives before they leave that upper room are bold and clear realities for us. Jesus *"will come again,"* and He *"will receive you unto [Himself]."* He *will.* And at this moment, He went to *"prepare a place for you."* He did that. For you. To be with Him again. There are *"many mansions,"* different degrees, all in glory, prepared for everyone. And because He *"lives, ye shall live also."* Shall—*will.* Those are sound truths, promises, and reality. Jesus, our Savior, is *in you,* part of you, He gives us an invitation and a plead to abide in Him, just as He does in us—*"and I in you,"*—thus never being *comfortless,* never truly alone. Jesus *is* the *"true vine."* Continued nourishment that leads to fruit and blossoms comes from abiding, remaining, staying, with Him. Without our Savior, with distancing ourselves from Him, we would be like the green branches that dry up and shrivel off. We'd become like those who turn back His outstretched hand. But because He offers Himself, we are meant to blossom and thrive. To have His *"joy fulfilled in themselves"*—in us.

And as Christ then says He can't keep talking much longer, because the *"prince of darkness, who is of this world, cometh,"* Judas with his kiss, He leaves us with *peace.* The crowning peak to His last teaching, is leaving us with His *peace.* In all the darkness and pain and weight He will suffer, and with all the darkness, and pain, and weight *we* will suffer, the Savior of our souls consoles us, *"let not your heart be troubled,"* spoken of twice in just a few short verses of each other. *"Peace I leave with you, my peace I give unto you; not as the world giveth, give I unto you. Let not your heart be troubled, neither let it be afraid."*

Leaving the intimate upper room, Jesus brings all eleven apostles to the Mount of Olives, where Jesus has continuously throughout His life retreated to for prayer and teaching. Heading to a special, private place where they often sought solitude and their Father and to be taught truths. This time, He lifts *"up his eyes to heaven,"* offers Himself as the great sacrifice for our sins, and prays. A prayer known as the Intercessory Prayer. We can read the intimate words of Christ Himself, speaking directly to His Father, and they are overflowing with dedication and love to Him and to us. I hate to break it into pieces because it's beautifully impactful in its perfect entirety. But listen to His honest report back to His Dad, the God of all, *"I have finished the work which thou gavest me to do."* He gave us all the words which God gave Him, He *manifested* God to us, and lived so that all *"might know thee the only true God."* He did it. He stayed dedicated to Him and to us. From the time of His birth in a stable, to the young age teaching in the temple, until His time on the cross, He has always been dedicated to Him and to you.

And as He is in the Mount of Olives, He then prays for us. The Mount of Olives of all places, to pray and to suffer and succor for us. Olives, oil, Gethsemane, (which in the Mount of Olives), meaning *oil press.* The Jews would put olives into mesh fabric bags and put them in a press to squeeze oil out of them. The first pressings would have the purest olive oil, prized for many uses, including giving light to lanterns and healing. The last pressing of olives, from the pressure of additional weight, created a bitter, red oil. The symbolism of Christ and oil for healing and light, is obvious and deep. The bitter red parallel to the bitter cup He drank from the pressure of what He had felt and suffered in that exact olive oil garden. And in this spot of profound symbolism for His sacrifice and atonement, He prays for us.

In His final moments before crushing agony and pain that causes Him to collapse directly on His face, He dedicates His time and love to *"pray for them,"* to pray for you—Please Father, protect them in this world *"from the evil. They are not of this world, even as I am not of the world."* Please, *"sanctify them,"* consecrate, and make them holy. Please Father, I pray that they *"might have my joy fulfilled in themselves."*

The only begotten is pleading to God Himself for us to be protected, to be holy, and to have His joy *in* us, to be part of us. His prayer of greatest desire is for us to *believe on* Him . . . to be with Him where He lives. For us to be *one* with Him, perfect oneness with the perfect one. To give us the *glory* that was given to Him from God. He wants us back. Reunited, sanctified with the same great glory that He has. That's huge. That's for us, that's what's meant and intended for us. That's why He is going to be taking His next steps into the garden, for this, for His greatest prayer to be able to come to pass. *"I kept them in thy name: those that thou gavest me I have kept, and none of them is lost."* You are not lost. He is with you with those same desires. Even in our Judas-betrayal and Peter-denial moments which He is aware of in perfect detail, He continued into the garden—and He continued to the cross—for us. Because *"it grieveth me that I should lose"*[1] you.

Near the bottom within this mount, is the garden of Gethsemane. Leaving His eight at the gate, He takes Peter, James, and John further in so they would be within a stone's throw of Jesus. And with His very first steps, He began *"to be sorrowful and very heavy,"* His *"soul"* was *"exceedingly sorrowful, even unto death."* To feel so painfully, and so deeply, it was a direct and immediate hit to His soul. So consuming and powerful, He collapsed *"on his face."* Which is also, in Jewish culture, the gesture of submission and humility.

I have absolutely collapsed under fatigue and pain from trials, absolutely I have struggled so long that my body physically aches, it hurts, it's sore because the burden I was asked to bear was too big, too heavy, too impossible, too unwanted. I have known loss so painful that it's caused me to yell so loudly at God, wondering where He is, that I lose my voice. I have felt empty. I have felt hollow and hopeless and consumed with darkness that seemed too thick to ever lift. But I have never bled from it. Not even a single pore. Jesus's bleeding *"great drops"* was not figurative, it was

---

1. Jacob 5:7

literal, and can also be found in both Mosiah 3 and Doctrine and Covenants 19, *"blood cometh from every pore, so great shall be his anguish."*[2] An average person has over five-hundred million pores. And every single one of them bled for you. What could He have looked like? Every pore meaning, He gave all that He had to give. He held nothing back. This sacrifice, which demanded everything from Him, incomprehensible agony that no human could withstand without dying, only a God was capable of experiencing, *"even more than man can suffer, except it be unto death."*[3] I know pain, I have suffered many times that caused me to literally drop to the floor, convinced I could not handle the weight, could not carry on. But Jesus. What is that weight and pain when it is magnified by every single soul that has ever lived, and will ever live, with each of their entire existences here, all at the same time. I try, but my finite mind cannot wrap around it.

Although hearing His agony and painful pleads to God, three times His three apostles fell asleep. Although they were willing, His chosen ones did not stand with Him fully in the end. Jesus would sorrowfully request them to watch again, yet in this deepest time of need when He wanted them most, they slumbered, returning to the agony of soul alone. Regardless of their best intents, *"their eyes were heavy."* What of Jesus's sleep? What of His fatigue? He who needed it the most did not get rest to sustain Him through not just in this garden, but the trials, the abuse, the march with cross, and nails to follow, there will be no rest. Could they not watch with Him *one hour?* He was saving them personally, and they couldn't focus on Him for that short of time? Wasn't He important enough for them? I catch myself in my criticism as I think of all the sacrament meetings I have sat with wandering irrelevant thoughts, or fatigue and desire to be elsewhere. Could I not be there for Him for *one hour,* with His blood and body under the cloth that only lay there to save me personally? Isn't

---

2. Mosiah 3:7; Doctrine and Covenants 19:18
3. Mosiah 3:2

partaking of His blessed and broken body and forgiveness important enough?

With so much He could have said or taught, *"watch and pray, that ye enter not into temptation,"* is what He says. Which is also what He chooses to say *twice* during His visit to the American continent, to *"watch and pray always."*[4] Though we may have dedication and good intentions like His chosen apostles, *"the spirit is indeed willing, but the flesh is weak."* During the Last Supper, Jesus even spoke to Simon saying, *"Satan hath desired to have you, that he may sift you as wheat: But I have prayed for thee."* The adversary's constant lures and traps to pull us away from God also pulls with *"the natural man"* which *"is an enemy to God and has been from the fall of Adam, and will be, forever and ever."*[5] Though we may feel strong, and though we may be chosen of the Lord, because the apostles could not stay awake, we must cling to His consistent plead to *watch,* to be mindful, to be aware, and to *rise and pray* always. Lest we slumber.

As the apostle's sleep, continuing alone to suffer through fear of death, through blood, sorrow, sins, pain, loss, Jesus Christ will make it so a new kind of rest for their souls possible. Jesus calls out with a personal and intimate term, *Abba.* Dad. *Let this pass. Take away this cup.* But if not, help me to *drink it.* Not only does this show the depth we cannot fathom of what He was experiencing, but a profound template of prayer and faith we should have in our times of pain and struggle. Knowing that our God is *not* a God of avoidance and prevention of hard, we can better remind ourselves that, like with Jesus and His miracles, in the times they are not taken away, they are used to bring us to greater magnifications. And while we are led through and not around, He sends us what and who we need. *"There appeared an angel unto [Jesus] from heaven, strengthening him."* Because Jesus is God's, He sent an angel to strengthen. Because we are God's, He sends angels to strengthen. *"Therefore, hold on thy way."*[6]

---

4. 3 Nephi 18:15, 18
5. Mosiah 3:19
6. Doctrine and Covenants 122:9

"*The people in darkness will see a great Light—Unto us a Child is born.*"[7] Getting us back and giving us everything is "*this cause came I into the world.*" This was the start of taking upon Himself the sins of the world, an act of sacrifice that will continue and finish to the next day on the cross at Golgotha. Three or four hours with "*which suffering caused myself, even God, the greatest of all, to tremble because of pain . . . to suffer both body and spirit.*"[8]

But not sins only, Jesus "*shall suffer temptations, and pain of body, hunger, thirst, and fatigue even more than man can suffer, except it be unto death.*"[9] "*He shall go forth, suffering pains and afflictions and temptations of every kind; and this that the word might be fulfilled which saith he will take upon him the pains and the sicknesses of his people.*"[10] He will feel and carry the weight, the consequences, and the pain of all that is mental, spiritual, and physical. All encompassing, all inclusive. There is not one thing you have suffered that He has not—not just physical, not just mental, not just spiritual, but of it all. Needing and lacking in all forms. Even if I tried my best to articulate, in the times I have felt hopeless and felt no one understands how I have felt, I remind myself, that's not true. The one that can help me best is the one who perfectly knows with exactness. "*The Son of Man hath descended below them all.*"[11] But because Jesus was *below*, because He was under it *all*, He then can lift us all higher! He can lift and lighten our load and our soul and elevate us out of thick darkness and to greater heights above the storm clouds into beautiful magnifications that are promised to us.

Infinite agonies, all-encompassing pain, and yet, it is overshadowed by His love. Love for His Father. Love for you. "*Nevertheless . . . I partook and finished.*"[12] And because He did, the plan of salvation became operative. Because He *partook and*

---

7. Isaiah 9, chapter heading
8. Doctrine and Covenants 19:18
9. Mosiah 3:7
10. Alma 7:11
11. Doctrine and Covenants 122:8
12. Doctrine and Covenants 19:19

finished, chains will be broken, change will be possible, and clean slates will be given. Because He was alone, we never will be. Because He descended below it all, everything that is bringing us down, weighing us down, holding us down, can be lifted up. Because He did, His greatest desires of unity and reunion in perfected glory is attainable to even you. Because He partook and finished, there will always be someone who understands perfectly, and we will never be truly alone. Because Jesus continued, He will never falter nor fail us.

"I, God, have suffered these things for all, that they might not suffer if they would repent."[13] Because they often sought solitude and a private place to seek their Father and be taught truths, so should we. Because He lifted up His eyes to heaven, so should we. Transgression, loneliness, guilt, weakness, failure, injury, sickness, fatigue, death, addictions, mistakes, pain, will all bring us to our personal Gethsemanes, but Jesus is there. Angels are there. And all are strengthening and leading us to magnifications here and hereafter. "If the bitter cup does not pass, drink it and be strong, trusting in happier days ahead."[14] Never-ending glory is available to you because Jesus partook and finished.

Jesus is driven by passion and purpose to save you. He wants us back. Reunited, sanctified with the same great glory that He has. That's why He stood calmly at the sight of approaching torches, and willingly awaited His arrest, for this, for His greatest prayer to be able to come to pass.

"Peace I leave with you, my peace I give unto you."

TONIGHT

Tonight, when you sit down for dinner,
think of Jesus,
Sitting down for dinner with His friends—
for the last time.

---

13. Doctrine and Covenants 19:16
14. Jeffrey R. Holland, "Like a Broken Vessel," October 2013 General Conference

Tonight, when you get up from eating,
think of Jesus,
getting up, making His way to a garden—
blood and betrayal.

Tonight, as we sleep,
think of Jesus,
who will be beaten and abused all night —
filled of illegal trials.

Tomorrow, when we awake to start our day
think of Jesus,
who will be suffering and striped, carrying His cross—
to end his.

how hard and heavy it must be,
how weak He must be.

Tomorrow, as we go about our daily tasks,
as we go to work, run to the store,
scroll on our phone, watch TV,
Think of Jesus,
who will have nails driven through His flesh—
willingly.

Tomorrow, think of Jesus
Because tomorrow,
He was definitely thinking of you.

Let's give our life to Him,
Who gave His life for us.

Finding Yourself in . . .

The Betrayal and Trials

Matthew 26 & 27, Mark 14 & 15,
Luke 22 & 23 & John 18

"*Sleep on now, and take your rest,*" even though there would be no rest for Him. "*It is enough, the hour is come; behold, the Son of man is betrayed into the hands of sinners.*" There was no use further watching Jesus in the garden as He knew in perfect exactness Judas was close.

"*Rise up, let us go.*" Prepared to fulfill, Jesus somehow was able to stand and continue after the infinite worth of souls stripped Him in all ways in the garden. With His eleven, Jesus, bloodied and weak, somehow standing, calmly awaited the reunion of His friend, approaching with *a "multitude"* of soldiers, "*officers from the chief priests and Pharisees,*" and "*the scribes,*" equipped with "*lanterns and torches and weapons.*"

There were many times, several shortly to follow, where Jesus opens not His mouth. But with the weaponized multitude that came in secret at night, He quickly and knowingly declares twice, "*I am he.*" I am who you want. I am Christ. I am He who saves, He who forgives, He who heals. I am the Messiah you all have been waiting for. And *"they went backward, and fell to the ground."* Their wickedness and weapons proved to hold little weight when in the presence of the Son of God. *"Master,"* Judas says, as he kisses Jesus who suffered for even him. A kiss was the token Judas chose for his sought-after betrayal. And Jesus responds to it by calling Judas, *"friend."* He who loves.

The apostle's lives were in danger of arrest, as well. *"If therefore ye seek me, let these go their way."* Turning Himself over with the agreement of their protection and safety. Yet regardless of peacefully, willingly, submissively offering Himself, they *"come out, as against a thief, with swords and staves."* Jesus goes on to say, *"When I was daily with you in the temple, ye stretched forth no hands against me: but this is your hour, and the power of darkness."* He recognized and knew those that came out to bring Him to His death. He has seen them, been with them often, and says to them, I have been among you so many times and you did nothing, but in your dark moment you have been long seeking, you treat me like a common thief who was trying to hide.

Peter in refusal to believe Jesus's life would end, knowing His power and growing population, Peter was overwhelmed in excitement with all the possibilities Jesus's future could look like! In protest and protection, Peter inaccurately strikes the *"servant of the high priest,"* taking off his ear. Jesus's response is similar to on the Mount of Transfiguration. When Jesus told Peter of His coming death and resurrection, Peter tried to *rebuke* His words, committing to making sure no one would hurt or take Him. His response to Peter then, was, *"Get thee behind me, Satan."* Meaning, anything that would prevent Jesus from doing what needs to be done to save us, is the sole drive of the adversary, and He will not heed.

Peter, now seen keeping his promise to defend his master's safety, Jesus again reacts in defense of His mission to save all. *"The cup which my Father hath given me, shall I not drink it?"* Should I not go ahead with the atonement? Doing so will fulfill *"scriptures of the prophets"* and the entire purpose of me and your Father. *"Thinkest thou that I cannot now pray to my Father, and he shall presently give me more than twelve legions of angels?"* Meaning, if He wanted to stop this, He could, *"but how then shall the scriptures be fulfilled?"* *"Thus it must be."* In other words, let them arrest me. It is not Him losing against darkness, it is the beginning of infinite triumph over it!

Jesus *"touched his ear, and healed him."* Jesus's last miracle performed was the healing of one who was weaponized to take him to His death. And just like they have been for the past three years, they choose to dismiss another miracle they've witnessed by Jesus, and they continue with their one-track-mind plan.

"Then they took him." And *"all the disciples forsook him, and fled,"* fulfilling prophesy which Jesus had given during the Last Supper just hours before, *"All ye shall be offended because of me this night."* Bloodied, hurt, and fatigued, Jesus walks further into the night and begins the secret and illegal after-hour trials, in direct violation of Jewish laws. And Peter followed Him *"afar off."* Jesus was sent *"bound,"* tied up, as He made his way to five so-called hearings against Him. Seeing first Annas, the father-in-law to Caiaphas, who hadn't been in office as the high priest for over twenty years but sought after Him in hope to win after and leverage his heavy influence. Jesus says He has done nothing in secret. He had taught *"openly to the world,"* in their *"synagogues,"* in their *"temples."* How dare He speak to Annas like that, was their response. Still bound, they continued to the high priest.

Meeting with Caiaphas already had scribes and elders assembled and waiting to witness the outcome of the end of Jesus. This wasn't a hearing or a trial, they weren't asking or listening to Jesus, they were meeting among themselves, conspiring up a specific false narrative that would *"put him to death,"* seeking and asking around for *"false witnesses,"* but *"found none."* They were in it too deep; they would not accept arrest or punishment alone, but death only. Then a *"fellow"* said he heard Jesus say He was able to *"destroy the temple of God, and to build it in three days."* Guilty of *"blasphemy."* "Jehovah was convicted of blasphemy against Jehovah."[1] They tore His clothes, said, *"He is guilty of death,"* spitting on Him, blindfolding His eyes and hitting Him. Taunting and mockingly asking who it was that *"struck him on the face."* The pride and irony of these nighttime and illegal trials is disgusting. Doing so at night so as not to be seen doing anything unclean so they can all continue and finish Passover worship, worship and gratitude for sacrificial lambs that saved them. Ironic indeed.

Peter was recognized among the crowd as he was following along to watch. He was asked by three separate people who were among the angry conspirators, if he were one of the *disciples,* one of them even being a *"kinsman whose ear Peter cut off."* Just as Jesus had prophesied only hours earlier, and like we saw with Judas, His knowing is down to the very detail, and Peter denied Jesus three times before the morning rooster crowed. *"I know not this man."* Perhaps it was because Peter was wanted for arrest among them, or perhaps because he was witnessing the brutality of Jesus in that moment and was trying to save himself from receiving likewise. Or perhaps it was something more than even those. Regardless, what pains me the most is knowing *"the Lord turned, and looked upon Peter."* Jesus heard his denials and they locked eyes. I think often what it would be like to look into the Savior's eyes, how overwhelming it would be, and how I long to do so. I feel anguish spin inside of me even, as I picture Peter locking eyes with His Savior, as He is in the very brutal act of saving Peter's soul. To look upon Him, with spit, with blood, with all the red hands that surround Him from the beatings they did to Him, I can't handle a sliver of what Peter, Jesus's right hand apostle and friend, must have been feeling. *"Peter went out, and wept bitterly."*

I sink at the thought of it as I become very aware of the too many ways I unintentionally deny Him to others, and I deny Him to myself, even. Because that brutality was for saving my

---

1. James E. Talmage, "The Trial and Condemnation," Chapter 34, *Jesus the Christ* (The Church of Jesus Christ of Latter-day Saints, 2006)

soul, too. I love Him so deeply, yet so did Peter. And in the very process of what Jesus was in the midst of during Peter's denial and Judas's betrayal, is the very act that will unlock forgiveness and change from *our* Peter and Judas moments, to be able to indeed, lock eyes with Him one day.

No Jewish tribunal had authority to inflict the death penalty, only imperial Rome could, which is why they made their way to Pilate, the Roman ruler. Wanting to dismiss the case and receiving warning from his wife, He sent Jesus to Herod, to try to avoid any responsibility. Yes, *the* Herod *the Great,* the one who gave the order for the massacre of infants, and who authorized John the Baptist's death. He was *"exceedingly glad: for he was desirous to see him of a long season, because he had heard many things of him; and he hoped to have seen some miracle done by him."* Both Pilate and Herod found *"no fault"* in Jesus, *"nothing worthy of death."*

Back again was Jesus sent to Pilate, who said some of my favorite things to self-reflect on. *"What hast thou done?"* Everything our Father gave Him to do. *"Art thou the Christ?"* The whole nation was looking for the Messiah, and Jesus says to him, *"To this end was I born, and for this cause came I into the world, that I should bear witness unto the truth."* Pilate asks, *"What is truth?"* He is. *"I am the away, the truth, and the life."* Saying multiple times, *"I find in him no fault,"* fell upon deaf ears. Using the custom to release a prisoner at the time of Passover, Pilate was hoping it would free Jesus, as His wife had dreamt Pilate should do. The *"chief priests and elders persuaded the multitude."* "Barabbas!" they yelled. *"Destroy Jesus"* and release the known murderer. Pilate's job involved two major tasks, collecting taxes for Rome and keeping the peace. The crowd would not be satisfied and there was no peace. Another favorite self-reflection question of mine, *"What shall I do then with Jesus which is called Christ?"* Jesus is who He says He is, not just a man, but the awaited Messiah. What are we going to do with Him? What are we going to do with what He has done for us? What will we do with what He has taught and offered us? Are we going to let it change us? Are we going to let that be our drive and our influence? Or will we allow it to fall upon deaf ears as we pursue our own personal path and desires with conviction and blindness?

Crucify Him. *"Why, what evil has he done? But they cried out the more, saying, Let him be crucified."* Willing to put the blood of Jesus upon themselves and upon their *"children,"* Barabbas is released, yet still their yells of crucifixion grew louder. Isaiah prophesied that Jesus would be *"despised and rejected of men; a man of sorrows, and acquainted with grief."* Pilate delivered Jesus to be *"scourged"* to satisfy their demands of His blood. Victims were tied to a column or frame with their arms pulled up tightly with strain on their back muscles and are then whipped with leather strips with sharp metal and bone attached. *"Surely he has borne our griefs, and carried our sorrows."* This was a severe punishment many prisoners did not live through. Forty stripes that ripped and tore into His flesh. *"And with his stripes we are healed."*[2]

Blood ran down His face as a crown of thorns pierced His head. Stripped of His clothes, He was mockingly draped in purple, symbolic of a king, as soldiers continued to hit *"the King of the Jews."* Bringing Jesus in front of the crowds after the metal laced whips tore at His back, thorns punctured in His head, and a *"purple robe"* draped disgracefully over his form, Pilate says the piercing words, *"Behold the man."* Hoping they could see Him for who He is, or at the very least, take pity on Him, *look at Him.* They could see Him, but they did not truly behold Him, nor take any pity; they did not have eyes to see. When we look at Him, what do we see? How do we view Him in our times of confliction or times of not receiving our own agendas? Do we see Him as who He truly is, and see His purpose to bring us to better things? *"Or canst thou run about longer as a blind guide?"*[3]

A conflicted Pilate goes yet again to the judgment hall to speak of his hesitations and ask further questions of Jesus, and with power to release or crucify, Jesus *"gave him no answers"* to which he was seeking. *"Thou couldest have no power at all against*

---

2. Isaiah 53:3–5
3. Doctrine and Covenants 19:40

me, except it were given thee from above." Similar response He had just given Peter and will soon give to the taunting while on the cross. Though Pilate *"sough to release him,"* He *"saw that he could prevail nothing."* We have no king but Caesar, they said, and if Jesus was let go, Pilate would not be loyal to Caesar. But even releasing Jesus to them, it did not save his place as a leader. Only a few short years later, the Roman empire removed him from position; he was banished, and followed in the path of Judas, into suicide.

The purple robe was removed, they led Jesus *"out to crucify him,"* alongside two criminals sentenced to death for robbery. Required to carry His cross to *"a place of a skull,"* Jesus's exit is a stark contrast to His triumphant entry only days previous, lined with the same people who once held palms of praise. There is nothing written anywhere that there was any man who raised their voice in love, protest, or pity. And to the women who followed Him crying and mourning, Jesus turns to them, saying, *"Daughters . . . weep not."*

Soldiers call on someone to help Jesus, not to make things easier for Him, but because time was counting down until the day changed to the Sabbath and bodies remaining on the cross is unlawful on the Sabbath. No Jew or Roman would have voluntarily offered because it was considered degrading to carry the cross of a criminal walking to their death. They chose a visiting passerby named Simon to *"bear his cross,"* to walk in His footsteps, to make the journey with Him. And the relation of this to Jesus and us is obvious but incredibly profound and often overlooked or misunderstood.

There will be times when will be too weak to carry the cross we are asked to bear; the things we will be asked to suffer through and carry will seem too much, too heavy, and it will feel as though we will not make it. Jesus is at our side; He does that which no one else would or could do, and He carries our cross that He has overcome and conquered already. *"Take my yoke upon you"*[4] has

---

4. Matthew 11:29

always been His invitation and plea, so that we may not suffer *"even as I, which suffering caused myself, even God, the greatest of all, to tremble because of pain."⁵* The suffering has already happened by Him, the victory has already been claimed, and He offers Himself more to us as He carries us and our weight.

Like a baby who is just born, and the parents hold their baby for the first time, they look down and are just so overwhelmingly consumed with love for them. And it wasn't because the baby did anything—it couldn't; it was just born. It's not that the baby accomplished anything to earn that love. The parents profoundly and deeply love that child simply because it is theirs. When I think of the times when I fail and I fall, and I betray and I deny, sometimes I wonder why the Lord would ever want to be yoked with someone like me. He reminds me that I am deserving simply and profoundly because I am His. "He knew that the price of those sins was death. And He knew the source of those sins was you. And since He couldn't bear the thought of eternity without you, He chose the nails."⁶ I'm not sure what part of that seems ordinary or insignificant or what part of it could make us feel anything but empowered. Because if that isn't empowering, then I don't know what is.

So then, what shall we do then with Jesus who is called Christ? *"Behold the man."* He who saves, He who forgives, He who heals. He who loves. He, the Messiah we've been waiting for. *"Surely he has borne our griefs, and carried our sorrows."* Just as He did to His sleeping apostles in the garden, He says to us, *"Rise up!"* Let us go. *"Weep not."* He has done the suffering and conquering. His plea is our invitation to take up our cross daily *"and follow Him."* Take up our cross, continue on that path, walk in His footsteps, make the journey *with Him*. Because He is there on that journey, He is helping, He is lifting, and He is leading us down a path that leads us to finally look into His eyes, reunited in perfect glory, and receive endless bliss.

---

5. Doctrine and Covenants 19:18
6. Max Lucado, *He Chose the Nails* (United States: Thomas Nelson, 2012), 34

Finding Yourself in . . .

The Crucifixion

Matthew 27, Mark 15, Luke 23 & John 19

I'm in the middle of a hard season of struggle right now, and it's been going on for so long, I'm just . . . so tired. It's taken so much from me, and it's left me just . . . so tired. I can't even begin to understand how tired Jesus was even in the garden. No mortal man could have withstood even a sliver of the weight that Christ felt in that garden. Feeling the weight and the consequences of every single soul to ever exist and will ever exist, I can't imagine, as I sit here overwhelmed with fatigued just with myself, how He was able to continue on. And from that moment when infinite pains and sorrows consumed His entirety, even more was required through the entire night. Being dragged from five locations like some sort of sick roadshow for mistreat and maltreat. He did that. I don't know how He did that.

"Upon the cross of calvary, they crucified our Lord."[1] Fulfilling scripture in Isaiah, *"he was numbered with the transgressors,"*[2] the long awaited and promised Messiah was recognized and killed

---

1. "Upon the Cross of Calvary," *Hymns*, no. 184
2. Isaiah 53:3

as a common enemy. On a hill, intersected at the most crowded roads, at a time of many visiting nations for Passover, Jesus was a spectacle of mockery, a target for stones, and abuse. Stripped of His clothes and arms stretched, great mallets in Jewish hands forcefully drove Romans nails into the sinless flesh of our Deliverer, centered between two thieves, at the place of *skulls*. *"None other nation on earth that would crucify their God."*[3] The most drawn out and most painful of all forms of death, spikes hammered through nerves and tendons, both through hands and His feet, making any movement excruciating throughout the entire body. Hours keep passing without companionship or comfort. Jesus willingly did that. I don't know how He did that. He did that for all those who believe on Him, and He did that for all those who do not.

He could have saved Himself from the cross, but He didn't. Betrayed, falsely judged, abused, and murdered. And in one word—in one single command—He could have put an end to it all. And yet, *"He opened not His mouth."*[4] What could have caused Jesus to allow Himself to endure all of that? *You.* Saving you. Getting you back. Giving you everything. He was motivated, strengthened, and dedicated to you. The only way to be saved is for someone else to rescue. It was always about and for you. And He never lost sight of that. He never lost sight of you.

"As a lamb to the slaughter,"[5] Jesus, the *Lamb of God,* was sacrificed for all mankind at the very hour when lambs were being sacrificed for Passover. Priests, elders, and Pharisees inaccurately thought that putting an end to Jesus would put an end to Him, His impact, and His work. Dismissing prophecies and teachings, they did not realize their actions were the very ones that enabled Him and what He did, and does, for humankind to be magnified infinitely—endless and everlasting.

The long-awaited moment they had sought after for years with such priority, was overshadowed by the sign Pilate hung

---

3. 2 Nephi 10:3
4. Isaiah 53:7
5. Ibid.

above Jesus, *Jesus of Nazareth, King of the Jews*—believed to be both revenge against their actions as well as Pilate's actual feelings. In three different languages to be understood by all during this holiday, the sign was no insult against Jesus, but against them. So distracting and upsetting to them, the chief priests journeyed to beg Governor Pilate to remove or change the title, but Pilate responds, *"What I have written, I have written."*

"Father, forgive them, for they know not what they do," Jesus prayed, showing compassion for the Roman who were crucifying Him, as opposed to the Jewish leaders who knew exactly what they were doing. But the same Jesus who forgives those who know not what they do, can also forgive those who know exactly that they do.

By how common crucifixions were, the crosses themselves were quickly and simply made using the most common wood. There was nothing grandiose about them, and Jesus's cross was no different, made only as big as needed to withhold his weight. Yet *so* painful and slow a death, potentially lasting up to several days, it was allowed to offer the victim vinegar mixed with myrrh as well as a few other ingredients, to work as a narcotic against pain. *"He would not drink,"* needing to fully feel and experience all pains up until death. The chief priests, scribes, and elders, *"sitting down,"* mocked and taunted Him to *"save"* Himself. If He really is who He says He is, then He should *"come down from the cross."* They mocked, *"He saved others"*—He who had risen the dead, calmed the storms, healed the terminal and the disabled—yet *"himself he cannot save."* Demanding to come off the cross so that they *"may see and believe,"* we know after the years of seeing miracles and healing, with their hardness of hearts, even if He did, seeing would not be enough for believing.

There will be times we'll wonder why Jesus does not exercise His power in our behalf. We can remember that He did not always exercise it on His own behalf. *"Ye shall be sorrowful,"* He said, and we can add pained, lonely, misunderstood, struggling, persecuted, *"but your sorrow shall be turned into joy . . . Be of good cheer; I have overcome the world."*[6] Though sometimes we try on our own to *"save thyself,"* as taunted to do by opposing forces, we can only truly be lifted up by the One who has been lifted up. He gave all so we could receive all.

Jesus spoke seven times while on the cross. After His plea to His Father to forgive, the second time is in response to the disputing thieves He hung between. One joining in the mockery and taunting, while the other *"rebuked him, saying, Dost not thou fear God, seeing thou art in the same condemnation?"* In other words, who are you to say anything when you are on the cross dying as well, except the difference is, *"we indeed justly; for we receive the due reward of our deeds,"* we are getting what we deserve, *"but this man hath done nothing"* wrong.

"Jesus, Lord, remember me when thou comest into thy kingdom." I am not one to easily tear, but reading that does it every time as I feel my soul within me desperately long for the same plea. Please, *Lord,* my Jesus, *remember me.* And He responds, *"To day shalt thou be with me in paradise."* After the cross, Jesus goes into the spirit world, where this man will also be, and able to accept all that is offered and taught to be with Him in His kingdom. That Kingdom, *paradise,* is offered to a criminal on death row, and it is offered to you.

"Now there stood by the cross of Jesus his mother, Mary, *and his mother's sister, Mary,"* as well as *"Mary Magdalene."* None of the apostles are mentioned to have been there, apart from John the beloved. *"Jesus therefore saw his mother, and the disciple [John] standing by"* and says, *"Behold thy son!"* Jesus speaking for the third time on the cross, says to John, *"Behold thy mother!"*

The pain of watching your most loved one suffer is indescribable. Is it any wonder that Jesus had spoken to whom He loved, to take His mom *"unto his own home"* immediately, to save her from watching His last breath? It is assumed that Jesus's father had passed since the charge to John, who *"was leaning on Jesus's bosom"* during the Last Supper, was to take care of her for Him.

---

6. John 16:20, 33

The nails were driven through at nine in the morning, and at noon, *"darkness over all the earth"* came. *"The sun was darkened."* Even the accounts in America on the day of His crucifixion says there was no light, and *"there could be no light, because of the darkness, neither candles, neither torches; neither could there be fire kindled with their fine and exceedingly dry wood, so that there could not be any light at all; And there was not any light seen, neither fire, nor glimmer, neither the sun, nor the moon, nor the stars, for so great were the mists of darkness."*[7] Among the Nephites, there was darkness as well as a *"great and terrible destruction,"* and *"many great and notable cities were sunk."*[8] Darkness covered the land, before Jesus died. And in this complete and total darkness that was so thick, it could be physically felt, without sight, all heard Jesus yell, *"Eloi, Eloi, lama sabachthani, . . . My God, my God, why hast thou forsaken me?"* "What mind of man can fathom the significance of that awful cry?"[9] Needing to experience all things, including the effects of sin, the dying Christ was alone; the Spirit and the help from God withdrew.

"After this, Jesus knowing that all things were now accomplished," having felt and experienced it all, all things were accomplished and accepted, He speaks for the fifth time, *"I thirst."* Which medically, actually signifies severe blood loss and shock. The nails, the leather and metal whips, the garden, it was too much blood. To a medical doctor, "when a patient goes into shock because of blood loss, invariably that patient—if still conscious—with parched and shriveled lips cries for water."[10] When He was again offered the vinegar mix for relief, having finished His mortal requirements, they *"filled the sponge,"* and put it to His dying lips. And after having drank, *"It is finished,"* He says, and crying *"with a loud voice,"* His

---

7. 3 Nephi 3:21–22
8. 3 Nephi 8:11–14
9. James E. Talmage, "Death and Burial," Chapter 35, *Jesus the Christ* (The Church of Jesus Christ of Latter-day Saints, 2006)
10. Russell M. Nelson, "The Atonement," October 1996 General Conference

seventh and final utterance from the cross, *"Father, into thy hands I commend my spirit."* Jesus *"gave up the ghost."*

There were violent earthquakes, *"graves were open,"* and the destroyed veil of their temple between the Holy Place and the Holy of Holies was exposed for all to see. The darkness that came and stayed with no scientific explanation, just fulfilled prophecy. The Great Jehovah, the *"light and life of the world,"* He who made heaven and earth and all things that are in them, is gone. "No wonder the very earth convulsed at the plight of this perfect child."[11]

And *"all the people"* that were there, *"smote their breasts."* In the silence of His death and the darkness, everyone that was there literally beat their chests, a cultural expression of doom and deep fear. A Roman centurion, a commanding Roman soldier over a hundred soldiers, has reat experience with crucifixions, but so different was the one of Jesus, *"he glorified God, saying, certainly this was a righteous man."*

"Upon the cross our Savior died, but, dying, brought new birth."[12] Jesus has died. But victory had been won. *"I lay down my life, that I might take it up again. No man taketh it from me but I lay it down of myself. I have power to lay it down, and I have power take it again."*[13] He did not die because of Judas, He died *for* Judas. He did not die because of Pharisees or any other Jewish leader, He died *for* them. And for you. That He *"may draw all men unto him."*[14]

If we were to make a list of all the things we wouldn't have if it weren't for Christ on Calvary, would it ever be finished? Because of Jesus, death is not the end, this life is not final, we are not done. *"In Christ shall all be made alive."*[15] Every single soul to have ever lived, even the most vilest of sinners, has been

---

11. Jeffrey R. Holland, "He Loved Them unto the End," October 1989 General Conference

12. "Upon the Cross of Calvary," *Hymns,* no. 184

13. John 10:17–18

14. 2 Nephi 26:24

15. 1 Corinthians 15:22

given the gift of resurrection, the gift of continued life. Without Him, sealed to our families and sealed to Him are not realities. Our bodies will rot in the grave and our souls that can never die would become subject to Satan forever. Jesus chose suffering all, for all, to remove the effects of sin from us, without so, returning to God would not be possible. Stained by our sins with no change or forgiveness or cleansing, *"our spirits must have become like unto him, and we become devils, angels to a devil."*[16] Never ending damnation. There would be no hope for anyone. Breaking the heavy chains that hold us to the grave and to the devil means suffering and loss is not final, our life here has purpose, and it is just the beginning. We are going somewhere with all of this! Which means He is not done with us, this is not it, there is so much more to come, and it is blossoming, and it is beautiful.

Jesus was the only one capable of doing this sacrifice and offering us everything. Because He was perfect, He was free from the demands of justice; He had no debt to justice. And because of Him, that clean slate is offered to us, to stand and receive all that He has as if we were all along as well.

With Jesus comes forgiveness, comes newness. From sin, from betrayal, from denial, from it all. *"As often as my people repent will I forgive them."*[17] He does not choose to look past, they are completely non-existent. Because of Jesus, we are always offered a clean slate. Like it never even happened, wiped completely clean, off-the-record kind of forgiveness. So readily available because that's precisely why He purposely died. He found that much importance in getting us back and giving us everything, He allow Himself to be murdered. Absolutely He stands ready with open arms and more chances. Because of clean slate restarts, He gives Himself again as He will stand shoulder-to-shoulder to us and advocates for us to God. Pleading our case, fighting for us, Jesus will say we are able, we are worthy, using His own life and sacrifice as evidence.

---

16. 2 Nephi 9:9
17. Mosiah 26:30

Because Jesus chose the cross means, what is, and what was, isn't what will always be. It means things can change; *we* can change—improve. And how awful would it be if we couldn't. With change comes growth, comes progress, comes healing, comes conquering. With change comes the gift to try again, to start again, over and over. Hope is not lost, all is not lost; we are not lost. We do not have to be who we were. We are not stuck; we are not stagnant. We are not living linear, this is not final, we are not done! It means we have a God of commas, not periods. Everlasting struggle just isn't in God's cards for us. We do not have to wait for a new day, a new week, a new chapter, a new season! Because of Jesus, every passing second is a chance to turn it all around.

With Jesus comes change and with change comes movement. Movement away from trauma, from pain, from heartbreak, from loneliness, from sin, from unfairness. And because of Jesus, that movement is onward and upward, to and through love, through forgiveness, through healing. And because of forgiveness, comes healing, inward cleansing, renewal, revival, and the ability to move on. We can let go, we can be set free. There *is* a love that satisfies. His love will heal you. His love *does* heal you.

Because Jesus descended below it all, there is nothing that is not covered. There is nothing He has not felt, there is nothing that He does not understand down to exactness. Which means we are never fully alone in them. There is no mistake, no addiction, no shame, no fear, no guilt, no loss, no weakness, no depression, no attack, no fear, no trauma, no loneliness that is not covered and met with perfect understanding and full resolve. Everything from broken hearts to broken homes. Because He has experienced and overcome all things, He has power over all things, and with Him, we have full access to that power. The adversary may have power to bruise. But bruises heal. Because of Jesus, we have power to *crush,* to conquer.

Because He descended below *it all,* everything that is bringing us down, weighing us down, holding us down, can be lifted up, He can lift us all higher! He can lift and lighten our load, elevate us to greater heights above the storm clouds into beautiful magnifications that are promised to us. And if this day that Jesus suffered the most brutal death as a criminal can be called *Good Friday*, our situations can all be turned for good, too.

Jesus Christ specializes in the seemingly impossible; He specializes in you. And because of it all, endless guidance and true purpose. Hope, and help, and light, and comfort are always there. It means He is always there with desire to bring us to Him with oneness of heart and mind. I have given too many reasons for Him not to love me and none of them has changed His mind. Having *"a perfect knowledge of all our guilt, and our uncleanness,"*[18] Jesus sees the real you. And He chooses to stay. To love, to cleanse, to advocate, to save. *Hosanna*. Save me.

As He was on the cross, He was thinking of you. As Jesus fell in the garden, He was thinking of you. As Jesus raised on the third day, He was thinking of you. The love of Christ has never failed. Not on the cross, not in the garden, not in this day, not now, and not ever. He gave all so we can receive all, never-ending happiness and endless bliss is your reality and your future. With Jesus comes better things that are endless and everlasting. *"Endless is my name;"*[19] endless is He, endless are we.

---

18. 2 Nephi 9:14
19. Moses 1:3

Finding Yourself in . . .

Silent Saturday

Matthew 27, Mark 15, Luke 23 & John 19

Their Sabbath fast approaching, not starting at midnight like how we track the start and end of a day, but beginning that evening at sun fall, around six. And as the sun was beginning to set, preparations for the Sabbath needed to happen, and according to the law, bodies could *"not remain upon the cross on the sabbath day."* Jewish religious leaders are very strict and concerned about the laws of the Sabbath. Getting approval from Pilate, the three on the cross had their legs broken, the shock of doing so had been found to be promptly fatal to those crucified. The soldier broke the legs of the two thieves, and when approaching Jesus, they marveled because He had already passed, and He had done so very quickly, as crucifixions were chosen for their lengthy time frame of suffering. So quick that when hearing of His death, *"Pilate marveled." "They brake not his legs,"* fulfilling two prophesies and scripture, *"a bone of him shall not be broken."* Making sure Jesus was actually dead, *"one of the soldiers with a spear pierced His side,"* making a hole large enough for a human hand to be thrust in, *"and forthwith came there out blood and water."*

When Elder Holland said Jesus "died from a heart broken by shouldering entirely alone the sins and sorrows of the whole human family," turns out it had literal meaning to it as well. Medically, blood and water are evidence of a cardiac rupture, the blood and water are a result from any part of the wall of a heart actually breaking. "Inasmuch as we contributed to that fatal burden, such a moment demands our respect," [1] and might I add, devotion.

Joseph, a counselor and member of the Sanhedrin, was a believer but only in heart. Though he kept his beliefs *"secretly for fear of the Jews,"* he threw all fears away as he boldly went to Pilate and *"begged"* for *"the body of Jesus."* If it weren't for Joseph, Jesus would have been discarded and lost among a pile of criminal corpses. Instead, we can picture Joseph removing His hands from around the nails that held Jesus up, allowing His body to drape over Joseph's shoulder as he brings Him down from the cross. Wiping His wounds, cleaning off His bloody body—it's such a beautiful and messy visual. But I love the humility that overwhelms as I wonder what thoughts I might have had if I were the one with my hands running over all those lacerations on His back, and the wounds on His palms, on His feet, on His side, and around the crown of His head, that were there because of, and for, me. I have yet to picture this without in return receiving a resolve to better live with Him and for Him.

Joseph dedicates his preparation for the Sabbath and his entirety by boldly and openly focusing on his Lord. But he is not alone. Out of all of Jesus's devoted and public followers, the two that are with Him in this moment are two secret and unexpected ones that would both suffer high consequences for doing so.

Here we reunite with Nicodemus, the great *"ruler of the Jews,"* master teacher of Israel. I love the wonder of him. Meeting originally with our Savior in great awe three years previous at the start of His earthly mission, Nicodemus comes at His end and serves

---

1. Jeffrey R. Holland, "Behold the Lamb of God," April 2019 General Conference

as a mortician for the Savior. Sitting in a powerful sect among the Pharisees, during this time of preparing for the Passover Sabbath, one of the most important days to Jews, so much was required of him. Yet he was not preparing himself for this high Sabbath by making sure he was meticulously and ceremonially clean, but by choosing to deliberately make himself ceremonially unclean by preparing a dead body for the grave. Throwing reputations and consequences aside, the two of them are here allowing their actions to be motivated by Christ. Nicodemus brought one hundred pounds of aloes and myrrh for anointing and embalming, a quantity and price only the very wealthy could do. Following Jewish tradition, together they wrapped the body in clean linen cloths, and they carried Jesus to a nearby tomb in a garden that belonged to Joseph himself. And there lay our Savior. What started in a manger, has ended in a borrowed grave.

Chief priests and Pharisees remembering Jesus saying He would rise on the third day, got approval from Pilate to have guards keep an eye on the tomb and to secure it with an official seal in place. And in guarded alertness they would wait. But Jesus's disciples are not plotting to steal His body, like they thought, but instead wallowing in the silence of Saturday. We know this because when Mary came to tell them of resurrected Jesus the following morning, they were found *"mourning and weeping."* Disciples and followers had been taught of His coming, but with lack of full understanding, the reality that they were facing was that the great *I Am* is dead. It was over, all was lost, He was gone. Done. Finished. I can only image what was going on in their mind. I always say passing time, waiting, is the hardest trial to go through. The silence and sadness of Saturday could have had them wondering in their weeping, had they been duped? Had what they hoped in, and been taught, not been true? When they were told He had come back that following morning, they *"believed not."* Doubt, disillusionment, maybe even anger, and the reality of a dead King.

Mary Magdalene and Mary, mother of James and Jose, were watching and following close behind Joseph and Nicodemus, but unable to intervene because sun had set, and darkness had come. Following the commandment and law to rest, they had to leave with their incompleteness as their devotion, and spices and ointments for entombment had to wait. Wait in their grief, wait in their loss, their void, in their pain, in the darkness. It was all unknown, all new. Strict laws forbid people from doing the smallest of things on the Sabbath, all the believers just had to sit and ponder it, face it, live with it, not knowing that their Sunday was coming. The darkest day the believers will have experienced, the in-between.

With hindsight and scripture, we know of where He was and what was to come, we know that He was preaching to spirits in prison, and that Easter was a day away, but they didn't. Not fully. When thinking of the Holy Week, don't leave Saturday only for the egg hunts during the in-between of cross and resurrection. We have *Saturday's*, too. Jesus could have rose from the dead instantly. That could have been the story. But He carved out a space for Saturday, He gave us that room to wait, to weep, to wrestle, to cry out to Him, and to lay our burdens at His feet.

I have been in a lot of seasons of waiting, weeping, and wondering. Times where I thought my faith and my God were failing me from the unwanted, unexpected, and the uncharted. I have had a lot of times where I felt I had nothing to show for my efforts. I have had a lot of Saturday's, sitting with pain, loss, doubt, and darkness. Writing this exact book has come at such a high price, the sacrifice of six months of rising before sun-up, and staying up far past sundown, as I dedicated every single day to deep research, to writing. Sacrificing other things that I love, staying behind from my kid's games, practices, outings. Having to place on the back burner other projects that will bring in much-needed income, just to follow out the deep prompt to write this book. In this exact moment, I am sitting here typing with little left in me. I'm tired. I'm so burnt out. My body physically aches. But *I am so close,* I keep telling myself, with fatigued tears in my eyes. Final stretch.

But the other day as I sat down to sacrifice just the little bit that was left of me, and of this book, I saw all my research was gone from my laptop. Months and months of sun-up to long past sundown, pages, and pages, and pages of all my sacrificed work and research to finish this book vanished. We have tried everything, calling upon all these experts proved to be fruitless, with all the talent to hack, it had vanished and was unretrievable. It's the week of my book deadline, and I have lost everything I needed to finish, all of it is just gone. Not just rewriting, but re-researching, everything.

I've lost my soul.

I feel stripped. I can't function. I can't focus. I am gutted. I am broken. Because it's not just my pages and pages of deep research that is gone and will have to be redone, it just sure feels like all of my sacrifices within home and family life have been in vain. *What for, what a waste.* What do I have to show for all that I gave up? And it's pushing everything that has been on pause back even further. I'm just so tired. And I don't know that I have anything left to redo, to try again, to start again. It's like I've lost part of me that I can never get back. I've lost part of what God and I built together so intimately. And the pain snatches the breath from my lungs, and I'm very much grieving over the sacrifice and loss.

This must be a sliver of what they must have been feeling on that dark, silent Saturday in their loss. But I am reminded that there is no suffering that we endure that Jesus Himself hasn't endured. As Heavenly Father watched His Only Begotten Son be falsely judged, abused, and murdered, it's said, *"it pleased the Lord to bruise him."*[2] Why? How? Because there was, in fact, something *so much more* to come. God is good even when our situation is not, because He knows something we don't. Something *greater*. As I am feeling lost over what I have lost, I'm reminded that the Good Shepherd finds, and brings us to new places, better *"pastures,"* filled with nourishment, protection, care, guidance.

---

2. Isaiah 53:10

He gives us *"life, and that they might have it more abundantly."*[3] Life more abundant! Something *greater.*

I think we forget that. I think we forget that the unexpected is God intervening. I think we forget that His whole purpose is to bring us to the best things. I think we forget that we don't truly want things our way. I think we forget how thrilling it is to live by faith. What would we do differently if we could see our own Sundays the way we can see these believer's? What kind of life could we be living if we stopped keeping God at arm's length? What could our life look like if we trusted Him completely? What could we receive if we see our seasons through and give God the chance to show us how great He really is? He knows something we don't, and there is beautiful closeness and meaning in it all. Sometimes we don't always know the what or the why behind things, but we do always know the Who. A Savior who gave all for us to receive all, and a God who is always good. A God who solely exists to bring us to the better and to make us better.

I know the weight that comes from not knowing how or when things will work out. But as we continue to turn and cry to Christ, we will find peace and forgiveness, change, rest, and a new start. Where we don't find an ending to a trial quite yet, we find ease and added strength. And where we can't find answers to prayers quite yet, we find comfort and reassurance. Where we don't see promised blessings quite yet, we find love and help and continued guidance. My Saturday season I've been in seems too long with little or no change and it's thinning. I've been feeling that I've done it wrong and that my right things are also fruitless things. And it starts to sting when others are in a season of reaping when you're still sowing, others are feasting and you're in a famine. I've been having to remind myself too often lately that every time I feel this way, a redirection is coming. Feeling like this causes me to dig deeper and I find a powerful and profound pivot from God Himself who really does only exist to bring us to better things.

---

3. John 10:10

Absolutely I feel like I am sinking right now but reminding myself that Peter knew safety does not come from reaching for the boat, but from Him—grabbing for the hand that has *me* engraven upon the palms. Reminding myself of Mary who returns to the grave, returns in the darkness, returns to Jesus, to keep going, to try again. Christ conquered death so I could conquer life. I am remembering all is not lost because He is still here. *I* am still here, *alive*! I have a heart that is beating and to have a God that is mine, and He fills our soul and breathes life back into our sunken spots.

Because there is a Saturday wedged in between the death and resurrection, shows me that we love a God who is close to the brokenhearted, close to the ones waiting, close to the ones in darkness, close to the ones that feel they have nothing left to give. God inserts Saturdays into our lives. If today is one for you, take heart. You are not alone in your darkness, He is not diminishing or dismissing. Even in our Saturdays, your Jesus sits with you at your well, weeps with you at the grave, carries back the lost, lifts the fatigued. He carves out space to have intimate moments with Him as we take to Him all that is broken and all that is heavy as He turns it into greater things. Like we see with Christ's life, as well as ours, our God is not one of avoidance and prevention, but He is one of intimate love, profound dedication, and greater magnifications to something greater.

We are not required, expected, or pressured to rush or push it away. God gives us space to grieve, to process, to rest, to seek, to listen, to turn to Him a little more. He doesn't rush us, He joins us. He comes and comforts with full understanding because He's felt that, too. He does not come with pressure; He comes with purpose. And healing. And full understanding. Because He's felt that, too. He suffered that, too. When my heart is turned towards Him, I can see life with a lens of hope, peace, strength, and stillness. Through loss and confusion, anger and anguish, because of Him my soul finds rest and promised *"peace in this world, and eternal life in the world to come."*[4] Whoever you are, wherever you are, you are not any less because of the stage and season you are in. You are not being punished and you are not less than. You are valued. You are loved. You are noticed. Your efforts, your hope, your faith is not in vain. You are His and that is everything! God knows something we don't, and it's full of deep purpose, and a commitment and a love *so deep* He dedicated His entire existence to it.

Like Mary and Martha at the loss of Lazarus, like the woman with blood disease, those born blind, those deteriorating from disease, it may seem like our Saturdays are never ending.

The fact that this book somehow was finished and made it to your hands means Saturdays do not last and strength is restored. That fact that you are still here with a heart that is beating means that Sundays do come. The fact that Jesus will rise means darkness will be lifted, all is not lost, and your efforts and faith are not in vain. The death of Jesus was not the end, it was only the beginning. Hold tight; Saturday is not the end, He is still here, so much more is to come, and it is beautiful.

Love and prayers to you who may be in a silent Saturday. A beautiful pivot and redirection is coming, and you too, will feast. *"Verily, verily, I say unto you, That ye shall weep and lament, but the world shall rejoice: and ye shall be sorrowful, but your sorrow shall be turned into joy."*[5] He is not dead. It is not over, all is not lost, we are not finished, He is not gone. Darkness may come, but the sun always rises.

---

4. Doctrine and Covenants 59:23
5. John 16:20

Finding Yourself in . . .

The Resurrection

Matthew 28, Mark 16, Luke 24 & John 20

The sorrow and silence of Saturday had moved on too slow, because before the sun had even risen, *"when it was yet dark,"* Mary Magdalene, *"the other Mary,"* and a *"certain woman"* already started to make their way back to the sepulcher with spices and ointments for the body of their Master. They ask among themselves while walking there *"who shall roll away the stone from the door,"* but when they arrive it has already been removed. There had been a *"great earthquake"* as an *"angel of the Lord had descended from heaven,"* and *"rolled back the stone,"* and the guards on duty *"became as dead men."* As Mary entered into the tomb, she saw two angels in *"long white, shinning garments."* As they *"bowed down their faces to the earth"* in fear, the angels spoke. *"Fear not ye: for I know that ye seek Jesus,"* but *"Why seek ye the living among the dead? He is not here, but is risen."* Alive. Living, active. Still, now. *"Come, see the place where the Lord lay."* You are seeking Jesus. Come. See!

As *"they entered in, and found not the body of the Lord Jesus."* The woman having been appointed to go and tell, they literally left running in *"fear and great joy"* to *"tell his disciples"* as directed by the angels. Peter in disbelief, hearing Mary's words only as *"idle tales,"* ran with John what could have been no more than a half mile back to the sepulcher. *"Stooping down, and looking in, saw the linen clothes lying."* And the burial cloth, the *"napkin,"* that was wrapped around His head was folded. They made their way back to *"their own homes"* as Peter was *"wondering in himself"* at what happened. Mary stayed looking into the tomb, weeping. While His apostles were not to be found at the crucifixion, Mary stayed for the entirety, and was the first one to the tomb, to honor and serve and worship. She wanted to be as close to Jesus as she could, even if that meant sitting by the tomb. After the severity of sorrow Mary had felt, now she was met with heightened loss as she now grieves His disappearance.

"Why weepest thou?" the angels ask.

Because He is gone; *"because they have taken away my Lord,"* and I don't *"know where they have laid"* Him.

"Why weepest thou?" Jesus asks.

If you know where He is, please tell me *"and I will take him away."*

Coming from a joyous reception in the spirit world, He's returned. Not recognizing it is Jesus could be because she was not facing that direction. It could be because it was *"at the rising of the sun,"* either it was still dark, or as dawn may have been finally breaking. If the light was slowly filling the sky, Jesus would have been silhouetted against the dim, approaching sun. Either in darkness, or the smallest dim of slow glowing light, as she was turned away, we hear the shortest sermon Jesus spoke, *"Mary."* The power of recognizing His voice when He calls our name, she *"turned herself"* as she called out *"Rabboni." Master.* I feel within myself a lifted weight I was carrying as I, in this moment, picture the lifted weight of relief and darkness she must have felt at the aid of her beloved. After saving her from *seven devils,* He had saved her again everlastingly, and here Jesus is, symbolically at the rise of the light, the Light of the World comes to her. As we seek Jesus, draw near to Him as she did; darkness will lift and relief will come, as He speaks from His living lips, the intimate one-word sermon, our name.

Mary becomes the first witness to the resurrected and perfected, glorified Jesus. And in His perfection, He has chosen to keep us engraved in His palms and in His feet and on His side. *"They may forget, yet will I not forget thee."*[1] Permanently engraved on His celestial body, He has chosen to keep us part of Him forever.

Appearing to many, not just the apostles but also woman, believers, and doubters were able to touch His feet, and at His invitation, to *"reach"* and *"behold"* His *"hands,"* to *"thrust"* their fingers *"into His side."* Come and see. The invitation to them and to us is one of personal, individual, intimate interactions with Him. Meeting all with the words, and ability behind them, *"Peace be unto you,"* the Prince of Peace Himself, says. Not just a saying, but an action, a verb. When He comes to all of us, whether in our doubts like Peter and Thomas, or pain, loss, and darkness like Mary, or mourning, weeping and waiting like John, or terrified with fear like others, He comes to us in personal and individual ways with peace to it all. With their plead to *"abide"* with them longer, to stay with them longer, Jesus does. He stays with them, He feasts with them. In true suit to Jesus, He *"stands in the midst"* of them, is among them, with them, with us, and their *"eyes were opened"* to all that He is. *"He goeth before you . . . there shall ye see him."* He is with us, and we can see Him. And He will speak to us in great intimacy of perfect knowledge and love of us. *"Why are ye troubled?"* You do not need to be, I am right here with you. *"Look at my hands and my feet."* I have chosen to have you part of me. You are mine. *"I am with you always, even unto the end of the world."* I will never leave you. I will stay. *"And he lifted up his hands, and blessed them."* With wounded hands, *we* are blessed.

As we read of Him, as we have these intimate moments with Him when we feel filled, we are sure that those will be enough

1. Isaiah 49:15

to become chains to tether us close to Him always. Yet with our idleness or with our business, we find ourselves on the sea fishing and failing. Those that lined the streets with palms, yet shortly lined with support or indifference to Jesus's crucifixion did not allow themselves to be changed by Him and what He did and taught. Those believing chief priests, the rich young ruler, and all those that did not turn away from their current ways, they did not allow themselves to be changed by Him. The five foolish virgins did not allow themselves to be continuously filled, the nine healed lepers did not turn to Him without a personal and immediate need to be filled. Peter, who has always been in active defense and protection and service of Jesus and His mission, and even after touching Him in His perfected state, decides to go fishing. And at least six others followed, *"and entered into a ship immediately."* They retreat to doing exactly what they were doing before Christ. On the same sea, on those same boats, exactly three years previous. And this skilled, professional fisher, had yet again caught not a single fish the entire night.

Symbolically, *again*, at the rise of the sun and the coming of light, Jesus, the Light of the World, comes. Almost identically as three years previous, Jesus comes and fills their nets enough to almost sink their boats. The difference from what they were doing all night as professionals to this morning was Jesus. Jesus is the difference. Most of us can say we love our Lord. Those five unprepared virgins who fell short, I'm confident they would all say they love their Lord, or else they wouldn't have been there with lamps waiting. Peter, we know He loves the Lord, because He walked with Him and served Him. Because He is literally telling us, *"Thou knowest that I love thee."* Then Peter, why are you here? Why are we back on this same shore, by these same nets, having this same conversation? Do you love *"me more than"* this? Do you love me more than fishing? Do you love me more than your old ways? Do you love me more than how life was before you had met me? Do we love Him enough to allow it to change us and our actions? Or do we find ourselves loving Him, but still on the water fishing, or on the wayside with an empty lamp?

Three years ago, when Peter was fishing, Jesus said to them, *"From henceforth thou shalt catch men."*[2] Men. People. Souls. Fish are nothing. And here we are, yet again, and Jesus's final documented teaching is the same thing. *"Go ye into all the world, and preach the gospel to every creature. Teach all nations, baptizing them in the name of the father, and of the Son, and of the Holy Ghost."* Up until now, His mortal ministry was limited to the Jews. His final documented teaching to His apostles is to take the gospel further! Jews considered themselves to be somewhat superior because they were direct descendants of Abraham. Not only is this teaching to further and expand the work, but also removing any and all social or racial barriers in all ways because *"the worth of souls is great in the sight of God."*[3] None are favored, all are equal, all are deserving, all are His. Which means you, regardless of where we are and what corrections and recommitment and changes need to be made, you are still His and you are still deserving. And if we think He will do anything to stop us from overcoming and conquering, we're wrong. *"I will in no wise cast out."*[4] He turns no one away, but invites and *pleads* for us to come to Him, to take advantage of exactly why He willingly died.

Sometimes we think, *well, this is all well and good, but this is a pipe dream. I've tried, but it's just not compatible with my life.* And you're right. It isn't. It's not compatible. When Peter was asked to leave everything behind three years ago, that wasn't compatible, that wasn't easy. But it *should* disrupt our life. It should disrupt our own plans. It *should* change us. We should allow Him to disrupt and change, that's the best part! To have the privilege for Him to come, to step in, to make better, and give us more. When we, like Peter and his failed fishing, can say, *"I will,"* and drop our nets at His command, magnifications happen. Both-our-ships-filled-and-sinking kind of magnifications!

So to Peter, what was more important than his entire career, trade and life's support? People. Souls. Your soul. And using it for

---

2. Luke 5:10
3. Doctrine and Covenants 18:10
4. John 6:37

many great things of greater importance and greater meaning! The departure of Jesus wasn't the end to Him, or His teachings and miracles, nor was it the end of Peter's calling. Peter lived on teaching and leading, and the church grew rapidly! He was able to leave the boat and himself become a man of miracles and healing. So great were the miracles Peter was able to perform with God, that afflicted ones would lay on couches in the streets in hopes that a passing of Peter would heal them. Seasons end. Things change. But through the evolution of life, with God things will continue to blossom in new, beautiful ways for us. An entire life full of great power and purpose and impact that will be everlasting is intended for us here. Fish are nothing. If He wanted fish, He could get fish. *He wants you.* And He wants to give you so much more than what's right here within reach. All that is better, all that is lasting, all that is good. *"This is the will of Him that sent me."*[5]

After Jesus was resurrected and was among His disciples, He *"breathed on them and said receive the Holy Ghost."* The same words are used in Genesis when He *"breathed"* on Adam and He became a living soul.[6] This breathing is one of giving additional life and *power.* That is what happened to us when were confirmed to receive the Holy Ghost. That is what we have right now. He is breathing into us additional life and *power.* To dwells *in* us, to drive us, to work with us from within. Then said Jesus to Peter, *"Follow me."* Then said Jesus to us, *"Follow me."* Trust me. Let me take you somewhere better. What a privilege it is to have the perfect One intervene, for He makes no mistakes.

MORE JESUS

"Then said Jesus . . . will ye also go away?"[7] Will we also go away into our own ways? Or can we allow what He has done for us

---

5. John 6:40
6. Genesis 2:7
7. John 6:67

be enough to stay? I want to be different and do better. I'm just gunna be honest here, last year I spent most of my time in weighted confusion and in deep self-reflection and soul searching and reevaluating. And through all the different feelings and different things to navigate, I've landed on . . . I want more Jesus. I do, I just want and need more of Him. It needs to be more about just Him. That's all. I want Jesus. Looking beyond the mark is such a subtle, subconscious thing. Getting caught up in the weeds with things that seem like they matter but aren't actually important, slowly causing confusion, distraction, and haze. Smoke and mirrors to intellectually, and blindly, fall victim to the adversary. After a lot of vain attempts, I finally have a *freeing fire* of redirection! To trim down, to cut back, to let go, to turn cheek, and to *run* with better *simplification* to Him. Because it really is about Him. I don't want to go back. I don't want to live a life without Him, I already did. He has changed me much too much that all that was before Him has become so foreign. *"Lord, to whom shall we go? thou hast the words of eternal life."*[8] More Jesus.

I know very well the times where we are losing our voice, losing hope, losing strength, those times that feel unheard, unanswered, unwanted, unfit, unworthy—to feel lonely, lacking, tired, tried—to wonder, to doubt, to guess, to struggle, to sink, to sacrifice. Like you, I know how it feels to think our faith is in vain with nothing to show for our efforts, to feel like you have to force yourself to use faith you don't even know if you have or not. I know it's easy to point fingers at God and easy to quit and to turn back. But I also know that He is giving us everything we need to move forward away from that. Small steps are still steps. And they are also steps backed with life and power. You may not understand what He is doing, but soon you will. What a *thrill* it is to stick with it and stick with Him and see it all unfold! To look back and humbly connect the dots, to look back in humble "ah-ha's" as we finally notice His strategic intricacies. Once you

---

8. John 6:68

AL CARRAWAY

realized what He was up to all along, you really will stand all amazed. The crying, complaining, confusing, turned to blossomed blessings. To look back and see my favorite things, *the best things*, stemmed from all that I initially was fighting against. To see all that was unwanted has brought me to all that is new—to see all that was different has brought me to all that is better.

Christ conquered death so we could conquer life. He rose, so we too, will rise. Not just hereafter but rise from the trials, from the weight. Hard times will always be there, but so will Christ and with Him we overcome everything—every feeling of loneliness, of pain, of darkness, with Him, we will overcome the world! Christ died so that we may live, so let us live well! For me, what has been helpful is: see your seasons through. See Him through. *Let Him* show you how great He really is. Let Him take you off the boat, on top of water, past the shores. Allow God to be God by embracing the unexpected knowing who is guiding you. Take chance on your good, reoccurring thoughts. Remove limitations we ourselves may have placed on a limitless God. I am learning the vastness and intricate details of God and I am certain God knows something we don't—about ourselves, about life, about our souls living within us. Prioritize goals to take care of a spirit living within us. Realizing, in deep ways recently, that stewardship absolutely includes my soul that can never die but still suffer.

Let's give this a real go at it! Every day. We've got to. This is it, you know? Let's make taking care of us and our soul a priority. Make Jesus a priority. Life . . . it just . . . blossoms when we invest in us, and we invest in Him. Effort? Well, yeah. Sacrifice and disruption? Well, yeah. When reading the scriptures all the way through, how many times did I read about endless torment, endless misery, endless damnation, endless darkness that *we* choose for ourselves by our actions, or lack of. Over what . . .? *Jesus?* Over an all merciful, all-loving, all-powerful, all-forgiving, perfect Being who stands with *"open arms to receive"*[9] us and give us the greater things?

---

9. Mormon 6:17

Is it that hard to *feed* my *soul*, to give my spirit living inside of them the self-care (no no, *spirit-care*) it desperately needs to thrive? Is it *that* painful to do the smallest and simplest things that literally revive and pump *life* and power into my soul? Is it *that* much of a chore to come closer to the most powerful Being to ever exist and become more intimate with the Creator of everything's existence? To become one with He who chose to wear my scars on His palms, He who only exists to bring me to the better things. Is there anything more important than endless life and eternal bliss?

This absolutely gives me reason to get out of the boat, to see it through, to allow God to be God. To give Him the chance to show me how great He really is. And run like I am on fire, living a life of great passion, knowing who's hands I'm in—doing what God has called me to do—those things that make me feel filled. Because I am only here once! *Alive*!

More Jesus.

Then times will come when the scary and the hard and the unexpected turn into exciting, thrilling new adventures that come with peace, knowing that we are in motion to the best-fit blessings. We can stop doubting and start embracing, and we can move forward, onward and upward and become lighter and stronger and happier in the new, in the different, in the unwanted. And we will find ourselves feeling at ease even among trials because from consistently acting, we will have experienced time and time again that we are being led to the greater things. And we'll be profoundly grateful things didn't go our own way because we will find ourselves living our best self *in* our best life, living and experiencing things we didn't even know were available to us, with new knowledge and talents we wouldn't have wanted to go any further in life without. Because we chose to trust the most powerful Being to ever exist.

With Him, the life of this world, we can truly *live*. And *ahhhh*, what a *life it is*! Different and new is not bad. One day we'll pause and look around, and we'll see where we are, what we've gained along the way and we wouldn't want to change a thing. And we'll wonder why we hadn't done better all along when we look around and see where we are and what we've gained along the way. And through it all, we'll know Him. Because of it all, I know Him; I love Him with a real love. And when you have that, could you trade it?

We will wonder if it is worth it. If it is worth the time, the painful sacrifice, problem solving, and struggling. *It is.* I am writing the last few words of this book, and doing so is *finally* bringing me to take my first step out of this hole of a trial I have been in for so long. This lifted weight I am feeling from this step out, is a lifting weight that gives us seasons to *soar*! I am in tears right now feeling my soul begin to take flight! *Oh my, what a feeling!* In this exact moment, I feel free. I feel revived and whole. My heart is racing so fast, yet I am enveloped with a release to rest, to breathe easy.

I know more unwanted and unexpected will come. To my future self, and to you: It is worth it! The view up here above the clouds is incredible! It is worth the disruption from He who gave all to us to receive all. The feeling and ability to *soar* is worth it. To have these moments that cause our spirits to jolt and dance within us! That is worth it. To have the chance, and power, and strength to be lifted up and lifted out, that is worth it. *He* is worth it. Endless life and eternal bliss is worth it. With the intensity of my soul, *come* and *see*! See it through. There is a liberating ecstasy for us! Allow His ways to disrupt your life; that's the best part! To be changed by Him. Because *"thou shalt see greater things."*[10] Greater. Full of purpose and passion and impact.

Sometimes we don't always know the what or the why behind things, but we do always know the Who. A God who *is* always good. And in the times we plead and wonder, He will lovingly

---

10. John 1:50

correct us, *"Of little faith, wherefore didst thou doubt?"*[11] Because *of course* He will. He's right there with you with outreached arms. Because Jesus conquered, we will in fact conquer. We will find peace to our soul. Everlasting struggle just isn't in God's cards. Death was the beginning, a better life and a better us *is* within reach. They will never give up on us, so let's not give up on Them.

"He is not here, for He is risen."[12] Alive. Living, active. Still, now. Your prayers have been heard, but greater is what he has in store for you. Right now, in this life, we are in motion to greater magnifications that leave us to stand all amazed! With wounded hands, *we* are blessed. He is here, speaking from His living lips, the intimate one-word sermon, your name.

So, what if we got it all backward? What if every step is the miracle? Enjoy living, friend. Because of Him, everything good is here just for you.

---

11. Matthew 14:31
12. Matthew 28:6

—Notes—

—Notes—

—Notes—

—Notes—

—Notes—

About the Author

Al Caraway is a writer, multi-award-winning international speaker, and author of the best-selling books *Wildly Optimistic*, *More than the Tattooed Mormon*, *My Dear Little One*, and *Cheers to Eternity!* Since 2011 she has traveled worldwide, inspiring others by sharing her conversion and faith through difficult times as well as traveling by bus or boat guiding Church history tours.

Her passion is to tell everyone that happiness exists. It comes from living the gospel of Jesus Christ and in finding and loving Him through the hard, the unwanted, and the unexpected challenges of life. Because through it all, with God, we have every reason to be wildly optimistic.

After a decade spent in Arizona and Utah, she is now living with her husband, Ben, and her three kids, back where she was raised, in New York.

For more, follow Carraway on instagram:
@alcarraway or alcarraway.com.

SCAN TO VISIT

www.ALCARRAWAY.COM